This book belongs to the
Visitation Monastery of
Philadelphia

GREATER PERFECTION

GREATER PERFECTION
Conferences

OF

SISTER MIRIAM TERESA, Litt.B. *Demjanovich*
of the
Sisters of Charity of St. Elizabeth
Convent Station, New Jersey

Edited by
Rev. Charles C. Demjanovich, A.M.

NEW YORK
P. J. KENEDY & SONS
1928

269
D36
Cop.2

Nihil Obstat:

THOMAS H. McLAUGHLIN
Censor Librorum

Imprimatur:

✠ THOMAS JOSEPHUS WALSH
Episcopus Novarcensis

Newark, N. J.
August 21, 1928

MY Beloved One! To the Father, Son,
And Holy Paraclete
Be all honor, praise, to the end of days
In measure full, replete.
—Sister MIRIAM TERESA

THE UNION OF LOVE

This *union of divinest love*
By which I live a life above,
Setting my heart at liberty
My God to me enchains.
But then to see His Majesty
In such a base captivity
It so my spirit pains,
That evermore I weep and sigh,
Dying because I do not die.

—Saint Teresa

FOREWORD

THE works of the late Sister Miriam Teresa of the
Sisters of Charity of St. Elizabeth, Convent Station,
New Jersey, having been given for inspection to me
as " Censor Librorum " of the diocese of Newark,
with a view to their publication, I wish to state that
in addition to granting the *nihil obstat* it appears
incumbent upon me to say a few words about these
extraordinary conferences of a novice.

These conferences were circulated and used in
communities throughout the United States, in Ireland, England, and even Australia. They have made
a profound impression upon everyone who has read
or heard them. The reason is not far to seek.

In a marvelous, yet simple manner, we have here
unfolded the means, in accordance with the principles of a most profound ascetical theology, of
achieving intimate union with Almighty God
through prayer that in nowise comes into conflict
with the duties of one's state in life. The depth of
love and knowledge of the workings of Divine
grace, in so far as these have been made known in
revelation and theology; the unction, as well as the
discernment of the tendencies of the human mind

[vii]

and heart; not to speak of the delicate and pleasant style, are astonishing in one so young.

A spirit of personal humility and breath of charity pervades the whole. They are intended that other hearts may strive to live in close union and intercourse with Almighty God, and burn with ardent love for all things dear to Jesus and Mary.

Although intended primarily for religious who in their sanctification must combine the spiritual with the active life, these writings will be found to be a source of enthusiasm for a more intimate union with Christ, together with practical indications of how to live in, by, and for Jesus, not only for the clergy, but even for the laity who amidst the turmoil of the world wish to be concerned effectively with the things of God in striving after perfection, according to the will of Jesus, " Be ye therefore perfect as your heavenly Father is perfect." No one who has an ardent desire to live a spiritual life in union with the Blessed Trinity can rise from these considerations without being refreshed in spirit, and stimulated to take up with joy and alacrity one's daily burdens in union with our suffering Lord.

The perusal of these works, begun as a matter of duty, became for the undersigned a source, not only of personal edification, but also of deep appreciation of the wondrous ways of God in His dealings with souls.

Without, in any way, anticipating the definite judgment of the Church, it would seem that the manner of the origin, the dissemination, and publication of these spiritual writings would indicate some particular purpose in the plan of Divine Providence for God's greater glory. Through the attainment of perfection, not only on the part of the spouses of Christ, but of all devout souls in the world, may this book continue the excellent work begun under obedience, by the hidden novice, for the sanctification of the religious-minded within and without cloister walls.

(*Rt. Rev. Msgr.*) THOMAS H. McLAUGHLIN, S.T.D.

February 11, 1928

TABLE OF CONTENTS

✠ TABLE OF CONTENTS ✠

PREFACE

IN THE plan of Divine Providence, each individual person born into this world has a definite mission to fulfil. For this end, to some God appoints a long life — others He calls to Himself in their youth. Whether the span of life be short or long, each individual leaves an impress, for good or evil, on his co-wanderers in this vale of tears.

The spiritual writings of Sister Miriam Teresa have deeply impressed those who have been favored in seeing them. Without a single exception, they agree that the conferences may further God's honor and glory in bringing souls, both lay as well as religious, into closer union with Him.

A Sister high in the council of her Order writes, under date of February 15, 1927: " I am overwhelmingly in your debt. Yesterday we received two more conferences, the last of the series. I cannot begin to thank you for your great kindness in sending them to us. They are a wonderful help to many communities, and I hope you will be able to continue them. I think it would be a great boon to many religious to have these conferences in book form. The Mistress of Novices in ———, Ireland, is delighted with them and is making copies to send to the other novitiates in England, Spain, and Australia. Sister

M. M. gave some copies of the conferences to a Sister M. M., and her superiors are having them copied and sent to all the houses of their congregation in that diocese. In this way they will reach nearly two thousand Sisters. It seems incalculable the amount of good that may be done by the conferences."

Likewise, letters written in a similar strain came from communities in Connecticut, Pennsylvania, Texas, Minnesota; from Australia and other places. All testify to the good work that the conferences are doing in the communities in helping souls on the path of greater perfection by a more and more intimate union with God.

The desires manifested in these letters, together with the wish expressed by those who, apart from the editor, were familiar with the facts, prevailed upon the latter, a brother of Sister Miriam Teresa, to prepare her written works for publication. Accordingly, though with great personal reluctance, he has addressed himself to this task, and begs the reader to excuse anything which may appear of a too personal nature.

In order that the reader may understand how these conferences came into existence and were distributed, the following brief notice of the life of Sister Miriam Teresa is presented.

The editor would take the reader, in retrospect, to the year 1901. On March 26th, in Bayonne, New Jersey, was born his sister, Teresa, the last of seven children. While not what might be termed a precocious child, she nevertheless manifested a rapidly maturing intellect, and entered, or rather scarcely could be prevented from entering, the primary school in the autumn of 1905. In a letter written shortly before her death, she notes that she remembers being conscious of possessing the use of reason before she was fully three years of age, and cites an incident in her life, occurring in January 1904, to substantiate this statement.

As valedictorian, she completed her grammar school education in January 1913, entered high school, and secured her diploma, with honors, in January 1917, being then not yet sixteen years of age. The next year and a half she spent in taking care of her mother during her mother's last illness until her death in November 1918. The following September, Teresa Demjanovich entered St. Elizabeth's College, Convent Station, New Jersey. During her college days she won the esteem of all by the manifestation of those qualities which later on endeared her to her companions in the novitiate. She received the degree of Bachelor of Literature, with highest honors, from St. Elizabeth's College, in June 1923. The following year she utilized her talents in imparting knowledge to God's children at St. Aloysius Academy, Jersey City, New Jersey. For many years she felt a call to the religious life, but it was not until the close of the year 1924 that God manifested clearly His will. She entered the novitiate of the Sisters of Charity at Convent Station, New Jersey, February 11, 1925. A coincidence which she considered noteworthy was that the day of her reception as a novice of the habit, and name in religion — May 17, 1925 — was the date of the canonization of St. Teresa, " The Little Flower of Jesus "; while the name she received was her own baptismal name, that of " The Little Flower," Teresa.

The conferences presented in this volume were written by Sister Miriam Teresa, while she was still a novice at Convent Station and at the request of her spiritual director, who recognized particular gifts in her. Writing later to him (August 7, 1926), she confessed: " I never knew what I was going to write or say, but when obedience imposed the task, He took care of everything."

With the approval of the Mother Superior, these conferences were used by the spiritual director in his weekly talks to the Sisters. Not until after Sister Miriam Teresa's death, though, was the authorship made public. The conferences were regarded so highly, that copies were sent to the different houses of the community. Convinced that the good contained in these writings should be brought to wider circles of religious, the director forwarded copies to Sisters in other sections of the country, from whom he received the responses already noted.

A very severe attack of tonsillitis in December 1926 was the forerunner of death. Our Lord's will, manifest in illness as well as in health, stayed the pen. The last four months of her life, Sister Miriam Teresa spent in St. Elizabeth's Hospital, Elizabeth, New Jersey, where, following an operation for appendicitis, she died, May 8, 1927.

Should the reception accorded this work indicate a desire for further compositions of the late Sister, it is the purpose to publish her other literary efforts, — poems and letters, as well as a biography.

Particular acknowledgment is due to Sister's spiritual

director, especially in the matter of the verification of
Scripture quotations; to the Rev. John J. Wynne, S.J.,
for his valuable helps and suggestions; to the Venerable
Mother M. Alexandrine and the Venerable Mother M.
Grata of St. Elizabeth's College for their gracious assistance in the preparation of this work; and to all others
who in any way contributed toward making the publication of this volume possible.

THE EDITOR

Immaculate Conception Seminary
Darlington, New Jersey
February 2, 1928

I. *The will of God: your sanctification*

GREATER PERFECTION

1. RELIGIOUS HUMILITY

"The Lord possessed me in the beginning of His ways" (Prov. viii, 22)

ONE of the important feasts of the Church is that of
"the Nativity of the holy Virgin Mary, whose glorious
life is the ornament of all the churches. Sprung from a
royal race, sprung from the seed of Abraham, from the
tribe of Juda, and from the noble lineage of David, Mary
shines forth to the world" (Antiphon 1 Vesp. of Feast
of Nativity of B.V.M.). This is she of whom Solomon
in prophetic vision sang: "Who is she that cometh forth
as the morning rising, fair as the moon, bright as the
sun, terrible as an army set in array?" (Cant. of Cant.
vi, 9). This is she, the peerless one, the powerful one,
the mighty woman God had in mind when denouncing
the serpent in the garden of Eden: "I will put enmities
between thee and the woman, and thy seed and her seed:
she shall crush thy head, and thou shalt lie in wait for her
heel" (Gen. iii, 15).

No wonder the Church rejoices with boundless joy
in this happy festival which is in truth the beginning of
our salvation. No wonder the Church shouts with exul-

tation in the Introit of the Mass of the Nativity of Our Lady: " Hail, holy Mother! giving birth to thy Child, thou didst bring forth the King, who ruleth the heavens and the earth forever and ever." Truly St. Anne in bringing forth the Morning Star brought forth through her the Sun of Justice, Christ, Who is our God. And if our joy be not so great as that of the Church, it is only because we do not understand the greatness of the mystery that has come to pass.

Because of the Word, Him " Whom the whole world availeth not to contain " (Gradual — Mass of Nativity of B.V.M.), Mary figured in the plan of creation from all eternity. She was to bear the Creator of all things; she was to bring forth Him Who made her, Who " being made man shut up Himself within her womb " (Gradual — id.). For this reason it is said of her: " The Lord possessed me in the beginning of His ways, before He made anything from the beginning. I was set up from eternity, and of old, before the earth was made. The depths were not as yet, and I was already conceived " (Prov. viii, 22–24). Ah, yes, Mary owes all her glory, all her marvelous privileges to her Divine Son, her Saviour and Redeemer and ours. From all eternity she alone, because of the dignity to which God was to raise her, was exempt from the curse of Adam by virtue of the anticipated merits of the Word. Her Immaculate Conception accounts for all her graces and dignities, her joys and sorrows. In itself it contains all her feasts, because the Lord possessed her from the beginning. Her nativity is so glorious only because of the splendor of her conception.

[4]

Some of us are too apt, however, in venerating the Blessed Virgin — and who among the creatures of God is deserving of higher honor? — to overlook one thing, very important, and recognized most clearly by Mary herself. She gave expression to this thought in her sublime hymn of praise and thanksgiving when she said: "He that is mighty hath done great things to me" (Luke i, 49). Why, we may ask? The answer comes back: "Because He hath regarded the humility of His handmaid" (Luke i, 48). Unlike Mary, we are too prone, in our admiration of the gifts, even the gifts we perceive in her, to forget the Giver, the bountiful Father of all. Mary never forgot. Mary never forgot because she was humble. It was this very humility that drew forth the Eternal Word from the bosom of the Father to repose Incarnate in the bosom of Mary. What an ineffable reward for profoundest humility! And now His delight is to be with the children of men, with us, for whom He is our sole hope of happiness and peace.

For us who are religious, who have left all things in the sole aim of seeking and finding in Him our fill of happiness and peace, must also be realized the truth of these words: "The Lord possessed me in the beginning of His ways" (Prov. viii, 22). They shall, if like Mary, we clearly understand and sincerely acknowledge that "He that is mighty hath done great things to me, and holy is His name" (Luke i, 49). Arriving at this truth, we shall have begun to quench our spiritual thirst in the bottomless well of humility, from which thereafter we can quaff deep, refreshing draughts, for "he that shall drink of the water that I will give him, shall not thirst forever " (John iv, 13).

Let us consider these great things. God created us. But for His loving thought of us, we should never have been. Do we appreciate the wonderful gift of life? God did more. He called us from earliest infancy to become His children by the grace of adoption. We were baptized, and received the gift of faith. We could just as easily have been born of semi-barbarous parents in the wilds of Africa, or of these super-civilized modern pagans. But God in His preventing mercy gave us the Church for our Mother. Have we ever thanked Him for this stupendous gift, lavishly bestowed? God did still more. He provided for us by means of a truly Christian and Catholic education that the virtues instilled into us at baptism might thrive and bring forth fruit. But for God's love, all this might just as readily never have happened. Even then God was not satisfied. God did yet more. He whispered to us " If thou wilt be perfect, go, sell what thou hast, and give to the poor, and come, follow me " (Matt. xix, 21). This, too, was not enough. We heard the call. We could have stopped our ears, and like the Jews of old, complained: " This saying is hard, and who can hear it? " (John vi, 61). In our blindness and pride we might have turned aside. Ah, but God's love for us knows no bounds. So He gave us the courage to leave all, father and mother and brethren, for His sake. What an excess of love! Surely " the Lord hath possessed me in the beginning of His ways " (Prov. viii, 22), for He had me in view from all eternity and counted out with generous hand the numberless benefits He was to pour out on me, a beggar.

In another sense, the novitiate is for you "the beginning of His ways" (Prov. viii, 22). He does not leave you in doubt as to what they are. He called you from the world that you might give yourselves wholly, unreservedly to His love and service. He called you to live the Christian life perfectly. "If any man will come after me, let him deny himself, and take up his cross daily, and follow me" (Luke ix, 23). And He adds: "Now, therefore, ye children, hear me: blessed are they that keep my ways. Hear instruction, and be wise, and refuse it not. . . . He that shall find me, shall find life" (Prov. viii, 32, 33, 35).

You came to religion to seek and to find — to seek life in its fullest perfection, and to find it in the one Being in Whom it exists perfectly, Christ Jesus, your Master and Model. To find this perfect life, you have only to keep the ways of the Lord. His way is the way of the cross which you must shoulder daily, cheerfully and courageously, if you wish to have realized in you the name of disciples. The way of the cross is the path of sacrifice and self-denial. Only a humble soul can walk this path securely. If you wish to understand something of Mary's humility, think of the sufferings she was called upon to endure — Joseph's doubts, the thirty-three years of anticipated agony with the shame of Calvary always before her, Bethlehem, the flight into Egypt, the pain of exile, the return, the loss of the divine Child, the sorrow of separation at the beginning of His public life, the passion, and the foot of the cross. She drank the chalice to the dregs with the ignominious death of her All, but it was humility that made it possible.

You must learn of Mary. At the start of your religious life, ponder over and assimilate these thoughts. Realize that everything you have you owe to God — life, faith, health, talents, virtue, vocation. Tell Him you know you are nothing. If nothingness has favors showered upon it, nothingness can, at least, and must, be grateful. But how can you manifest this gratitude? By carrying the cross willingly. For you the cross is the rule. Only a humble soul can shoulder this cross. The proud man will rebel. But remember, it is the keeping of the rule, not the donning of a distinctive habit, that makes you a religious. You came to religion to keep the ways of the Lord — to become perfect. Keep the rule perfectly and that is all you need do. This applies to every detail of the rule, not only to such as appeal naturally. Every detail of the rule is the will of God: you honor Him as much in keeping one as in keeping the other; you dishonor and offend Him in breaking one as in breaking another.

It may be to your liking to spend the prescribed time of prayer in chapel. You would not for a minute think of omitting it or shortening it. But with regard to — let us say — silence, your sense of obligation is not nearly so keen. You talk when you please and as long as you please. Now bear this in mind: the violation of that silence, that is by breaking it altogether, habitually, or by shortening the period of silence, that is, speaking without absolute necessity even one minute or one second before the time enjoined by rule, is just as serious in God's sight as omitting or shortening your prayers of adoration. The same thing holds true with regard to duties — recreating, retiring, eating, rising, meditating. You give God just as much glory in eating, or recreating, or going to bed according to the rule, as you do in meditating, in praying, in adoring before the tabernacle. Why? Because the rule in every detail is God's will. You cannot say you are doing God's will and pleasing Him when you choose what you like and do it, and at the same time omit what you dislike. If you wish to say in all sincerity, and you must if you are to fulfil the end of your vocation, " the Lord possessed me in the beginning of His ways," you must above everything else, and always, keep the rule, and keep it perfectly. Otherwise you are not a religious but a sham and a hypocrite in the sight of Almighty God.

Why does the Church sing of Mary that her glorious life is the ornament of all the churches? Because she obeyed the will of God in all things perfectly; she kept the rule as it was laid down for her in the decrees of Divine Providence. And she was able to do this because she was humble. If you, too, are to become the ornament of the churches, and you must since you aspire to be the spouses of Christ, learn humility of Him Who was meek and humble of heart, and of her who conceived her Creator, by humility calling down upon herself the overshadowing of the Holy Spirit. You who aspire to be the spouses of Christ, the spouses, remember, of a crucified Christ, are also called by humility to draw forth the

Word from the bosom of the Eternal Father to repose in the secret tabernacle of your hearts. To accomplish this end, the desire of Him whose delight is to be with the children of men, subordinate your will to His in all things, in the perfect keeping of the rule and the commands of superiors. So imitate her, " the Virgin Mother of God, whose nativity was the herald of joy to the whole world; since from thee arose the Sun of Justice, Christ our God, Who, destroying the curse, bestowed the blessing, and, confounding death, gifted us with life everlasting " (Antiphon at Magnificat 2 Vesp. Nativity of B.V.M.).

2. RELIGIOUS CHARITY

"Thou shalt love the Lord thy God with thy whole heart, and with thy whole soul and with thy whole mind — and — thou shalt love thy neighbor as thyself"

(MATT. xxii, 37, 39)

IN OUR first conference we saw that the foundation upon which our religious life is to be built is humility, which for us means in particular the cheerful and ready acceptance of the self-denial and mortification imposed by rule. It is the faithful observance of rule that makes us religious. Let us never forget this important truth if we wish to be religious after Christ's own Heart. But surely we had no other motive in view when entering religion than to fulfil, as perfectly as we could, the counsel of our Saviour: " If any man will come after me, let him deny himself, and take up his cross daily, and follow me " (Luke ix, 23). And by accepting generously from the very first this yoke, which by His grace, is sweet, and this burden, which by His love, is light, we disposed ourselves in all sincerity to repeat what the Church places on the lips of Our Blessed Mother: " the Lord possessed me in the beginning of his ways " (Prov. viii, 22).

But the true life of a religious does not consist in mere external conformity to rule. No. To act thus would be to place ourselves in the same class with the Pharisees, of whom Our Blessed Lord said: " This people honoureth me with their lips but their heart is far from me " (Mark vii, 6). We have a very striking instance of their conduct in this matter as narrated in the Gospel. We read that one of the Pharisees came to Jesus, tempting Him, saying, " Master, which is the great commandment in the law? " (Matt. xxii, 36). He asked this question, wishing to ensnare Jesus into a statement that would get Him into serious difficulty with one or the other of the numerous pharisaical sects. To the law which Moses had received from God, these men had added successively so many minor and minute details relative to its observance, that the original principles had long since been lost sight of, and they individually prided themselves on the scrupulous exactitude with which they conformed to the *letter* of these individual laws, even to the last comma. This was their religion. For the spirit of the law they had no regard. As long as they appeared holy and edifying in the sight of men, nothing else mattered. Indeed, they performed all their so-called good actions only to be seen by men. It was this hypocrisy that merited for them the scathing rebuke from the lips of the gentle Redeemer, when He called them " whited sepulchres, — full of dead men's bones " (Matt. xxiii, 27).

Our Lord knew their hearts, and the purpose of the question. By His answer He swept aside all their carefully planned human legislations, and restored and perfected the spirit of the Old Testament. " Jesus said to him: Thou shalt love the Lord thy God with thy whole heart, and with thy whole soul, and with thy whole mind. This is the greatest and the first commandment. And the second is like to this: Thou shalt love thy neighbor as thyself. On these two commandments dependeth the whole law and the prophets" (Matt. xii, 37–40).

By these words Christ clearly laid down the law of charity, of love, manifested in His own life from the moment of His conception. This principle of charity is the supreme law and quickening spirit of the New Covenant, taking precedence and holding absolute sway over the law of fear of the Old Dispensation. It is the heart, then, the intention, the will, that gives life to our works — not the exterior conformity to established custom, or the mere outward performance of matters of obligation. Or, as Christ said on another occasion, " It is the spirit that quickeneth: the flesh profiteth nothing " (John vi, 64).

Hence it is not sufficient for us to adhere solely and strictly to the letter of the rule. We must acquire its spirit, if we wish to be religious deserving of the name. And what is this spirit? It is the spirit of charity, of mutual love, — the vivifying spirit of every religious rule.

St. Paul in his epistle to the Ephesians stresses this thought most emphatically: " I . . . beseech you that you walk worthy of the vocation in which you are called. With all humility and mildness, with patience, supporting one another in charity, careful to keep the unity of the Spirit in the bond of peace. One body and one Spirit; as you are called in one hope of your calling " (Ephesians iv, 1–5).

[13]

As you well know, all the faithful form one body, with Christ the head. And this Supreme Lawgiver Himself pointed out in very definite terms the mark by which the body of His faithful would be known. "By this shall all men know that you are my disciples: if you have love one for another" (John xiii, 35). "Mutual love," says Abbot Marmion, "is the distinctive sign whereby the members of the Christian family are infallibly recognized, the sign given by Christ Himself. It is the same for the monastic family, and the true mark of the protection of Christ Jesus over a religious community is the charity that reigns between its members." "Charity," he continues, "is the cement that joins together its different members" (Christ, the Ideal of the Monk, Chapter iv, No. 5).

Charity is humility in blossom. It is more. It is the fruit of humility. Without humility there can be no charity. This is self-evident. The proud man loves neither God nor his neighbor; he loves only himself. All his actions, even his seemingly good ones, begin, develop, and end in himself. And self-love is neither love nor a virtue: it is superlative selfishness. Only the humble man is capable of real love that is not sentiment, but the strong, faithful, devoted love, supernatural love, the love Christ teaches in His gospel and above all in His life. And it is this life, this love, the essence of this life, that we try to perfect in ourselves by living the common family life of the community under a common rule, the expressed will of God.

Note that I have said "a common rule." The rule

was intended to be, and should be, common to all. But what happens only too often? Individual members, like the Pharisees in the Gospel previously quoted, set up individual rules for themselves. As was mentioned before, certain religious may choose for themselves certain points of rule to which they adhere because they feel so disposed; for example, the prayers of rule, or the appointed time before the tabernacle; and ignore other points, as silence or community recreation, because these do not coincide with their natural inclinations. What are they really doing? Like the Pharisees, they are setting up for themselves a code differing from the prescribed law, and if they persist in following out their own tastes they will eventually think it better to spend an hour in chapel than at recreation; to recreate during the time set aside for recollection; or to shorten the duties of obedience to follow out the fancies of their own imagination. And so, because they have set up their will for the will of God, and perverted His law, God will, little by little, allow them to fall. And all because of their pride. If pride, then self-love, and lack of charity.

Please remember that you came to religion not to develop individualism, but to lose it. In accepting a garb common to all the members of your community, you thereby renounced your rights to individualism, and gladly professed to follow the common life, to eat the common food, to do the common work, to sacrifice your interests for the common interests, to sacrifice your will to the common will, the will of God made known to you in the rule and the commands of superiors. The person who fails to live the common life, the family life, the community life with the community as prescribed by the rule in the spirit of the rule, " the cementing bond of charity," is a failure in religion, and does not possess the first idea of how to achieve the end supposedly had in mind when entering religion.

This divine charity which is not only of counsel but of commandment is one in its essence, yet twofold in its aim. It is a supernatural love directed toward God and through God to our neighbor. It is a supernatural love arising in God, born of " One God and Father of all, Who is above all, and through all, and in us all " (Eph. iv, 6). It is that " unity of Spirit in the bond of peace " (Eph. iv, 3), for which Christ in His sublime prayer to His Father on the eve of His passion prayed: " That they all may be one, as thou, Father, in me, and I in thee; that they also may be one in us " (John xvii, 21). For love is born of God and resteth not but in God. For love is God. And God is Life. And Life is Love.

This supernatural love, this life born of God, is the soul of the religious body, the community. Without it the body is only a corpse. How does this love, this " unity of the Spirit," this oneness of intention or will manifest itself? First, it is directed toward God in keeping the rule, which is the manifestation of His will, perfectly; not to be seen by men and esteemed thereby, but because His will is the Only Good toward which we should reach out, the accomplishment of which is the sole reason of our existence. A religious at the very beginning of his following of Christ, the Beloved of his soul, should in truth be able to apply to himself the words of his Spouse at His entrance into the world: " Behold I come . . . that I should do Thy Will, O my God . . . Thy law in the midst of my heart " (Ps. 39, 8–9).

Possessing this divine love in his heart, the religious must necessarily show great love for his brethren, and prove this love by the works of charity he performs for them. St. John says that the man who claims he loves God, yet hates his neighbor is a liar. Love is life. And life is activity. So love, if it be genuine, ever seeks new ways of reproducing itself. Remember, too, that the charity Christ wishes us to practise, especially in community life, is not only negative charity — that is to refrain from uncharitable thoughts, words, and acts — but above all positive charity — the doing of kindnesses toward our neighbor because in him we see the image of Christ, and what is more important, putting ourselves out in the doing.

If we really desire to know the measure of our love for God, we can easily determine its intensity and quantity by asking ourselves just how much we actually do by way of charity toward our neighbor. That does not mean the person toward whom you may naturally feel an attraction; one easily and cheerfully performs acts of natural virtue in an instance such as this. But we are speaking not of natural, but of supernatural virtue. What was it that Our Lord said? " If you love them that love you, what reward shall you have? Do not even the publicans this? But I say to you, love your enemies,

[17]

do good to them that hate you, and pray for them that
persecute and calumniate you: that you may be the
children of your Father who is in heaven, who maketh
his sun to rise upon the good and bad " (Matt. v, 46, 44,
45). According, then, to Our Lord's own words, you
are the children of your heavenly Father inasmuch as
you do your good works in the spirit of that same
Father, " who maketh his sun to rise upon the good and
bad." Does the sun of your charity diffuse its beams in
equal intensity of heat and light upon both the good,
those who are agreeable and striving to become perfect,
and upon the bad, those who are disagreeable and indifferent? You love God exactly as much as you love
this latter class. Remember love proves itself in deeds;
otherwise it is not love that springs from the heart, but
love that springs from the lips. Love such as this is not
love but a delusive echo protesting its fidelity in honeyed
phrases that are as " sounding brass and tinkling
cymbal " (I Cor. xiii, 1).

If, as St. Paul entreats, you are to " walk worthy of
the vocation in which you are called " (Eph. iv, 1), you
must support one another in charity in the spirit of your
rule. As exteriorly you form one body in the organiza-
tion of your religious community, so interiorly you must
be " one spirit, as you are called in one hope of your
calling " (Eph. iv, 4). If it is the soul that gives life to
the body, then it is only the cement of love, supernatural
love, that will preserve in your community " the unity
of the Spirit in the bond of peace " (Eph. iv, 3). Walk-
ing thus through life in the perfect love of God

and your neighbor, you will be that blessed " nation whose God is the Lord " (Ps. 32, 12); Who will pour on you in abundance the blessings of " the undefiled in the way: who walk in the law of the Lord " (Ps. 118, 1).

3. RELIGIOUS PERFECTION

"I give thanks to my God always for you, for the grace of God that is given you in Christ Jesus" (I Cor. i, 4)

OUR first conference was concerned with the necessity of living from the very start of our entrance into religion in a manner conformable to these words from the book of Proverbs: " The Lord possessed me in the beginning of His ways " (Prov. viii, 22). We saw then that if this truth were to be accomplished in us, we would have to submit cheerfully to the way of the Lord marked out for us — our rule. In our second conference we learned that it is not sufficient to live up to the letter of the rule. The Pharisees did that with regard to the law of God, and they were far from being found acceptable in His sight. We must strive to acquire what the Pharisees lacked, and for the lack of which they were so severely condemned by Our Lord: the *spirit* of our rule, the cementing spirit of charity. This fundamental law of love was expressed by Incarnate Love Himself: " Thou shalt love the Lord thy God with thy whole heart, and with thy whole soul, and with thy whole mind, and with thy whole strength; — and — thy neighbor as thyself " (Matt. xxii, 37–39).

[20]

You entered religion responsive to the invitation of the Son of Man: "If any man will come after me, let him deny himself and take up his cross daily, and follow me" (Luke ix, 23). Your presence here proves your generosity in heeding the call to perfection, for that is the meaning contained in these words of Our Lord. To become perfect, you must keep the rule perfectly; that is, strive to develop in your lives, with the help of God, the spirit of your rule, the bond of love in all its perfection. In other words, to keep your rule perfectly, you must keep the one commandment perfectly. "If any one love me," says Jesus Christ, "He will keep my word, and my Father will love him, and we will come to him, and will make our abode with him" (John xiv, 23). The word to be kept is the one commandment on which "dependeth the whole law and the prophets" (Matt. xxii, 40). The sole condition and reason for its observance is — "if any one love me." And who is more worthy of love than God, Infinite Love? The reward — beyond the understanding and power of man to conceive — is union with God. "My Father will love him, and we will come to him, and will make our abode with him." There is no possible doubt as to Our Lord's meaning here. "We will make our abode with him," that is, dwell with him continually, unite ourselves in the fulness of the Godhead to his soul, made to our own image and likeness, so that we two shall become one spirit. Do you begin to understand the sublime end of your vocation, an end not impossible of achievement, but desired with desire by your Divine Spouse Who has called you from the world for this one, only purpose? His promise of the reward, union with Himself, is infallible; but it depends on your keeping His word *perfectly*.

How are you to acquire this spirit of divine charity in the plenitude of perfection? Of ourselves we can do nothing, for we are unprofitable servants. Saint Paul, however, answers this question in his epistle to the Corinthians: " I give thanks to my God always for you, for the grace of God that is given you in Christ Jesus " (I Cor. i, 4). All grace, then, that is given us, all the graces we need for the fullest development of the life of the soul, are found in Christ Jesus, the fountain of grace, and flow into our souls through Him by the directing hand of the Father. Christ came on earth to lead men to the Father: " That all may be one, as thou, Father, in me and I in thee: that they also may be one in us " (John xvii, 21). You will attain to the Father, arrive at the union of love, only through Christ, Who is for you " the way and the truth and the life " (John xiv, 6). He is the Way that you must follow; the Truth that you must believe; the Life that you must possess.

What does this mean? It means that if you aspire to keep the *one* commandment perfectly, and this Christ expects you to do, you must put " on the Lord Jesus Christ " (Rom. xiii, 14) as the apostle tells us. How then are you to go about clothing yourselves with Christ? " Ask, and it shall be given you; seek, and you shall find; knock, and it shall be opened to you " (Matt. vii, 7). Ask. For what shall you ask? For one thing only, that for which Our Lord taught us to pray, " Thy will be done" (Matt. vi, 10). And what is this Divine Will for you? Again St. Paul has the answer ready. "This is the will of God, your sanctification" (I Thess. iv, 3). Asking for the accomplishment of this adorable Will, you shall certainly receive, "good measure, and pressed down,— and running over" (Luke vi, 38). Seek. Whom shall you seek? God, the First Beginning and the Last End. The beginning and the end of your creation, the cause and triumph of your existence. Whom shall you seek? The Father, by means of the Word Incarnate, Who for this very reason took upon Himself human flesh. "And I, if I be lifted up from the earth, will draw all things to Myself" (John xii, 32). Seeking God through Christ, you shall certainly find Unity in Trinity. Knock. Where shall you knock? At the door of Christ's Heart, His human Heart. How shall you knock? Gently, lovingly, persistently, by keeping His word. And so knocking, it shall be opened to you, for He tells us "I am — thy reward exceeding great" (Gen. xv, 1.) "My delights were to be with the children of men" (Prov. viii, 31). Truly you have cause to sing aloud with the Psalmist: "Let the heart of them rejoice that seek the Lord: seek ye the Lord and be strengthened; seek His face evermore" (Ps. 104, 3–4: Introit, Friday in Ember Week in September). And the echo of this your joy finds renewed expression in the words which the Church uses: "I rejoiced at the things that were said to me: we shall go into the house of the Lord" (Ps. 121, 1: Gradual, 18th Sunday after Pentecost).

Where is this house of the Lord which you are to enter

rejoicing? It is within you — it is your soul. " Know you
not," says St. Paul, " that you are the temples of God? "
(I Cor. iii, 16). And why do you enter? To find God;
for the apostle continues, " the spirit of God dwelleth in
you " (I Cor. iii, 16). To do God's will, to keep His word
perfectly, to clothe ourselves with Christ, all of which
are identical in meaning, you must give your soul an
opportunity to grow freely, unstintingly. You must
live a life " hid with Christ in God " (Col. iii, 3), " for
save Thou be with us, O Lord, we avail not so to live
as to be pleasing to Thee " (Oration, 18th Sunday after
Pentecost). Only when Christ is with us in all we think,
say, and do, even in the most trivial matters — and yet
hardly trivial, but rather sublime since He is their mainspring — are we living lives pleasing to the Father. This
is the work of a lifetime; it is the first and principal work
every religious, cloistered or uncloistered, has to perform;
it is the primary object and aim of every order and
community.

In order never to lose sight of this sublime task, you
should keep, therefore, like Mary your Mother and
model, these words in your heart, pondering over them
within you: " Let this mind be in you which was also
in Christ Jesus " (Phil. ii, 5). To have the same mind
with Christ, means to think in all things as He thinks;
to speak always as He would speak; to will, that is to do,
what He wills, what He wants done at all times; to desire ever only what He desires — His glory, your sanctification, and the sanctification and salvation of all mankind. A tremendous and exalted privilege this; and yet

[24]

it is but the true realization of the title "spouse" to which you all hope some day, God willing, to lay claim.

There are Catholics who pride themselves on being Catholics, yet who are such in name only, the sacrament of Baptism having enrolled them among the children of the Kingdom. Aside from that, religion has no part in their lives. Unfortunately, there are some "spouses" of Christ, who became entitled to the name on the day of their profession, the day of their second baptism, and who pride themselves on their exalted dignity, yet for whom the actual realization of their vocation clearly manifested in their condition of "spouse" means nothing, and has no part in their lives. These are so absorbed in striving to become excellent teachers, nurses, book-keepers, cooks, what not, that the affairs of the soul are relegated to a minor level, and eventually almost to oblivion. Christ looks in vain into such hearts to find His image reflected therein . . . a growing and daily increasing likeness to the Crucified. "O souls, whom I have espoused," He seems to sigh over them, "seek ye, therefore, first the kingdom of God, and His justice, and all these things shall be added unto you" (Matt. vi, 33). Why are you so solicitous about what you shall eat, or wherewith you shall be clothed? "Consider the lilies of the field, how they grow; they labor not, neither do they spin. But I say to you, that not even Solomon in all his glory was arrayed as one of these. And if the grass of the field. . . . God doth so clothe, how much more you, O ye of little faith?" (Matt. vi, 28–30).

It is just because they are lacking in faith that these

indifferent religious have become obsessed of the material and so pitiably blinded with regard to the spiritual, to their one true Good, Christ Jesus, Who weeps over them as He long ago wept over Jerusalem. " If thou also hadst known," He grieves, " the things that are to thy peace " (Luke xix, 42). This is the cutting lash that rips His Heart in jagged shreds, " thou wouldest not " (Luke xiii, 34). Can it be possible? What is it we see? A God sorrowing in the bitterness of rejected love over the wilful blindness of His creatures, His spouses. " My Beloved to me, and I to him " (Cant. of Cant. ii, 16). But " thou wouldest not." " We will come to him and will make our abode with him " (John xiv, 23), but " thou wouldest not." " My delights were to be with the children of men " (Prov. viii, 31), but " thou wouldest not." " Arise, my love, my beautiful one, and come " (Cant. of Cant. ii, 13), but " thou wouldest not." " This day thou shalt be with me in paradise " (Luke xxiii, 43), but " thou wouldest not." " Have I been so long a time with you, and have you not known me " (John xiv, 9), but " thou wouldest not."

Ah, no. " Thou wouldest not." But I, your God, *would* become a fool for your sake, a leper, a worm and no man, despised of men; hoping against hope that some day you who call yourselves My spouse would esteem it a privilege to become a fool for My sake. But no. That would cost something. That would hurt. And nature dislikes hurts. Out of love for you, My spouse, I gladly gave up heaven and came down to earth to suffer and labor that you, who by sin had become My enemy, might be redeemed.

And you, whom I chose to raise to the closest intimacy with Me — but you would not — find it too much to give up the baubles of earth for the true and lasting delights of heaven. Remember that " not every one that saith to me Lord, Lord, shall enter into the kingdom of heaven; but he that doth the will of my Father Who is in heaven " (Matt. vii, 21).

But, Lord, " we have left all things and have followed thee " (Mark. x, 28).

" All things? " In word, yes, in theory. Repeating this often, you delude yourself into thinking that you are fulfilling it in practice. Are you honestly, sincerely, striving to please Me alone in all things, even the very smallest? Are you giving Me alone the complete love of your heart, using all creatures — persons, places, things — only as I destined them for your use, that they should lead you to Me? You revolt at the thought that a bride, who has vowed fidelity to her bridegroom, should deliberately let her affections rest in another. It is perfectly wrong, you say; and so it is. And it is perfectly right for you, who are My bride, to let your affections, according to your estimation and actions, rest in a miserable creature, whom I drew out of nothing; and give to Me, your God, to Whom you vowed fidelity, to Whom you gave yourself absolutely body and soul that I might do with you as I chose, only second place, if that, in your heart. If you loved Me, you would think of Me as often as possible, " for where thy treasure is, there is thy heart also " (Matt. vi, 21). If you loved Me, you would visit Me in your spare moments. If you loved Me, you would think of Me first in every difficulty, in every temptation. But you come to Me for advice and consolation only after seeking it in vain from creatures. If you loved Me, you would exert yourself to become more like Me, so that with My vessel of election you could truthfully say, " The world is crucified to me, and I to the world " (Gal. vi, 14). How great, then, is your love?

God grant that this reproach may not apply in all its severity to any of you. Yet even some of you may be afflicted, perhaps, with the palsy of indifference, or sloth, or carelessness, or a purely sensual affection for some created object — yourself, too, for that matter. Whatever it is that is holding you back from seeking God alone, through Christ Jesus, His Son and your Master, be generous. Give it up for Him Who gave up His life for you. " Bring up sacrifices, and come into His courts " (Ps. 95, 8). Seeing your faith, and the desire henceforth to serve Him only, He will say to you as to the one who was sick of the palsy: " Arise and walk " (Matt. ix, 5). Since He is God, His words produce the result they signify. If each day you walk before Him holily, you shall become perfect, thanks to the " grace of God that is given you in Christ Jesus, that in all things you are made rich in Him " (1 Cor. i, 4–5) ; " Who through the Communion with Himself will make you to be sharers in His own supreme Godhead " (Secret of Mass of 18th Sunday after Pentecost).

4. PERFECT LOVE OF GOD

"And be renewed in the spirit of your mind, and put on the new man, who according to God is created in justice and holiness of truth" (EPH. iv, 23–24)

YOU have already seen how vital it is for the accomplishment of your vocation to acquire the spirit of your rule, the spirit of supernatural love. This can be achieved only by the grace of God that is given you in Christ Jesus, Our Lord. He clothed Himself with our humanity to bridge the void between the Infinite and the finite. He came upon earth not only as the Redeemer of mankind, but also as its incomparable Teacher. He willed to live in the world for thirty-three years to give us an example, to hold up before us an ideal.

Nor did He intend that the ideal should be viewed merely in the abstract, as something worthy of admiration, but hardly of imitation. Jesus Christ, God Incarnate, lived, and toiled, and suffered, and died, that you and I might know how He wishes us to live, and toil, and suffer, and die. He did vastly more than simply give us an example; He bought for us at the price of His blood all the graces we need to live the life He would have us lead. That is why we ask for all good gifts through His mediation. " If you ask the Father anything in My name, He will give it you " (John xvi, 23). That is why the Church in all her supplications to the Father

[29]

ends her prayer " Through Jesus Christ, Our Lord — *per Dominum Nostrum Jesum Christum.*" For us, Christ is the open door to heaven; we have but to enter if we so will.

I have just noted that Christ is the open door to heaven. I made a mistake: Christ *is* heaven. For Christ is God. And what is heaven? God. The beatitude of the blessed in heaven consists in their possession of God. Beatitude is perfect happiness. And happiness is what every soul craves, because it is the end for which it was created. Our happiness in this life — our imperfect beatitude — can consist in one thing alone: the possession of God, which for us means Christ. You will tell me that as long as you are in the state of grace you possess God; but this is not enough. According to your ideas it may be; according to Christ it is not so. The life of grace must be developed, perfected, as Christ intended it to be. " For I have given you an example, that as I have done to you so you do also " (John xiii, 15). And what did Christ do? " Father," He says, " I have glorified Thee on the earth; I have finished the work which Thou gavest Me to do " (John xvii, 4). We, too, if we are to be worthy followers of Christ, must glorify Him on earth, and finish the work He has given us to do. It is precisely in striving to finish this work that we shall glorify Him on earth.

What is this one work of such supreme importance? It is the answer to life. It is the first cry of the Incarnate Word on His entry into the world: " Behold, I come . . . that I should do Thy will, O my God; . . . and thy law in the midst of my heart " (Ps. 39, 8–9). Why did the Father send the Word upon earth? To sanctify men. So that the apostle truly says to us: " This is the will of God, your sanctification " (1 Thess. iv, 3). This can be done only in one way. We must be renewed in the spirit of our mind, and put on the new man, which is Christ Jesus, our God. To put on the new man means that the old man must be destroyed. The essence of Christ's teaching consists in living a supernatural life. The natural, then, must be overcome before the supernatural can be developed to its fullest perfection. Subduing nature is not an easy, nor painless procedure. Yet, it must and can be done. It must, because Christ demands it: " And whosoever doth not carry his cross and come after me, cannot be my disciple " (Luke xiv, 27). And it can. " Ask, and it shall be given you; seek and you shall find; knock, and it shall be opened to you " (Luke xi, 9). If you ask, you shall certainly receive. Our Lord's promise holds good always. " If you ask the Father anything in My name He will give it to you " (John xvi, 23). If we ask only for that which is dearest to His heart, that for which He labored and suffered while on earth, that which He yearns to see accomplished in every soul He has created — to see His own image reflected in the full splendor of its beauty — how can He do otherwise than speedily grant our prayer, which is His also? We must ask him then in all confidence to sanctify our souls.

For religious, this striving after perfection is a duty not slightly to be foregone. Speaking to Benigna Consolata, during the retreat which He ordered her to make in preparation for her death, Our Lord " instructed her concerning the obligations of a consecrated soul to become holy, not so much for her own sake, as for the increase of the glory of God. ' This is of obligation,' He said, ' and not left to free choice; thou and all the other religious are obliged thereto. But in what should this sanctity consist? In this, that thou ever strivest to become the living image of thy Bridegroom. Thou must always imitate Me and therefore in spirit ever look upon thy Jesus. For this imitation thou art to use no other means than the faithful observance of thy holy rule. If thou dost apply thyself to the faithful observance of thy rule, in the right spirit, it will not be difficult for thee to imitate Me in all things, but this requires a deep interior disposition. Count, if thou canst, thy actions of the day; if thou dost animate all with the interior spirit, what merits thou wilt amass until evening.' "

According, then, to Our Lord's own words, made known to this favored soul, to keep the rule in the right spirit, to imitate Him in all things, requires a deep interior disposition. And it is just by aiming to acquire this interior disposition that we shall divest ourselves of the old Adam and put on the new man, who is created in justice — that is sanctity — and holiness of truth. But, perhaps, you may not quite clearly understand what is meant by a disposition of soul. To be properly disposed, or, in other words, to have a proper disposition, simply means this: that we have the knowledge of that which God wishes done plus the firm and resolute intention of doing it. To have the intention does not consist in vaguely wishing for a thing, however good in itself; to have the intention means to be determined, to will, to struggle, to fight. The trouble with a great many religious is that they do not possess the knowledge of the chief obligation of their state; not understanding, they cannot, of course, efficaciously desire that of which they are ignorant: namely, their own perfection. Thus they are utterly lacking in the prime essentials laid down by Our Lord himself — the proper disposition. With others, however, the knowledge is evident.

What then is their chief difficulty? They are wanting in a firm and resolute intention. Their will is weak; they recoil at the thought of the sacrifices they will certainly be called upon to make. They yield to nature and disdain the promptings of grace. Foolish mortals! How great is their blindness! They are fettered by pride and realize it not. They shrink from sacrifice because they rely on their own strength, forgetting that nature cannot be conquered by nature, but by grace alone. This grace is in Christ Jesus, their Spouse, Who purchased it for them by untold sufferings, Whose whisper in the depths of their soul they thereby reject. The guilt of such as these is great; ignorance may excuse the former class. To turn one's back on the wounded, pleading Saviour; to close one's ears to the voice of the Holy Spirit — what ingratitude, what folly! They forgot that to whom much has been given much shall be required.

It is not necessary, then, to feel an intense desire for perfection. Knowing that God demands it of you by the very fact of your call to the religious life, and being fully resolved to fulfil the will of God with the help of His grace, you can hinder your advance in putting on the new man only by your deliberate turning back, your giving up the task. He could not ask less. He asks only the essential for the ordinary accomplishment of any work whatever. Without coöperation, cheerful and sustained, nothing even in the way of temporal affairs can be brought to a successful close.

Thinking in the same strain, the holy Thomas of Kempis has clearly said: " Blessed is he who understandeth what it is to love Jesus, and to despise himself for the sake of Jesus. We must leave what is beloved for the sake of the Beloved; for Jesus will be loved alone and above all things. The nature of thy Beloved is such that He will not admit of a rival; but He will have thy heart for Himself alone, and sit as a King upon His own throne " (Imitat. II, 7). This is the full meaning of the second petition of the *Our Father*: " Thy Kingdom come " (Luke xi, 2). And the *Our Father*, remember, is God's own prayer. So that in trying to imitate the Bridegroom of your soul, you are doing exactly what He wills, in the manner He wills it, and laboring to make His sufferings fruitful in their application. You yourself realize how it cuts, when, after having, at a great cost, done a kindness to one you love, the act is not appreciated and even despised. It is the same with Our Lord. Only the pain is infinite. He has a human heart, and loves with a human love. How His Heart must be gashed by the wounds of ingratitude inflicted by His indifferent spouses!

If only religious deeply realized that the Spouse of

their soul is not only God but man besides, what a difference this would make in their lives! Christ Jesus, Who has loved each one of you with a love of predilection, is a living human being, the Man-God, who loves with a divine and human love. It was for this that He came down to earth — to win the love of His creatures. The Old Dispensation was a law of fear; the New Dispensation, the perfect fulfilment of the Old — " I am not come to destroy, but to fulfil " (Matt. v. 17), is the law of love. Christians are to worship God with a reverential love. That is the one and only commandment laid down by the great Teacher. Yet " the fear of the Lord is the beginning of wisdom " (Ps. 110, 10), says the Psalmist. Are we then to forget the majesty of God entirely? Certainly not. We acknowledge the majesty of God best by acknowledging in His sight our own nothingness. We proclaim our nothingness in a practical way by submitting our will to His in everything — especially in the manner of our worship (using " worship " in a restricted sense). God wishes from us the adoration of love — pure, disinterested, unselfish love; a love that seeks not any created thing in which to rest, but God alone. " Thou hast created us for Thyself, O God, and our hearts are ever restless until they find rest in Thee," says St. Augustine (Confess. I, 1).

Love is the only thing God asks from us. After all, that is not surprising. We ourselves crave one thing alone — love. This yearning of our souls is but an imperfect reflection of the intensity of the desire for love, for the love of His creatures, which is found in God; for the soul

[35]

is made to the image and likeness of God. The beginning of our wisdom is the love of God. Love does not exclude fear; it contains it in its essence. But the fear born of love is not the slavish, abject fear of the Jews — the fear born of the dread of punishment. The fear born of love is the holy, fruitful fear that dreads to displease the Beloved just because He is the Beloved, and alone worthy of affection and supreme adoration. And if we do not possess this love, it is because we do not understand what it is to love Jesus; we do not really understand what love really means. And note this well: without a deep, personal love for the sacred humanity of Our Lord, you will advance very little on the path of perfection. You will lag very far behind the Bridegroom.

If, then, you wish to be renewed in the spirit of your mind, and put on the new man, Christ Jesus, your God, you must combat self. You can never overcome self save by the grace of God which is in Jesus Christ. This grace will be given in proportion as you coöperate with the inspirations of the Holy Ghost. You will not be able to coöperate efficaciously, unless you love. To conquer nature, to imitate Christ, a strong selfless love, a tender, personal love for your Spouse is necessary. Why is this so, and how can you acquire this love?

Man, as he is created by God, needs companionship. " It is not good for man to be alone " (Gen. ii, 18), God said, so He made him a helpmate, Eve. The word of God has not changed in the course of ages; neither has man's nature. Even religious crave companionship, for we are men, not angels. It is here that so many religious go

astray. They feel in themselves this need for companionship — a legitimate need — since it has been implanted
in them by God Himself. But — and this is the important thing — they do not satisfy this legitimate craving
in a legitimate way. They seek and find their support in
creatures, instead of in all things seeking and finding
God alone. Being consecrated to the service of the Almighty, they are vessels of election, chosen by God Himself from all eternity to accomplish on earth as perfectly
as human beings can, what is fulfilled perfectly by the
angels and saints in heaven — the rendering to Him
eternal honor, glory, praise, thanksgiving, and love. To
them has been accorded the wonderful privilege of singing with the four and twenty ancients prostrate before
the throne of the Most High: " Salvation to our God,
who sitteth on the throne, and to the Lamb " (Apoc.
vii, 10).

Such is the end of their holy vocation; to seek and to
find God; to perfect in themselves the image of their
Bridegroom; to offer to God by a life of perfect self-
abnegation all the homage that is His due, which is denied Him by so many of His creatures. Instead of thus
fulfilling the *one* commandment perfectly, by seeking
the companionship of the Well-Beloved of their soul,
preferring His good pleasure above all else, these foolish
virgins tarry in sleep and forgetfulness outside the bridal
chamber, with no oil in their lamps, because the unruly
affection for creatures has dried them up. But recall:
" And at midnight there was a cry made: Behold the
Bridegroom cometh, go ye forth to meet Him " (Matt.

xxv, 6). " And they that were ready went in with Him
to the marriage and the door was shut " (Matt. xxv, 10);
for they that were invited to the marriage were called
even by the son of the King — and they would not come.
" The marriage indeed is ready, but they that were invited were not worthy " (Matt. xxii, 8).

It is certain that you love Our Lord too much ever to
cause Him this great grief. But you must go on increasing in love, otherwise the source will dry up. Love feeds
only on sacrifice. If you feel that your love is not as
strong as it should be, there is only one reason for its
weakness — sacrifice has been neglected. Here again let
me remind you that love for the Spouse of your soul is
not a matter of sentiment, but of will. It makes no difference how you " feel "; but it makes all the difference in the world how you " will." If, then, you wish
to acquire a strong, devoted, pure love for Jesus Christ —
and this is essential, if you wish to follow in His footsteps, by putting on the new man who " is created in
justice and holiness of truth — " (Eph. iv, 24) — you
must first be resolved to do His will in all things, even
the most trivial, and unseen by men.

Look to the intention with which you do everything;
strive to act always from a motive of pure love; that is,
do all just to please Him alone. This is not an easy matter, for though one may very easily say this with his lips,
God judgeth the heart. Do you know when you do all
from pure love of God? When in all things, those you
like and especially those you dislike, you attend to the
least details with the greatest possible care, doing all as

perfectly as you know how; when you are not cast down
by criticism nor puffed up by praise; when you are cheerfully ready to stop *instantly* anything you may be doing, and with equal readiness and minute attention to
take up another task not half as agreeable (that means
without making a face, even interiorly) ; when you are
scrupulously careful to will only what He wills, and refrain from offending Him in the smallest things; when
you honestly confess that you think more of the opinion
which God has of you than of the opinion of men (and
this is proved not by words but by acts) ; in a word,
when God, and God alone, means everything to you, and
creatures, above all, yourself, mean absolutely nothing.
No doubt some of us have a little work to do on that
score! But " now is the acceptable time, now is the day of
salvation " (II Cor. vi, 2). This is the hour of life that
has been given to us to achieve this end. Let us use it well,
" for the night cometh when no man can work " (John
ix, 4). And cultivating Christ Jesus as your companion,
your friend, your father, your lover, you will use this
moment of life as He intended you to; but a good will
and sacrifice are necessary. Since the measure of your love
is the measure of your good will, beg Him constantly to
strengthen your will; do so especially after Holy Communion. If you really will, you shall certainly be renewed in the spirit of your mind, and will " put on the
new man, who according to God is created in justice and
holiness of truth " (Eph. iv, 24).

5. PERFECT PURITY OF INTENTION

"But be ye filled with the Holy Spirit, . . . singing and making melody in your hearts to the Lord" (EPH. v, 18-19)

YOU will recall that according to the writings of Our Lord's " Little Secretary," Benigna Consolata, it is a matter of obligation to every religious to conform himself to his crucified Spouse; to develop clearly in his soul the image of the Bridegroom. This work should occupy his first and constant attention, for it is the special duty of love assigned him by God, when He called him from the world to devote himself to His service. And to devote oneself to anything whatsoever means to give oneself up to it heart and soul. Worldlings devote themselves to a multitude of interests; with some it is the accumulation of a fortune; with others, the desire for fame in some particular field; with a third class, a complete absorption in self-seeking, in pleasure.

Whatever the object on which they have fixed their fancy, they pursue it diligently, " for the children of this world are wiser in their generation than the children of light " (Luke xvi, 8). You know very well that to attain their ends they do not spare themselves any sacrifice. He who desires a fortune or a name spends many a sleepless night in devising schemes for its achievement, and gives up many an hour of even necessary relaxation. He who gives himself up simply to the enjoyment of this world's goods, who spends all his time in exerting himself to reap the questionable benefit of a so-called " good time," very often sacrifices his own health, and what is more, his real happiness and peace of soul. So that to arrive at the goal of any desired achievement, both persistence and sacrifice are indispensable. If — as in the case of all religious — the goal is God, what energy and fidelity in self-abnegation should not be evinced!

But all these words about sacrifice — which means pain of some sort, and self-denial, which in the end means death to self — do not sound very pleasing or cheerful to human nature. That they do not sound very pleasing is only to be expected. Nature is pleased only when her demands are satisfied. The more we satisfy the demands of nature, the more demands she will make, until some day we awake to the realization that we are the absolute slaves of our own passions and whims, having practically no power to resist them because we despised their presence in their early beginnings as trifles hardly worthy of notice. The very fact that all this insistence on the subjugation of nature is not pleasing to nature, certainly makes it far from being a cheerful subject to it.

But we must ever remember that nature is another name for the animal part of us, and that there is something higher than the animal in each of us, namely, the soul, the spirit, made to the image and likeness of God; redeemed by the infinite sufferings of God made Man, and now stained by the indelible dye of His precious Blood; the soul, destined by the power of grace for intimate union with the Father, from Whom it received the breath of life, and thus destined to become partaker in His very Divinity. Did not Our Lord promise, " We will come to him and will make our abode with him? " (John xiv, 23.) And the one condition he laid down — He could not ask less — " If any one love Me " (John xiv, 23). On the measure of our love, then, is going to depend the measure of our conquest of nature. Love of self is very deeply ingrained in man, and it can be overcome only by love — a higher, purer, worthier, more exalted love, the sole love to be sought — love of God.

It is a truth that the best way to root out a bad habit is to set to work to acquire the contrary good one. That is the principle we shall apply here. The bad habit to fight against is love of self; the good one to be put in its place is love of God. The point to be remarked is this: that we are not to be occupied so much with self — we do that only too expertly, continuously, and quite perfectly, somewhat like breathing, for example — but, and this is very important, we are to occupy ourselves with thoughts of God. It is going to involve a struggle, because the mind is ordinarily occupied with a thousand and one vain and useless ideas, distractions of all kinds that creep into our minds almost without our knowing how they reached there. You all know how difficult it is at times to keep your mind on some study — history, for example. You are just crossing the Delaware with Washington, when the first thing you know the ice-blocks have disappeared, and you are figuring up the days to Christmas, and wondering with what the family is going to surprise you.

But if you ever expect to get to Trenton with the General, you will have to return to the ice-blocks, or someone else will share all the glory of the victory. If you have so much trouble in acquiring a few historical facts, why expect a miracle when there is a question of learning a little more about God?

With most people, prayer is easy, and really the best thing in the world, and the only essential — until the sugar plum of consolation is withdrawn, and then the tide turns, " Oh, what is the use of praying? My prayers are never heard anyway. And, besides, I am no better for it. In fact, I am worse. I used to be able to pray, and to keep my thoughts from running around, but now — I might as well give up as try to remain in God's presence only to show Him irreverence." Reasoning thus, these poor deluded ones work themselves the greatest harm at the very time that God wills to do them the greatest good. They were willing to serve as long as they received an immediate reward. But the minute God wished to test their loyalty and courage, they showed the white feather. To such as these apply the words addressed by Our Lord to the ruler whose son was sick at Capharnaum: " Unless you see signs and wonders you believe not " (John iv, 48).

Why? Because they were ready to conquer self, and did truly begin in earnest; they earnestly strove to think of God and holy things, whenever their work permitted them a free moment, and, rather to their surprise, they found it not half as hard as they expected; in fact, it was very sweet, and they felt at last that they were really becoming good. Then something happened; what had formerly been agreeable and easy suddenly became bitter and difficult. To try to keep the thoughts fixed on God was an almost insupportable burden; distractions of all sorts abounded; temptations heretofore unknown began to torment. Just because they were forced to realize that one must earn even one's spiritual bread by the sweat of one's brow, they threw up their hands and did just what the devil was waiting for, with the discouraged " I am through. This spiritual life was never meant for me; I was a fool even to think of beginning. This business of seeking God always may be designed for religious in a cloister, but it was never meant for those engaged in an active life."

How absurd! Yes, " unless you see signs and wonders you believe not " (John iv, 48). While God was doing the work, and you were enjoying the fruits of His labors, everything progressed splendidly, but the minute you were put to the test, and asked in return to do a little work yourself, the tune of your song changed entirely. If you know that without work, and hard work at that, you cannot acquire a thimbleful of secular knowledge — a good deal of which you will sooner or later forget — and yet spend an enormous effort in so doing; why argue differently because the knowledge to be gained is spiritual? Nothing really worth anything is ever acquired without an effort; and ordinarily the more we prize the object we wish to attain, the greater and more earnest the effort we put forth. Now, it is hardly necessary to mention that of all things worth striving for, God, the one Supreme Good, the First Cause and Final End of all created beings, should hold chief place. If men in the world do not begrudge sacrifice and struggle in order to gain a miserable bauble, we, who are religious, should certainly stop at nothing in order to attain God Himself. Remember again, it is the special end of our vocation.

This is what it means to be " filled with the Holy Spirit " (Eph. v, 18), of which St. Paul speaks; to seek God persistently, in season and out of season, in the midst of hope or fear, in temptation, in darkness, in doubt, in vexation, in difficulties spiritual and temporal, in sickness and in health. A soul that is truly filled with the Spirit of God, the Holy Spirit, the spirit of patient and trustful submission to the will of the one Supreme God, cries out at all times and in all places: " My heart is ready, O God, my heart is ready: I will sing and rehearse a psalm " (Ps. 56, 8). For " the eyes of all hope in Thee, O Lord; and Thou givest them meat in due season. Thou openest Thy hand, and fillest with blessing every living creature " (Ps. 144, 15–16). In truth, everything that comes from the hand of God, every single circumstance of our lives, is a blessing of Almighty God, which He permitted to happen with one only end in view: our sanctification. But we do not see it that way, because we are filled, not with the Spirit of God, but with the spirit of indifference, the spirit of sloth, the spirit of self-love, the spirit of laxity, the spirit of the world. Had we really the spirit of the children of the Father, we should long since have advanced very far on the path of perfection, because all things work together for our greater good. What do worldlings do when their plans fail and troubles of all kinds arise? They rebel exteriorly and interiorly against the judgments of God, Who in His merciful wisdom sees that these things would not be for their advantage. But acting thus, they try to establish their human reason and judgment as superior to the Divine, and instead of taking the trial as a blessing, and as a means of drawing closer to God, they turn it into a curse by their worldly-wise folly, and only increase their sins and the punishment due them.

What about religious in a like circumstance? They may be given a command which they find hard to obey; they may be beset by temptations for which they themselves are responsible, because of the absence of self-denial in their lives; they may meet with failure in their works; they may meet with misunderstanding in their superior; they may be worried about affairs at home and abroad — and quite often these are of their own and the devil's creation under the widespreading cloak of a misdirected charity. These and a hundred other things may harass and vex them. And how do these religious, who have professed to follow the Master, then act? Very much like worldlings, I fear. If they do not openly refuse to obey the repugnant command, they obey exteriorly only, inwardly fussing and fuming, and making no attempt to bring their wills into submission to the will of God. Obedience such as this is no obedience at all, and will bring down on them the severe judgment of God, for the Lord judgeth the heart. This does not mean that one is going to find every command pleasant; nor does it mean that one cannot do, in a cheerful and willing manner, work that is naturally repugnant. On the contrary; to obey willingly for the love of God, when the thing commanded is hard to weak man, is the cream of obedience and the strongest proof we can offer to God of the sincerity of our love. It is just because a real love for God is wanting to these religious that they rebel and murmur. And they act the same in the other instances cited — for they are not filled with the Holy Spirit. And you know the name of the father of all rebels.

St. Paul warns us on this very point: " See therefore, brethren, how you walk circumspectly," he says, " not as unwise, but as wise; redeeming the time, because the days are evil. Wherefore become not unwise, but *understanding what is the will of God* " (Eph. v, 15–17). If only we could make ourselves realize that the will of God orders and directs every moment of our lives, we should become saints before we knew it. For sanctity does not consist in visions and revelations, but in the perfect conformity of the human will with the Divine. This is not easy, for the liberty of our free will is our dearest possession. For this reason also it is the choicest gift that we can offer to Almighty God. And to bring that will into submission requires persistence and sacrifice — a constant, resolute effort in the monotony of daily tasks, and amid frequent failures; a daily struggle to conquer and subdue self. Only one thing in the world is strong enough to overcome love of self — I am speaking from a supernatural viewpoint always — and that is love of God. All grace has been given us in Christ Jesus, our Mediator with the Father, who yearns to pour out upon us the

abundance of gifts He bought at the price of His precious
Blood. But without our coöperation He can do nothing,
for there is one thing which even God will never take
away from us, and which He, so to speak, respects, and
that is our free will. We are sanctified in precisely the
exact proportion in which we will to attain sanctity, in
which we will to submit to God's action in us.

As noted before, it is easy enough to submit when God
makes the spiritual path smooth and delightful by giving us an abundance of sweetness and consolation —
when we have feelings of sensible devotion. That is when
we make generous resolutions, persist in prayer and mortifications, and regret the time we are forced to give to
active labor. Then it is that we unconsciously take complacency in ourselves, for we feel that at last we are making progress in the spiritual life, and have entirely lost all
relish for the things of earth. We do not understand that
God sends us this sensible fervor, because we are not yet
strong enough to bear the things of the spirit in a purely
spiritual manner; that this consolation is a concession,
although a very necessary concession, to our weakness.
It is the way God entices souls to abandon the delights
of the flesh for the greater and only real joys of the spirit.

But in order that God may strengthen the soul, and
wean it away from any admixture of sensible pleasure,
that He may unite it more closely to Himself — for remember, God is a pure spirit — He has to feed it with the
dry crust of desolation and temptation. To do anything,
rather than pray and perform spiritual exercises, is then
a pleasure, though to do anything at all is a torture.

Everything is hateful. We are disgusted with ourselves and with all around us. We feel as if we would like to eat people alive: only being polite, we do not do it. But this feeling is not a hindrance. Even St. Teresa felt that way at times. Only the sad thing is this: instead of continuing to seek God in the desert, into which He has been pleased to lead us, by faithfully keeping up our mortifications, giving the customary time to prayer, performing all our spiritual exercises with exactness, executing our active work with fidelity, we do just what the devil desires: we give in to our feelings. Giving in here means giving up. Do you know why we give up? Because we are not humble. We feel that our service is not pleasing to God, whereas, the truth of the matter is that it is not pleasing to ourselves; and since it is hard — and nature does not like hard things — we yield to nature.

Oh, if you would only realize that it is in seeking God in the midst of aridities that you sing and make " melody in your hearts to the Lord " (Eph. v, 19). Crushed violets, you know, smell sweetest. " My thoughts are not your thoughts, nor your ways my ways, saith the Lord " (Isaias lv, 8). And our infallible guarantee that we are pursuing His way, fulfilling His will in our regard, lies in the very fact that that way is one excessively displeasing to nature. It is the way He has chosen for us to root out self in the *quickest* possible manner, and indeed, the *only* possible manner. But in our pride, our will refuses to yield to His, because we are blind. Only the humble have clear vision, and the more humble they become, the clearer becomes their vision. It often happens that even

when we are told what the trouble is, and what course
we are to pursue, the devil stirs up that accursed pride
still further, and we refuse to obey, arguing that the
director does not understand our case — it is so different
from all others! Of course, we understand ourselves perfectly. What sick person is there that does not think he
knows better how to prescribe for himself than the physician who has ordered a bitter medicine? Like the Jews
of old, " upon the rivers of Babylon, there we sat and
wept: when we remembered Sion " (Ps. 136, 1). We
should like to remain with Peter on Thabor forever.
" Lord, it is good for us to be here " (Matt. xvii, 4).
God, however, knows better. We forget that the glory
of Thabor lasted only for a moment, and Gethsemani, a
lifetime. We forget, and the serpent lends hissing assistance, that we promised to follow the Master, Who in-
sisted time and time again: " Follow me " (Matt. xvi,
24). That following leads in one direction — up the
mountain of Calvary.

Yet we delight in calling ourselves His spouses, and
expect in heaven the reward of spouses. Your Bridegroom was crucified. Are you? In so far as you are crucified, dead to self, will the image of the Beloved be un-
veiled in your soul, will you " put on the new man, who
according to God is created in justice and holiness of
truth " (Eph. iv, 24). Then will you " be filled with the
Holy Spirit, . . . singing and making melody in your
hearts to the Lord, giving thanks always for all things,
in the name of our Lord Jesus Christ, to God and the
Father " (Eph. v, 18–20).

[50]

II. *The Sacrifice of the Mass: the greatest means of sanctification*

6. THE HOLY SACRIFICE, OUR STRENGTH

"Put ye on the armour of God . . . in all things taking the shield of faith'
(EPH.vi, 11, 16)

W E HAVE been studying the necessity of making our lives conform to the image of the crucified Spouse, if we wish to attain to the end of our vocation, and walk worthy of the calling God has marked out for us. To clothe ourselves with Christ is the object in view, which, with the help of God's grace purchased for us by our Divine Lord, we aspire to achieve more or less perfectly. To so vest ourselves with Christ, we must divest ourselves of self — a painful procedure. One thing alone is strong enough to overcome love of self, and that is love of God. The more we advance in the love of God, the more we shall conquer nature; and conversely, the more we persist in subduing self, the farther we shall advance in the love of God. For as we approach nearer to God the more ardent is our love; and as we love God with the will, this statement simply means that we progress in sanctity according as we will to coöperate with the working of the Holy Ghost in our soul. And the earnestness with which we will our sanctification is going to depend on the measure of our faith. And as we believe, so shall it be done to us. " Be of good heart, daughter, thy faith hath made thee whole " (Matt. ix, 22). And she but

[53]

touched the hem of His garment! A look into the Gospel will convince us that Our Lord made faith in Him an absolute necessity for the cures He effected. And we, too, are sick with divers diseases — we are the blind, the deaf, the dumb, the halt, the maimed, the crippled of today. Only when we shall have put on Christ shall we become whole. And our healing can be wrought only through faith in the Divine Physician. So we must see to it that our faith in Him is healthy and vigorous, else our spiritual life will be crippled and infirm.

The virtue of faith is given us in Baptism, but not in its plenitude — only in its germ. The seed requires careful and constant nurturing if it is to develop into a hardy plant, capable of withstanding the winds and storms of life. God has given us in the Holy Sacrifice, the sacraments, and prayer, the means of developing this faith to a perfect maturity. These means have been at our disposal since we came to the use of reason. Why, then, is our faith so weak, so inconstant, so irresolute? Why is our spiritual life still in its infancy? The answer is obvious. We have not made proper use of the means.

You will notice that the instruments that are to be employed in the culture of our faith are the ones the Church holds out to us for salvation and sanctification. This is necessarily so. The Christian who is perfect differs from the Christian who is imperfect only in this: — (but what a difference!) — the latter possesses the germ of life; the former, the fruits. The latter has buried his talent in the ground; the former has traded with his to the utmost advantage. And to make good use of our talent, to cultivate perfectly our faith, means exactly the same as to cultivate perfectly our spiritual life, or to clothe ourselves with Christ. By putting on Christ we live the life of Christ; that is, we practise all the virtues perfectly. Or rather, we do not then live at all, for God Himself lives in us. The conclusion to be inferred is this: in striving to perfect myself in one virtue, I correspondingly strengthen all the others, for the soul is a simple substance, and whatever food is given it, invigorates the entire spiritual being.

Christ is the cornerstone of this spiritual edifice of ours, the temple of the soul; and our faith in Him is the foundation. If the house is to be raised to its greatest possible height and beauty, the foundation must be very deep. The house must be built on rock, not on sand. With a sandy sub-structure, the building sways with every wind that blows, and trembles at the rattling of every vehicle. With a rock-bottom, the temple faces the storm intrepid and secure. Let us then stop a minute to examine foundations.

Before we begin we must understand clearly the full significance of the virtue. Faith is our unconditional belief in the veracity of God. It must be unconditional — there can be no limitations attached. Otherwise the integrity of the virtue is denied, and an impaired faith, an incomplete faith, is no faith at all. This faith in God has been bestowed on us by God Himself in the sacrament of Baptism. Mark well: it was bestowed, that is, given freely, conferred without merit. In other words, it is a gift, the gift of gifts. Here is generally where the trouble begins for the majority of souls. Most of us are too prone to take our faith as a matter of course, something to be expected in the natural order of events, almost as if we had a right to it. Accustomed to look at the virtue in this light, we pay very little attention, if any, to its growth. Not that we do not make acts of the virtue daily, nor practise our faith according to the teaching of the Church. We do; but just the same, our faith is not as flourishing as it should be, more the pity! We have grown up in the faith, but it has not grown up with us. Why? Because we have not made good use of the means at our disposal.

There is the fundamental reason why in the very act of using the means, we have been abusing them. It comes from the habitual attitude of mind with which we regard the faith. We forget that it is a gift, a gift to which we have no title, to which we can lay no claim, the overflow of God's bounty on sinful man. Forgetting the gift, the natural consequence follows: we forget to return thanks; we are ungrateful. Ingratitude of our fellow men cuts us, and cuts us deeply. Yet we are but men, and thereby are punished justly for our own misdeeds. If we feel hurt, let us remember the countless times we have inflicted pain on another. Calling this to mind will take out the sting. But God has never hurt anyone. From eternity He has loved us with an everlasting love, and unceasingly has done us good. Yet only all too often we have replied to this tender love of the heavenly Father by rendering evil for good. " If I have spoken evil, give

testimony of the evil; but if well, why strikest thou
Me?" (John xviii, 23.) We strike Jesus a cruel blow
every time we fail to say "Thank You"; or say it half-
heartedly, for the sake of form. We take care to give at
least a lip "thank you" to one who has done us a kindness. We do not wish men to consider us impolite, or ill-
bred. But no matter how heavy the veneer of polish may
seem to be, our real character shows itself when we are
not on parlor inspection, when we are taken off-guard in
the midst of the family circle. Then one can readily see
whether we are civilized interiorly, or just on the surface.
In the family of God's children I wonder how many of
us are barbarians!

Oh, if we could begin to appreciate the marvelous
treasure entrusted to our care, how different would not
our lives be? Try to imagine for a moment what it would
mean to be without the faith — no infallible guide; no
Church; no sacraments; no Mass; no Real Presence; little
or obscure knowledge of God; no real understanding of
the reason of our existence — hence revolt at the sorrows
and trials of life; hence very often, despair. There are
millions of souls today who are living in utter ignorance
of the truth; millions who know nothing of God as He
really is, or of Christ; millions who have never been
baptized. But for the mercy of God, but for His love of
predilection, you might have been one in those millions.
Woe to us if we do not make every effort to unearth
this treasure entirely; if we do not cherish as we ought
this pearl of great price. Unto whom much has been
given, from him much shall be demanded. Unless we

are watchful, some soul may rise up on that last dread day, and, pointing an accusing finger at us say, "If I had been given the graces you wasted, I should not be where I am now." Though God gives every man grace sufficient for salvation, yea, for sanctification, still, will not the abundance of helps we have received, weighed in the balance of our niggardly coöperation, give some lost soul opportunity for complaint? And if, as the Gospel tells us, we shall have to render an account for every idle word uttered, how much more severe the judgment for the opportunities cast aside, or only half grasped!

Of the three great instruments offered us for our sanctification, for the perfection of our faith, the Holy Sacrifice is unquestionably the greatest. It is our use of the Mass, as a means of strengthening our faith, that we shall now consider briefly. Faith is an infinite gift, for it embraces God Himself. Now, the first way by which we show that we at least try to appreciate a gift, though we may not be able to fathom it, is to return thanks. And the Mass is at once the greatest act of thanksgiving and worship we can render to God, and the best exercise of our faith. By it we acknowledge our absolute dependence on God — the Mass is the Sacrifice Incomparable — and at the same time prove our unwavering submission to the words of Eternal Truth: "This is My Body; This is My Blood" (Matt. xxvi, 26, 28). We are those blessed ones who have not seen and have believed. But our submission, our participation is passive, not active; and hence, what we profess with our lips, we often unconsciously deny by our actions. Therefore, our little growth.

The Church is a living organism, being composed of living members, the faithful, and having a living head, Christ Jesus. She offers to the Eternal Father, a living Sacrifice, His Eternal Son, the Lamb immolated for the sins of His people. The Victim, Christ Jesus, offers Himself, through the hands of His consecrated ministers, with all the efficacy of His oblation on Calvary. Not one of us but would have esteemed it an unforgettable privilege to have witnessed that bloody and agonizing expiation. Certainly the impression would have been lasting. And we daily witness the Unbloody Expiation, and go on living apparently unmoved — indifferent to the miracle that takes place under our eyes. Yet each daily impression should be lasting in its effects. But our faith is inactive. We do not share in the sacrifice as the Victim intended. The Head and members form one body. If the Head is immolated daily, hourly, momently — " From the rising of the sun even to the going down . . . there is offered to my name a clean oblation . . . saith the Lord of Hosts " (Mal. i, 11) — the members must act in like manner, else the unction of the life-giving Spirit that flows from the Head does not invigorate the members, and the loss is almost irreparable.

This does not imply only that we are to offer Christ our Redeemer and Mediator as an infinite adoration, thanksgiving, reparation and impetration to the Father; we can and must do so, for according to the prince of the apostles, St. Peter, we are constituted " a kingly priest-

hood " (I St. Peter, ii, 9). It means also that we are
called upon by our life of sacrifice, in union with our
Lord's, to " fill up," as St. Paul says, " those things that
are wanting of the sufferings of Christ " (Col. i, 24).
We are all called upon to participate in the work of Redemption, for Christ in taking a human body willed to
become the second Adam, the Father of a spiritual race.
And as in the old Adam all sinned, so in the new Adam
all suffered, died, and rose again unto newness and fulness of life. " God became man that man might become
God " (St. Augustine).

Had we been on Calvary, the picture of that awful
scene would never have left our minds, and its lessons
would have borne fruit in our lives. Did our faith penetrate the mystery of the daily Calvary of the altar, the
image of the uplifted Crucified, the pleading, expiating
Just One, raised aloft in the hands of the priest to satisfy
the justice of the Father, would ever be before our eyes,
and its lesson would show its stamp on our lives. The
Lamb is being sacrificed every moment; and we are the
followers, brethren, spouses of the Lamb. He sacrificed
Himself for each one of us individually, and for all men
together, with ineffable love, compassionating forgiveness, exquisite agony of body and mind and spirit. And
we, whom He desires to be sacrificed through Him and
with Him and in Him, how do we comply with His
wishes? If our faith be strong, our sacrifices will be
many. Each day should increase, if not their number, at
least the purity of the love with which they are offered.
Looking back on our life of yesterday, last month, last

year, five, ten years ago, can we truthfully say that our spirit of sacrifice has been steadily increasing? Do we appreciate more, that is, do we understand a little better, the wonderful gift of our faith? The test is simple. To-day, when trifles vex, when difficulties threaten, when misunderstanding arises, when misrepresentations occur, when repugnant duties press heavily, when discouragement weighs us down, when plans are upset at every turn, when everything seems to go wrong and nothing right, do I more readily, more cheerfully, more selflessly than I did last week, last year, ten years ago, say from the bottom of my heart, " My Father, I believe. Thou knowest what is best; Thy will be done? " If I do, my faith has grown with my growth. Or do I complain, and murmur, and grow impatient and irritable, and make those around me miserable by my whining, by my unkind words, by my temper? — just the same as I did last week, last month, five years ago — or perhaps am I a good deal worse? If so, I have grown up in the faith, but that is all. My faith has not grown with my growth. My action gives the lie to what my lips profess. Faith for me is rather a formula than a principle to be lived.

The abiding principle of this our faith, its every essence, is found in the Mass — is the Mass. And the Mass is the Sacrifice Incomparable. Our lives should be molded on the Mass, on the life of the Victim therein immolated. The word " Victim " tells all. Sacrificed by Him, with Him, in Him, daily, hourly, moment by moment, our life becomes one unceasing holocaust, one perpetual immolation, one holy sacrifice unending. Then in us shall

be realized the words of the prophet: " From the rising
of the sun even to the going down . . . there is offered
to my name a clean oblation " (Mal. i, 11). So, united
with our Divine Saviour, the Spouse of our souls, our
actions take on an infinite value, because the Father,
looking at us, sees only His Beloved Son, in Whom He is
well pleased. The Son does always the things that please
the Father. Let us remember this word of the Only-
Begotten: " I do always the things that please Him "
(John viii, 29). If we earnestly try to fulfil this word in
our lives, to live the life of the Lamb who is constantly
slain on every altar of propitiation, we shall begin to
mean actively, not passively, that prayer of intense faith,
which we repeat at every consecration, and often, let us
hope, during the day: " Divine Heart of Jesus, Victim of
Love, make me for Thee a living sacrifice, holy and pleasing to God." Then shall we be accoutred in the armor of
God; we shall " be able to resist in the evil day, and to
stand in all things perfect; Stand therefore, having your
loins girt about with truth, and having on the breast-
plate of justice " (Eph. vi. 13–14).

7. THE MASS, OUR SANCTIFICATION

" Render, therefore . . to God the things that are God's " (MATT. xxii, 21)

YOU should have acquired, thus far, a clear understanding of the basic law of the spiritual life: constant
self-denial. Without this continual hammering away at
the seemingly-beautiful statue of EGO until it is completely destroyed, no spiritual progress is possible. True
advance in perfection consists in breaking down this
work of art, this apparent masterpiece, piece by piece.
For the statue is only a plaster cast — the interior is hollow. But once this sham is demolished, a wonderful image
stands revealed — the resplendent image of God, which
had been hidden under the false and ill-fitting casing.
This is the work of a lifetime, the special work to which
we are obliged by the vows of religion. We freely take
upon ourselves the duty of perfecting the image of the
Creator in our souls, in response to the invitation of our
Guide: " Be you therefore perfect, as also your heavenly
Father is perfect " (Matt. v, 48).

After all, God has a right to expect this of us. All
creation exalts the Omnipotent with its full capacity of
unconscious praise and glory. " The heavens shew forth
the glory of God: and the firmament declareth the work
of His hands " (Ps. 18, 1). Man is the only creature of
God who can refuse and does refuse to render Him the

greatest possible glory a creature can offer: the conscious praise and honor due His infinite perfections. Since man is the lord of creation, his homage to God must be and is superior to the combined glory given to God by all other living but unintelligent beings. Each individual act of worship on man's part incomparably outweighs the combined worship of sentient and inanimate nature. Yet the homage of nature to the Author of nature is invariable, perpetual, entire. And the homage of man, finite intelligence, to the Author of man, Infinite Intelligence, is changeable, fleeting, incomplete. You will admit the difference from your own experience. Just the same, man by his reason and free will is almost as highly exalted above nature as God is above man. Therefore God, in exacting from us the work of our sanctification, is only asking us to return Him in justice what He receives from insensible creatures according to their capacity.

We are therefore bound by our position as dependent beings to render " to God the things that are God's " (Matt. xxii, 21). The very first and most important thing we are obliged to render Him is ourselves; our being, our life, our will. This offering He demands, and yet it is not acceptable in His sight. Man has sinned, and the gift is horribly stained — it is repulsive in the sight of the Divinity. The case seems hopeless. Can man do nothing? Nothing. But God can do and has done everything. He has become Man, and the Word made flesh is our Mediator, our Saviour, the salvation of His people. Washed in the blood of the Sacrificial Lamb, we are made pleasing in the sight of the heavenly Father,

Who now beholds in us the lineaments of His Beloved
Son. So that this being, this life, this soul, purified by the
expiation of the God-Man, becomes an oblation acceptable to the Father, when offered to Him in Christ,
through Christ, with Christ Himself. " For in Him we
live, and move, and are " (Acts xvii, 28).

Man, then, of himself can offer God neither an adequate nor an acceptable holocaust, but He can render
to God the Sacrifice of His Eternal Son, Who clothed
Himself with our humanity for this very end. " Sacrifice
and oblation thou didst not desire: — behold I come —
that I should do Thy will, O my God " (Ps. 39, 7–9).
The Son's accomplishment of the will of His Father and
ours, was not to last only for the space of His lifetime: it
was to be perpetual. " Do this for a commemoration of
Me " (Luke xxii, 19). It was and is always the same,
invariable. " Till heaven and earth pass, one jot, or one
tittle shall not pass of the law, till all be fulfilled " (Matt.
v, 18). It was and is always whole, entire. " I do always
the things that please Him " (John viii, 29). " Father,
. . . not my will, but thine be done " (Luke xxii, 42).
The God-Man, Jesus Christ, Only-Begotten Son of the
Father, is the only Son of Adam Who has rendered, and
still continues to render to the Father, that perfect honor
and glory expected from man in creating him; that fulness of praise and adoration His justice seeks to receive
from man in exactly the same measure as He receives it
from all other creatures according to the plenitude of
their capacity.

In the mystery of the Incarnation, then, God Himself,

commiserating man, gave to us at once an Exemplar, a
Saviour, and a Sacrifice. In being our Exemplar, our
Model, our infallible and perfect Teacher, Jesus became
our Saviour, and because of His condition of Saviour, He
is necessarily our Sacrifice. In giving us a pure and acceptable oblation, God has bestowed on us the greatest
means to attain our sanctification; He has given us Himself, that we may reach Himself: " God became man in
order that man might become God " (St. Augustine).
These are tremendous words. ' Do I dare to aspire to this
close intimacy, to this participation in the very life of
the Divinity — very Life, Activity Eternal? Surely I am
deceived; it is not for me. I am too presumptuous; it is
an illusion.' Yes, you are mistaken. There is here no
question of your having to decide for yourself a matter
of everlasting importance. Were it so, you would indeed
be wise in hesitating, in fearing, in rejecting the thought
as almost blasphemous. It is a question here of faith in
God, in His commands, in His promises and threats.
Concerning this subject, let us now say to Him in all
sincerity what the Pharisees said in their cunning: " Master, we know that thou art a true speaker, and teachest
the way of God in truth, neither carest thou for any
man: for thou dost not regard the person of man. Tell
us, therefore, what dost thou think? " (Matt. xxii, 16–
17). And Jesus answering says to us: " Abide in Me, and
I in you " (John xv, 4). You shall so abide by rendering
to God the things that are God's. " Now this is eternal
life: that they may know the Father, the only true God,
and Jesus Christ, Whom He has sent. Do you now be-

lieve? " (Adapted). And we answer: " Lord, to whom
shall we go? Thou hast the words of eternal life " (John
vi, 69). " Now we know that thou knowest all things.
By this we believe that thou camest forth from God "
(John xvi, 30). And Jesus hearing our profession of
faith prays for us to the Father: " Sanctify them in
truth: Thy word is truth " (John xvii, 17). And we continue: ' Verily, Father, Thy word is truth, for He Whom
Thou hast sent, Who came forth from Thee, is the Word
Incarnate, Thine Infinite Utterance, spoken from eternity to eternity, the Everlasting Truth. He is come into
the world; again He leaves the world, and goes to Thee,
the Father. But through our hands He returns to Thee,
for Thou hast given Him to us that in Him we might
see salvation.'

Therefore, let us render to God the things that are
God's — His Eternal Son, and ourselves with Him. At
every moment He is born anew into the world by the
consecrating words of His priests. " Who for us men and
for our salvation came down from heaven; and is incarnate by the Holy Ghost; and is made Man " (Nicene
Creed). But let us not forget that this consecration, this
mystical Incarnation, is effected in our name, for we are
all constituted a kingly priesthood in Christ, the consecrating priest and Victim, our living Head. And the
members of the mystical body, the Church, participate
always in the activity, the life of the Head, as long as
they are in communication with Him; as long as they
are living members. The mystical Incarnation, like the
Incarnation in time, is effected for each one of us in-

dividually, and for all collectively. God gives me His Son at every moment of the day to atone for my sins, to make perfect my imperfection, to return to the Father a worship worthy of Him — in brief, to cancel all my debts, to present Him with that perpetual, invariable, entire homage He in justice demands from me and all living creatures.

God holds out the Gift — His Well-Beloved Son. He wills to blot out everything. Why is it not accomplished? Why is not the union He so ardently, so vehemently desires, achieved? Ah, we do not will to give the Son back to the Father — for He must return to Him with our message. He is our Mediator — we do not will with intensity of faith, with earnestness of purpose, to give Him back, to let Him leave the world and go to the Father, bearing with Him our royal message of good will. We believe, yes, but our faith is half-hearted, because we are cowards. We believe in theory, but shrink from the practice.

We return the Gift to the Father, but withhold the giver, ourselves, and still somehow expect that fulness of life shall be ours. Of course, the real Giver is Christ, but by becoming the Head of our race, He lets us act through Him and in His name. We know that the gift without the giver is bare. Therefore, our share in the sacrifice is almost meaningless; therefore, our spiritual growth is so small. Christ offers Himself for us, but we do not will to offer ourselves with Him. We hold back. There is no oneness of mind, no close union of will. So the life of the Head does not flow in all its invigorating power through us, the members of His body; the connection is injured. We desire to reap the harvest, but dislike putting our hands to the plow. God looks to the love of the giver — the love that is in our hearts. The Gift, Christ Jesus, is Infinite, is God, and worthy of the Father; but we must offer it with Christ, and through Christ, and in Christ. We must identify our lives with His sentiments, with the intention wherewith He offers Himself to the Father in our name. For He offers Himself to the Father with ineffable love for us, and the sacrifice of ourselves is pleasing and acceptable to God only when made in union with that of His Beloved Son. The more we conform ourselves to the image of the Word, the more precious in the sight of God will be our gift, and the more meritorious. And as we believe, so shall it be done to us. If we do not offer ourselves in good earnest to the Father, with the oblation of Christ Himself, our Propitiation, we cannot reap the harvest God wishes us to gather.

We expect God to do everything, and for ourselves we prefer to choose only the enjoyment of His bounty. But man is born to labor even spiritually. God Who reads the heart sees in us only a lie, if what we profess by our lips, namely, our oblation of self with Christ, in Christ, and through Christ, we do not attempt to achieve in our lives. " Be not deceived; God is not mocked " (Gal. vi, 7). As we believe so shall it be done to us. Christ our Pasch is sacrificed — and we let Him hang alone on the cross in the gathering darkness. We look to the fleshpots of Egypt, for they are more to our taste. " I thirst " (John xix, 28). " This saying is hard, " we murmur, " and who can hear it? " (John vi, 61). And so we turn our back on the quivering Victim in the throes of His death agony, and run down the hill to the hustle, and tumult, and transitory pleasures of the city below, in order to shut out the harrowing scene. We seek our pleasure and delight in the things of the world, forgetting that we vowed to strive after Him alone, to seek Him always in all our actions. We prefer to grasp rather at the easier of two things, and reject the hard. We gratify nature, our body, the sensual man, and forget that the Master, Whom we say we are following, said again and again: "If any man will come after me, let him deny himself and take up his cross daily, and follow me " (Luke ix, 23).

Yes, we must follow; we have vowed to do so, even to Calvary — that is where His footsteps lead. But we are cowards and run away. We are cowards, because our faith is weak and our confidence small. We do not remember to ask for strength and courage. And he who relies on his own strength is destined to immediate failure. Nature cannot overcome nature. Grace alone can. And that necessary grace drops down on our heads in great drops of blood from the Heart of the Lamb. But unless we are standing beneath the cross, the Blood will flow down, only not on us. But alas for us! In spirit we are all too often far removed from the cross; in spirit we are still in the world, looking for creature comforts.

Yet somehow, even in the midst of the sensuous din, we hear a strong cry echoing and re-echoing until it finds rest in the paternal bosom: " Father, forgive them, for they know not what they do " (Luke xxiii, 34). And the Father's just anger is stayed, and again He pours out new opportunities and graces. And we? Again we refuse. Again the pleading sob of the Lamb: " Father, forgive them " (Luke xxiii, 34). And again pardon, and renewed grace, and mercy. How long in your life has this been going on? God and you know. How long will it continue? God alone knows, for He will not be mocked forever, and the next chance may be your last. The day of reckoning will come inevitably, and we shall all have to render a strict account of our stewardship. We are that servant who owes his king ten thousand talents. As we have not wherewith to pay it, the Lord commands that we be sold, and all that we have. But we beseech Him, and being moved with pity He lets us go and forgives us the debt, because of our elder Brother Who intercedes for us. Then we, going out, find a fellow-servant who owes us a hundred pence. We throttle him, saying: " Pay what thou owest " (Matt. xviii, 28). And our fellow-servant, falling down, beseeches us to have mercy, but we will not. Then the Lord, calling us, says to us, " Thou wicked servant, I forgave thee all the debt, because thou besoughtest Me: shouldst not thou then have had compassion on thy fellow-servant, even as I had compassion on thee? " (Matt. xviii, 32–33). And the Lord, being angry, will deliver us to the torturers until we pay all the debt, because we have not forgiven our brother from our heart.

What is it to forgive our brother from our hearts? It

is to love him as ourselves. It is to strive to accomplish the *one* commandment perfectly: " Thou shalt love the Lord thy God with thy whole heart, and . . . thy neighbor as thyself " (Matt. xxii, 37, 39). It is to mean efficaciously, that is, to will with determined effort, to live our share of the sacrifice of the Mass, in union with Our Lord and Saviour, Jesus Christ; and to participate in that Sacrifice as frequently as it is offered — " from the rising of the sun even to the going down " (Mal. i, 11). Only in trying so to live, to make the Mass a vital thing in our daily actions, to live our faith in practice, to perform our tasks in the spirit of our living Head, and according to the principles He, the Eternal Truth, the Word of the Father, laid down for us — only in trying so to do shall we be rendering to God the things that are God's: our being, our life, our soul, with the full capacity of our measure as creatures of God. Only then can we say with St. Paul in all sincerity: We are confident in the Lord Jesus, " that He Who hath begun a good work in you will perfect it unto the day of Christ Jesus " (Phil. i, 6). This exhortation can be closed with no better prayer than the prayer of the same apostle: " And this I pray, that your charity may more and more abound in knowledge and in all understanding; that you may approve the better things; that you may be sincere and without offence unto the day of Christ; filled with the fruit of justice, through Jesus Christ unto the glory and praise of God " (Phil. i, 9–11).

III. *The Sacraments: the second great means of sanctification*

8. THE PURPOSE AND AIM OF BAPTISM

"But our conversation is in heaven" (PHIL. iii, 20)

WE HAVE been considering in the last two conferences the vital part the Mass should have in our spiritual
life, since God has given it to us as the greatest means of
our sanctification. The Holy Sacrifice is Christ, and Jesus
Christ is our only hope of salvation and sanctification.
Without Him we are nothing. But " in Him was life, and
the life was the light of men " (John i, 4), and the more
we identify ourselves with Him, the more we live in
Him, conforming our least thoughts, words, and actions
to His standard, the more abundantly shall we participate
in that life which comes to us, as members of His mystical body, from our divine Head. And the more earnestly and steadfastly we will to acquire Christ, which
involves the constant casting aside of self, the demolish-
ing of the super-statue EGO, the more clearly shall we be
given light to see, that is, to understand the manner in
which this transformation is to be brought about. For
Christ is God; and God is Life; and Life is Light; and
Light, for us here below, is the obscurity of faith, and
hereafter, glory.

It has been remarked in a previous conference that
Christ is the cornerstone of the temple of our soul, and
faith in Him, the foundation. And the higher we wish

[75]

to build, the deeper must the foundation be laid, because according to the measure of our faith — and this cannot be repeated too often — shall be the measure of our spiritual growth, our perfection. In exactly the same proportion as we believe, so shall it be done to us. This gift of faith, this infused belief in the veracity of God, in Eternal Truth, is bestowed on us in Baptism. It is not by chance, but of necessity, that Baptism is the first of the sacraments, and hence the most important. It is so absolutely essential that without it man cannot obtain the Beatific Vision. " Unless a man be born again of water and the Holy Ghost, he cannot enter into the kingdom of heaven " (John iii, 5). These words of Our Lord are very plain; there is no possibility of misunderstanding their meaning. And since Baptism is the chief of sacraments, and the sacraments the second great means of sanctification, we shall reflect a little while on its purpose and end.

No doubt, the very instant the word " Baptism " is mentioned, the majority of you immediately read printed on the pages of memory ' original sin, sanctifying grace, sacrament of the dead.' This is very good and very true. But the trouble is, we are too apt to emphasize in our thoughts the part about original sin, and sacrament of the dead, just because it was so hammered into us in childhood. We are not to blame. But if we only had realized the marvelous life that was offered to us in the purifying action of that sanctifying grace, how differently we should have lived till now. Our conversation would in very truth have been in heaven, as it was destined to be. But God is never in a hurry, and all time with Him is present, so all vain regrets over the past are not only useless and a wasted effort, but actually dangerous and harmful. Every day, as you know, should be considered as a new life, so that what we learn now we have but to apply henceforth.

I am going to begin with a statement that may sound strange. Recall that Baptism, and hence the life of grace, has to do primarily with the soul, not with the body of man. I do not mean to infer that any one professes the opposite. To do so would be unorthodox, and rank nonsense; but just because the soul animates the body, and is to a certain extent affected by its moods and wants and humors, many of us act with regard to the soul, the things of the spirit, as though nothing availed us except that which is tasted and touched and felt and seen and heard. Yet since we are men and not angels, we are stimulated to moral, intellectual, and spiritual growth by means of sensible, or material, impressions; those conveyed to us through the bodily senses. And it is certainly true that we can more readily grasp ideas, immaterial impressions, if presented to the mind in a concrete illustration than if conveyed through abstract explanations and definitions.

For example, a child who lives in intimate relationship with his father during all the years of infancy and adolescence, knows from personal experience what a father is. Nobody need give him a definition of the term; nor is it necessary for him to resort to a dictionary, were you to ask him what is meant by the term ' father.' But take a child who has no recollection of its father, because he has been dead so long. To such a one, father stands for a beautiful imagined relationship, which falls far, far short of the reality, because the knowledge of contact is lacking. All the explanation and illustration in the world will never atone for the deficiency. Therefore, it is because of our constitution as *rational animals* that we understand the spiritual better by comparison with animal, or sensible experiences. The danger with all such comparisons is not so much that they are at times very imperfect, but that all too frequently we forget that they are only figures of speech, and instead of extracting the *idea,* the spiritual truth, we confuse the metaphor with the immaterial reality, and attach to things of the spirit purely animal qualities or characteristics. With this warning before us we shall proceed.

Long ago you were all taught that all men are made to the image and likeness of God. Again let me remind you: it is the soul, not the body, that is created primarily to this divine resemblance. In the formation of our body, our parents had an active share; in the creation of the soul, they had absolutely none. Every soul made by God — your soul and mine, all the souls that have gone on before, and all those that will come after us, — requires on God's part an act of the will distinct in term. No two souls are ever made at once. Remember that it is the soul that gives life to the body. Our parents, in the order of nature established by God, provided us with a body, which is the house inhabited by the soul. But God alone created the soul, and created it to His own image and likeness.

The expression "image and likeness" (Gen. 1, 26), does not mean that we are to picture God as a human person, a rational, or reasoning animal, such as we ourselves are. No. God is a pure spirit. You cannot put your bodily finger on your soul; it does not occupy space, although it is clothed with a body; it is not a material substance, though your body is. Neither can you put your bodily finger on God; though He fills all space, He does not occupy any. It is this soul of mine, this spiritual substance, this real I, that is created by God in His own image and likeness. The Uncreated Spirit, Eternal, Life-giving, wills to create in time children like unto Himself, partaking in a measure of His nature. He has always existed, and will live forever; we did not always exist, but we shall live forever. He is Infinite Intelligence; our intelligence is finite, or limited. He is the Sovereign Will of the universe; our will is free, but subordinate. And all this is true of every soul; it is a child of God by its very nature; it owes its origin solely to God. And God, remember, is Life; and Life is unceasing Activity. Here on earth we see that all living beings are continually reproducing themselves. This perpetual generation is a shadow of that creative power which is God. God, Who is Life, creates. Each soul is an impulse of Life, of Creative Power, of God, and is a child of the Father, the Author of its being.

All that has just been said applies to every single soul as a child of the Father, according to its nature, no matter how it uses or abuses that intelligence, no matter how it uses or abuses that free will, whether it be in union with the Sovereign Will or in revolt against it. But there is another and more exalted manner in which we are children of the Father, and that is by the grace of adoption conferred on us in Baptism, wherein we are made brothers of Jesus Christ, the co-eternal Son, and heirs of heaven. It is this supernatural, superabundant life of the soul, the germ of which is implanted in us in the regenerating sacrament, of which we shall treat.

You will recall that God in creating our first parents bestowed on them natural, preternatural, and supernatural gifts, which they were to transmit unimpaired to their descendants. But they failed in the test — obedience — and hence forfeited for themselves and their posterity these gifts of Divine bounty. The natural gifts — understanding, free will, the immortality of their soul — remained; otherwise, man would cease to be man, for these gifts make man what he is. The intellect, however, was obscured; the will was weakened and inclined toward evil. In the preternatural order, the immortality of the body, and its freedom from pain and suffering were destroyed; the passions were no longer under the control of reason, but waged war against it; the full and clear knowledge of created things, possessed by Adam and Eve, was clouded. But it was in the supernatural order, the life of grace, that the greatest disaster manifested itself. Man lost forever that sanctifying grace which rendered him Godlike, and thereby lost his title to sonship and the inheritance to the kingdom of heaven.

Yet God was moved to pity, and was not angry forever. "The Word was made flesh" (John i, 14), and by His death we again became free men and not slaves. Our title to the eternal inheritance as adopted children of the Father was restored. And He Who redeemed us, willed that through Baptism this supernatural life of grace be again conferred on man.

Grace is to the soul what the soul is to the body. You know that a body stripped of a soul is a corpse. So a soul without sanctifying grace is lifeless in the sight of God, so far as its supernatural activity is concerned. Its natural life continues; it must, because God created it immortal. A soul without sanctifying grace is a disinherited, disowned child of the Father. Such are the devil, and all his associates; such are all they who by deliberately choosing mortal sin will to reject the Father as their Parent. And you know how repellent to us is a son who disowns, denies that father to whom he owes his earthly existence and maintenance. And yet the indignity, the ingratitude, the hideous insult is offered, after all, to a man like himself. But when the Father is God, Infinite Sanctity, who can measure the insult, the ingratitude? Not man, surely, with his limited intelligence — man who cannot comprehend his own nature fully. God, only, Who alone comprehends Himself perfectly, can fathom the corruption, the malice of sin. And it is to this greatest of evils, this one existing evil, that the life of grace is opposed.

This supernatural life is freely bestowed on us in Baptism. It is a gift which after a life-long effort we can begin but dimly to appreciate. And what if we do not earnestly try to appreciate it? Who can measure our ingratitude, our culpability? Only God, against Whom the insult is directed. And what is this supernatural life that is thus opened up to us? What is it to possess sanctifying grace? To be a brother of Christ, and so an heir to heaven?

The answer to these questions, or rather to this one question expressed in different forms, will be found in the answer to another, which is this: What is heaven? Since the end, the goal of the supernatural life is to enter into full possession of the kingdom of heaven, the matter resolves itself into the definition, or explanation of the term ' heaven.' What is heaven? Heaven is God. Take God away from heaven, and heaven is at once hell. Hell is the absence of God — not in His power, for He essentially supports all created things, and fills all space by His immensity — but in His Beatitude. Put God in His state of blessedness, His glory, into hell, and hell becomes paradise. Very well. If then, the end, the aim of the supernatural life is to enter into the full possession of heaven, then the goal of that life of grace is to possess God fully — and to possess Him whether the soul live in the house of the body here, or out of it hereafter.

Sanctifying grace, then, is the possession of God. It admits of degrees, or stages, of development. This is necessarily so. In the natural life of the soul, in the activity of my understanding and free will, I can trace from personal experience a steady development. I have to apply my mind to the acquisition of knowledge of any kind. For instance, my mere looking at the cover of an arith-

metic text would never have sufficed for my learning
how to make figures, and so on through the simple and
complicated problems. I had to apply myself closely, and
bit by bit acquire the knowledge I now retain. So, too,
with the will; it is free. I can choose one thing or another, yes. But my mere wishing to construct, let us say,
a house, would never have caused it to rise an eighth of
an inch above the ground. Only with God is the mere desire an effective act. I must exert myself, and either go
about building the house myself, or else get others to do
it for me. What holds true in the natural order, holds
good in the supernatural. Such is the usual plan God has
in mind for each of us, a steady development in the life
of grace. Not that He never deviates from the usual
order. He does, but rarely. Neither is this inconsistent.
Since He is the Author of all law, He can dispense with
His own rulings, if He so chooses. There are numerous
cases: Magdalen, the penitent thief, Saul. In an instant
God perfected in them that supernatural life which ordinarily he accomplishes, provided man consents, only
in a lifetime. He had His own motives in so doing; it is
for us not to question, but to admire and glorify.

For the majority of us, therefore, the supernatural life
is a constant growth, a steady development. In what does
this growth consist? We have seen that sanctifying grace,
without which no supernatural life is possible, is the possession of God, that is, the participation to a lesser or
greater extent, in His divinity. This means to share in
the activity of God, for God, remember, is Life, ceaseless Activity. Let us see in what this activity of God

[83]

consists, and then we shall understand a little better what is required of us to develop ourselves spiritually.

We are intellect and will, and thus are images of the Father by nature. God is the Intellect and Will of the universe. Our supernatural life of grace is the perfect adornment of the natural life of the soul, through the sanctifying power of Infinite Holiness. The closer our spiritual occupations resemble God's, that is, the more fully we permit Him Who dwells in us to operate in us, unimpeded by the great obstacle ' self,' the more fruit-fully shall we participate in the Divine perfections. Now, what has occupied God from all eternity? What is to occupy us for all eternity? With what are we to occupy ourselves now, here on earth, to prepare for that eternal, beatific activity? If we once firmly grasp this important truth, we shall have little difficulty in living these few moments of life as God wishes us to do, for we shall see the things of time from the viewpoint of eternity, of God, and so adjust all our labors according to the Divine perspective. We shall then see how futile and how foolish it is for us not to give our first and constant attention to ground ourselves in the foundation of that exercise, that labor which we are destined to perform for all eternity, forever. God, as you know, did not create us that we might labor feverishly at those perishable things that go down into the grave with us, for vain is the knowledge of man. We exist, we live here, only that we may effectively study how we are to live hereafter. Any-thing else is folly, and folly is the wisdom of this world.

God is Infinite Intelligence and Will. There is only one

object that is capable of satisfying the operations of that infinite intelligence; and that object must be and is necessarily infinite, is God. From all eternity, then, God has contemplated Himself, and perfectly comprehended His divine attributes, His perfections. He is the only Being capable of comprehending Himself; and since understanding is truth, He reveals Himself to Himself as infinite sanctity, essential perfection. Seeing in Himself incomparable holiness, He loves Himself with ineffable love, for that vital force, which is His will, reaches out and perfectly embraces that Goodness, which is Himself, manifested to It by His Intelligence. But with Him this comprehension and embrace are simultaneous, and constitute the essence of His Activity; or rather, this comprehension and embrace are Activity, Life unending. In loving Himself in all His perfections, God by that very act renders Himself the perfect and full measure of glory due His divine Majesty, the plenitude of homage and praise.

And we are children of this Almighty Being both by nature and by grace. His claim on us is a double one. We recognize that it is eminently fitting and proper for a child to pay reverence, love, and obedience to its earthly father. A child who acts otherwise is brutishly unnatural, and justly condemned. And the law holds good with regard to our heavenly Father, only its binding force is a million times greater. Why does a child reverence its father? Because it recognizes him as its greatest good in life. Why does it love? Because its will reaches out and embraces that good as its understanding reveals it. Why does it obey? Because obedience is the pledge, the external manifestation of love. It is the only effective way in which the child renders homage, gives glory to its father. This is the very thing we are to do with regard to our heavenly Father.

From all eternity God has contemplated Himself, loved Himself, and thereby willed His eternal glory. For all eternity we shall contemplate God, love Him, and glorify Him by perfectly accomplishing His will. God grant that for all time that remains for us on earth, we shall apply ourselves with full determination to contemplate God, to love Him, and to prove that love by glorifying Him through the obedience of our will; striving daily with greater purity of intention to submit our will to His adorable Will in every least detail; and keeping our interior gaze riveted on Him, the one Supreme Good, that understanding better we may more perfectly will, which is the more fruitfully to love, and the more divinely to glorify.

This God, this unfathomable Being, dwells in me in virtue of the sanctifying grace bestowed on me in Baptism. Sanctifying grace is the possession of God. I have God, — Father, Son, and Holy Ghost, — living in me constantly. To seek Him, I need only to fix my interior gaze on the Real Presence of the Divinity in my soul. I carry heaven around with me, and act as though I knew it not. And to fix my interior gaze on Him means simply to apply my mind with earnestness of effort to the consideration of His goodness. And the increasing knowledge of His goodness will reveal to me my own misery, my nothingness as a creature. And this truth will make me adore Him, love Him, glorify Him. He is my Father, and I am His child. The interests, the work of the Father, should be the interests, the work of the child, And little by little, if I am zealous and persevering in seeking Him, He will manifest Himself to me in His perfections; and in proportion as my knowledge comprehends His holiness, my will will reach out and embrace that Eternal Good with increasing ardor of love, which will externally manifest itself in the fidelity of obedience. Thus will my life become more divine, more Godlike; thus will my supernatural life unfold and develop; thus, if I am faithful and persistent, will He bring me in His paternal love, through the utter submission of my intellect, to the perfect blossoming of faith; and through the utter submission of my will to that all-consuming love, the invigorating flood-tide of a fiery sea. And this is the end here below of that supernatural life of grace, the germ of which is implanted in me in Baptism. Through this perfect faith and love He will have united me to Himself in the closest union possible here on earth, when, as a reward for my steadfast cleaving to Him in all things, always, God will have made me one spirit with Himself.

9. THE INCREASE OF SANCTIFYING GRACE EFFECTED IN PENANCE

"Brethren, We cease not to pray for you . . . that you may walk worthy of God . . . who hath . . . translated us into the kingdom of the Son of His love, in whom we have redemption through His blood, the remission of sins"

(COL. i, 9-14)

IN THE last conference we made a broad and general survey of the supernatural life of grace, imparted to us in its first beginnings in the sacrament of Baptism. We saw that without sanctifying grace, which is the possession of God, no supernatural life is possible. We also realized that for us, life of grace is a steady development, depending for its growth on our measure of coöperation with the workings of the Holy Ghost in our soul. Let us also recall that we are studying the sacraments as the second great means of sanctification held out to us by Almighty God; the Holy Sacrifice, the immolation of the Man-God, being the instrument chief among all others. Of the sacraments, we first considered Baptism, because it is the essential condition laid down by Our Lord for being admitted into His Kingdom, both here and hereafter. His Kingdom here is the Church, and it is she who holds out to us as a further help in our sanctification, the complement, so to speak, of the sacrament of Baptism: Penance, also called the sacrament of the dead.

[88]

The sacrament of Penance, as instituted by Christ, restores the soul who has forfeited God's friendship and sonship to its supernatural inheritance by investing it again with sanctifying grace. The soul thus once more possesses God, its First Beginning and Last End. Or, if the soul is free from mortal sin, penance increases its sanctifying grace, increases its measure of the possession of God. It is this latter alternative we shall discuss today, and see if again in our use of the means we have not been guilty of some abuse, and hence have retarded the spiritual development God so earnestly desires from us.

We all understand very well that the only sins one need confess and must confess are mortal sins: that mortal sin alone constitutes the necessary matter of confession. The Church has clearly defined, however, that it is a good and useful practice, especially for those who aim at conforming themselves more perfectly to the image of the Creator, to the life of Christ, to resort to this sacrament frequently, even though venial sin be the only subject of accusation. And this is because the Church, who is the voice of Christ, in her inspired wisdom recognizes the effective stimulus to sanctity contained in this sacrament. We shall limit ourselves, then, to the consideration of a soul who lives habitually in a state of grace, as it is to be hoped all religious do.

Here, then, we have the case of a religious who has been going to confession week after week, for many years — five, ten, fifteen, twenty, and as many more as necessary. God has held out to him grace upon grace, and yet in His sight, and even in that of thoughtful men, there is no proportionate increase in virtue; in fact, he seems to be and is in a worse state than at the beginning of his religious life. What is the trouble? The sacrament is of Divine institution; it is God Who forgives, Who gives the increase of grace; therefore, the trouble must be, and certainly is, with the soul. It is just this: he presents himself week after week before Christ, his Judge, with improper dispositions, which, through force of habit, have virtually become no dispositions at all, and hence not only prevent that outpouring of grace with which Christ wills to flood his soul, but in some cases it may even happen that, as a result of continued *deliberate* indifference, he may be in a certain measure guilty of sacrilege. And the pity of the trouble is — " It's only a venial sin." *Only a venial sin!* Ah, if we looked at the matter from God's point of view rather than from our own, we should be forced to say in all truth: " It's all of a venial sin." We have no idea of the malice of sin, and therefore we go on our way cheerfully piling up insult after insult to God, and heaping up for ourselves mountains of fuel to be consumed in the weary, slow-burning fire of purgatory. If only we had that clear knowledge of the evil of sin which the saints had. St. Aloysius, St. John Berchmans, St. Gabriel — all would rather have suffered untold tortures than be guilty of the least imperfection. Their hatred of sin was intense, because they realized, better than we do, something of the majesty and power of God. And they proved their principle by living a life of continual death, in the avoidance of even the shadow of sin.

[90]

A good many of us are inclined to smile at this scrupulous purity of conscience as — well — a pious exaggeration. And when we read of the intense sorrow with which the saints bewailed their faults of frailty, faults which we consider of no moment, in fact, no faults at all, and how they called themselves the greatest of sinners, unworthy of life itself, we, in our superior wisdom wave all this admission aside as humility stretched beyond its natural bounds — a trifle overdrawn, just a trifle. Yes, we are wise, too wise, but our wisdom is of this world. And the wisdom of the wise, our wisdom, is folly in the sight of the Almighty God.

The truth is, we seek self, and the saints sought God. " Seek," says Our Lord, " and you shall find " (Matt. vii, 7). We, seeking ourselves, find only ourselves, and the finding brings us no great measure of happiness or peace. But the saints, seeking God, found Him Whom their soul loved, and the finding brought them that perfect happiness and peace which surpasseth all understanding, and which the Beatific Vision alone can augment. Yet in our eyes they committed follies while on earth, preferring death to life. But what sweeter folly, and what greater glory than to be esteemed a fool for Him Who died, mocked as a fool, for our salvation?

I said a moment ago that the truth is — and the sad part lies in the fact that it is a truth we hate to confess, or even to face, for that matter — we seek ourselves in what we profess to do for God. Why are we so indifferent to the great danger and real harm of venial sin? Why? Because as long as we keep out of hell we are satisfied;

that is, as long as we know we will not suffer eternally. "*It is only a venial sin.*" Yes, I am still a friend of God. But just what kind of a friend am I? I wonder if it is one He is pleased to acknowledge? Remember His words: " I will not now call you servants, . . . but I have called you friends " (John xv, 15). When I deliberately commit a venial sin with the idea, " It's only a venial sin," which is the same as saying, " There is no eternal punishment attached," am I seeking God, or am I seeking myself? Not God, surely. If I were, I would take care not to do anything that would offend Him in the least. No, I am seeking myself. I am looking to see just how far I can allow myself forbidden liberties and pleasures, without straining my relations with God to the breaking point, and running the risk of being hurt in punishment for all eternity. I do not like pain, I am afraid of suffering. But just the same, I will indulge myself this once today. I will go just so far in gratifying my eyes, my ears, my tongue, my taste, my mind, my imagination, my temper, but I will go no farther. Just this once today. Tomorrow it is the same story. And the day after. Only it is more than once, and the number of falls goes on increasing daily. Some day, one of these horses, through our gradually relaxing hold, will break the reins, and rush us madly much farther than we ever expected or intended to go, down the length of the infernal precipice, to the foul abyss below. And all because "*It's only a venial sin.*" Nor is this another exaggeration. History affords us only too many instances. Luther did not become a heretic over night, nor Judas a deicide; neither was Peter's denial the result of a momentary weakness. No. All these betrayals had their origin in scarcely perceptible beginnings. And because the shadow of sin was not persistently dispelled, the storm of passion eventually broke in all its fury.

And how does such a soul, steeped in this poison of erroneous judgment, make its confession? Rather from habit than from the conviction of its usefulness, or from appreciation of the efficacy of the sacrament. Week after week, the same sins are recounted; year after year the tale never varies. Why? The confession is not entire; the contrition is not sincere. And contrition is the most essential part of the sacrament. It is impossible for a soul possessed of true contrition not to advance in the path of perfection; not to root out its faults one by one. But what is contrition?

Contrition is sorrow for sin, and sorrow that springs from a supernatural motive. This motive may be a love of God, whence arises that contrition called perfect; or it may be a fear of losing heaven or of gaining hell, whence arises that contrition called imperfect. And imperfect contrition is sufficient for a valid sacramental confession. Perfect contrition is sorrow for sin because a loving Father has been offended. Reward and punishment should have no place in its thought; the soul should grieve solely because it recognizes that God is love, the one Supreme Good.

True sorrow implies always a firm resolution of amendment. If sorrow be lacking in this essential characteristic, it is pharisaical sorrow, a sham, and no sorrow at all. To be sincerely sorry for one's sins, to have a super-natural contrition for them, it is not necessary to have the gift of tears, nor is this even desirable. Neither is it necessary to be penetrated with a vehement emotion of grief, nor is it desirable. And it is precisely on this point that the devil leads many souls astray.

What, then, is necessary? Simply this: to will an efficacious sorrow, a determined regret. Since the one evil in the world is sin, and the one force in the world capable of making me participate in this evil is my own free will; since, in brief, it is my will that causes sin, it is my will that repents. Certainly, my understanding assists the will by presenting to it the motives for regretting its bad acts — love of God, the reward of heaven, the punishment of hell. But all the consideration in the world will avail me nothing unless that will of mine acts in accordance with the truths presented to it, and acts efficaciously. My will is a power, a force. And if a power, a force, is going to accomplish something, it must be exerted against the object that offers resistance. Here is a high-pressure steam boiler. Properly applied, that steam may heat a house or move a locomotive; it may also be allowed to evaporate. And this boiler of my will is given me to heat the house of my soul perfectly by the quickening steam of love. Only if misdirected, the steam will evaporate. So this power of will, then, must be exerted against the one existing evil, sin. It is not sufficient simply to say vocally or mentally, or in the depths of my heart, " I am sorry "; I must mean what I say; I must be determined never to do it again.

For instance, take a child who has offended its father. Either by punishment, or rebuke, or kindly instruction, he is made to realize his disobedience. "I am sorry, father," he says. And the father forgives him because he thinks him sincere. A half-hour later he finds the child deliberately engaged in a similar offense. Did the child mean what he said? He may have thought he did, but his subsequent actions proved that his sorrow was lip-sorrow, because it was lacking in a prime essential: the determination to avoid the evil; the efficacious resolve henceforth to be obedient.

And this is why the soul that habitually says, "It's only a venial sin," cannot have sincere contrition, because of its affection for the evil. If the will embraces the evil, and it certainly does, because it finds repeated delight in it, it cannot at the same time embrace the opposite good, namely, God. It may at the moment of confession try to do so in an irresolute, half-hearted manner. And since it is impossible for a soul, while continuing in this state, to elicit an act of perfect contrition, its contrition is thus necessarily imperfect. And this is why its condition daily becomes worse instead of better; this is why, because the soul is so indisposed, that Our Lord is hampered in the work He is yearning to effect through the operation of His Life-giving Spirit, for even He cannot perfect us unless we give our consent.

And remember, it is impossible for a soul who makes a constant and proper use of the sacrament of Penance not to advance in perfection. And the abuse of it may be traced to one fundamental cause: lack of earnestness in prayer, failure to beg the necessary grace. To avoid the evil of venial sin, of all sin, one must act contrary to nature. And nature cannot overcome nature. Grace alone can. " Ask, and you shall receive " (John xvi, 24). But here again we must mean what we say, else the judgment for our rejection of proffered graces will be doubly weighty. And again, the whole question of perfection may be resolved thus: To conform myself to the image of my Beloved, Christ Jesus, I need but to will so to do. That will, however, shall not and cannot rely on its own strength; it can effectively act only through the strengthening power of grace, poured in great abundance on those who seek it in this holy sacrament of Penance.

10. REMOTE AND PROXIMATE PREPARA-TION FOR HOLY COMMUNION

" I will utter things hidden from the foundation of the world "
(MATT. xiii, 35)

IN ONE of the previous conferences it was said that of the three instruments held out to us by the Church for our sanctification, the Mass is unquestionably the greatest, because the Mass is Christ, our Head, sacrificing Himself again in a mystical manner for us, the members of His mystical body, His very brethren; and being offered by us to the heavenly Father as a sovereign, and therefore, sufficient adoration, thanksgiving, reparation, and petition. It was also said that to reap the full benefit of the wonderful harvest of graces which the Holy Sacrifice holds for each of us individually, it is necessary to be closely united to Christ Jesus, our Divine High Priest and Victim, in order that the unction of the Life-giving Spirit may flow and overflow in constant, invigorating, unchecked streams of grace, from the Head to the members of the body. This union with our Saviour consists essentially in reproducing within us His character of Victim, in conforming ourselves to Him absolutely, in every least detail — to Him, the Immolated Lamb. This is the work of a lifetime, the special work of the religious, that tending towards perfection, which is the obligation voluntarily assumed the day we pronounced our holy vows. In other words, we are bound to sacrifice ourselves with Him on the altar of propitiation.

Left to ourselves, or relying on our own efforts, we should speedily grow disheartened, and should be pledged to certain failure, for this task of overcoming self is beyond the natural strength of man. The less we confide in self, the more we shall accomplish; the more steadfastly we determine to die, the more effectually shall we begin to live. The spiritual life, as you realize, is one of seeming paradoxes, which may all be reduced to one word of Our Lord: " Without me you can do nothing " (John xv, 5). And so here. Knowing our weakness, and our great desire to imitate Him, the Atoning Victim, He gives us Himself, that He in His omnipotence and love may transform us into Himself, and so accomplish what we alone should not even dare to desire. And the wonder and mystery of it all is that this sublime gift of Himself is necessary for the integrity of the Holy Sacrifice; unless the Victim be consumed, there is no *complete* sacrifice. And our participation in this Divine Gift is the receiving of Holy Communion. Verily " God becomes man that man may become God " (St. Augustine). If we are to realize in full measure that we constitute a " kingly priesthood " (I Peter ii, 9), then, in order to make the oblation of Christ to the Father entire, we too must consume the Victim, must sit down at the Holy Table, to share in the sacrificial meal which the Father has prepared for us in the Person of the Incarnate Word. And in this, the partaking of the Blessed Sacrament, the sacrifice-banquet, we have a most powerful aid to sanctification. God Himself comes to perfect us, if we but so will.

Here again in our use of the sacrament we may be guilty of unconscious abuse. Because of this abuse we do not receive the full measure of graces which our Divine Master brings with Him for our healing; we do not develop spiritually as He would desire; we halt on the path of perfection.

Holy Communion! What better name could have been given this sublime repast? *Holy*. Who more holy than God, the Author and Fountain-Head of Sanctity? *Communion*. A " oneing." " God becomes man that man may become God." He gives Himself to us under the appearance of bread, common food, in order that we may be assimilated unto Him. This Sacred Host, this Gift of the Father, is that Divine Leaven which works secretly in the recesses of our soul, until the whole is leavened; until we have become sweetened, enlightened, purified, exalted; until we have in very truth put on Christ; until the Father sees in us the features of His Well-Beloved Son.

But in the natural order, leaven is inactive until heat is applied. Keep in mind that all comparisons between the natural and the supernatural, the material and the spiritual, are necessarily imperfect. With regard to the Divine Leaven, Holy Communion, there is this difference to be noted: Since it is God Whom we receive, whole and entire, in this ineffable mystery — and the same is true with regard to the operation of the other sacraments —

the Holy Ghost works in our souls independently of any action on our part, for the sacraments of themselves, being of Divine institution, produce the effects they signify.

Just the same, we can, and only too often do, hinder the operations of the Eternal Spirit by setting up barriers, now of one kind, now of another, which prevent that plenteous outpouring of graces He desires to lavish upon us. We do not dispose ourselves properly; that is, the heat of an active love, a resolute will, is lacking, and this in the way of preparation, reception, and thanksgiving. And so, because of the imperfect heat we supply, the action of the Divine Leaven, our sanctification, is therefore retarded; our spiritual growth is negligible, for we do not exert ourselves to submit fully to the precious embrace of the Eternal Word, the Gift of the Father to us, our sacrifice-banquet. Nor should there be any difficulty in seeing the necessity of increasingly-good dispositions. A shower of rain falling on rock or gravel produces no fruit; that same shower watering a carefully prepared acre brings forth copious vegetation.

We shall, then, consider the preparation, which is one in intention, yet twofold in direction: remote and immediate. It is a mistake to think of this preparation as being of two kinds. The immediate is but the compression of the remote; the remote, the extension of the immediate. By that I mean only this: All the earnestness of purpose, the fervor of desire, the cleansing of compunction, the ardor of love, the intensity of faith, which we experience in our prayer of anticipation before we receive the heavenly Food, should permeate as a delicious perfume all the remaining actions of the day. For the remote preparation, after all, may also be called a continued thanksgiving.

But the reason why our immediate preparation is faulty is because the remote is not vigorous. And why? We are not in earnest. We are not strongly determined. In our hearts we do not truly, sincerely, resolutely mean what our lips profess when Our Lord makes His abode with us. We partake of a Divine *Victim*, and He finds in us very little resemblance to Himself, or maybe none at all. If, then, I wish my communions to bring forth the hundredfold fruit Our Lord intends they should, my intention must coincide with His, must be identical with His. And this not only momentarily, but during the entire day, for " now is the acceptable time; now is the day of salvation " (II Cor. vi, 2).

To make my prayer of anticipation that heartfelt cry which finds immediate echo in the bosom of the Father, I must live the life of Christ the entire day. I must try to think as He would think; to speak as He would speak; to act as He would act. And thus doing, what more natural than that at my time of prayer, I should pray as He prays? For it is impossible for any one who makes proper use of his daily intimate contact with Sanctity Itself, not to become holy, perfect; not to be clothed with Christ, to be conformed to His image. Let us then think for a moment about ourselves; let us look at ourselves impersonally, from the point of view of our neighbor. Today, after five, ten, or more years of frequent, yes, daily com-

munion, does our neighbor begin to recognize in us another Christ? Are we really becoming Christlike? Are
we more patient, more meek, more humble, more zealous,
more charitable; in brief, more holy than we were at the
outset of our religious life? And this answer, to be can-
did, must be disinterested; it must have our daily actions
toward our neighbor as the basis of examination, not our
preconceived ideas of the size and durability of our
virtue.

Virtue is eminently practical. If it be the real thing
and not a sham, a make-believe, virtue is incessantly active, ever seeking new outlets for its consuming energy.
And the greater the amount of energy expended, that
is, the more frequently and determinedly virtue is prac-
tised, the more flourishing and vigorous it becomes. And
we who have the exalted privilege of being intimately
united every day with Christ, the Fountain-Head of
virtue, what should not the strength of our virtue be!
How invigorating its expellent sweetness! We, who in
Holy Communion have so long been the intimate friends
of God, the Life-giving Ether, should continually exhale
the sweet odor of Jesus Christ.

But perhaps our examination tells us that such is not
the case. We are still prone to anger, and the uncharitable word, and criticism, and love of the world, and
contempt of so-called trifles, and self-interest, nearly as
much as we were at the beginning of our conversion.
There has been an improvement, yes, but so slight that
it is hardly perceptible; nothing at any rate to correspond
to the innumerable graces Our Lord holds out to us each

day in the breaking of bread. And why? Because we do not think enough of our Divine Guest during the day. If we thought of Him more frequently, the majority of our troubles would vanish as the fog before the powerful sun, and the number of our falls would markedly decrease. For who could criticize, and speak the angry and unkind word, and give in to sloth, and vanity, and pride, remembering God, remembering the meek and humble Saviour, Whom he is professing to follow? Ah, no! We do not recall His early morning visit; we do not press Him to stay and assist us: " Stay with us, because it is towards evening, and the day is now far spent " (Luke xxiv, 29). For who, no matter how young he may be, can say with certainty that the present hour may not be his evening of life? And so during the entire day we continue cold and distracted and careless in the performance of our work, in the exercise of our spiritual duties.

Is it to be wondered at, then, that with such a remote preparation, the few moments spent in anticipation of the coming of Christ are far from being what His Heart desires? Are we not just a little like the Jews who, expecting the Messiah, the One promised to redeem them, had, by reason of their worldliness and self-absorption, become so blinded to the real, the spiritual significance of His advent, that they deluded themselves and others into a greedy expectation of a temporal kingdom? Do we not look forward to His advent chiefly from a material viewpoint? Are we not principally, perhaps even solely, occupied with thoughts and prayers for material advantages: success in our work; the good opinion of superiors and fellow-religious; aye, the approval of the world with which we come in contact, to the detriment sometimes of our character as religious; and a thousand and one favors of a purely temporal order? Not that it is wrong, or even unnecessary to ask for these things — health, success, good friends; — but all this should be subordinated to the one great interest we have vowed to pursue, the one end for which our beloved Master comes into our hearts — our sanctification.

We act thus because our faith, our confidence and trust, are weak. We do not take Him at His word. "Seek ye therefore, first, the kingdom of God and His justice," He, the Eternal Truth, tells us, "and all these things" (such is the *promise* of God) "shall be added unto you" (Matt. vi, 33). But He cannot add all these things unto us, He cannot fulfil His promise, because we do not fulfil the condition, no, not even in Holy Communion, to seek *first* the kingdom of God. And where is this kingdom? Within. "For, lo," says Our Lord, "the kingdom of God is within you" (Luke xvii, 21).

And because we do not care about our perfection, because we do not view the things of time from the standpoint of eternity, because we do not seek God all day long in all that we do (we say we do, but if we looked into the matter, we would discover we are after all seeking only our miserable selves), the immediate preparation for Holy Communion, the great "oneing," is cold, full of distractions, even distasteful at times, and bears little or no fruit. We hardly lift a finger to help ourselves, and then expect God to work a miracle for our benefit. Is it not unreasonable to expect to acquire a close bond of intimacy with God in a few brief moments, when we have not been striving to remain united with Him in thought, word, and deed the remaining twenty-four hours? Why wonder that the sublime participation of the Sacrificial Lamb (an act which is denied to the angels) becomes a formal round, a monotonous routine? The fault is purely our own — we do not mean our religious life earnestly; we are lacking in firm resolution.

And to help us to prepare to receive Our Lord in a manner becoming His Infinite Majesty, think reflectively on Mary's years of preparation before the Word was made flesh in her virginal womb. Her Divine maternity was a reward of her fidelity in seeking first the kingdom of God. From her earliest infancy she sought only Him Whom her soul loved. Had Mary done otherwise, the Incarnation might never have been according to the plan God had in mind from all eternity. Mary was determined; Mary was courageous; Mary was generous; Mary was faithful. And so when the perpetually-wound clock of eternity chimed the hour of the world's salvation, the angel found Mary ready, waiting on God, Who Himself waited for her consent to the ineffable union. Only at her *fiat* did the Word live on earth. And our daily, hourly *fiat* is necessary for the mystical advent of Jesus. So living, our prayer of anticipation for His coming will be the eager, generous, spontaneous love and desire of a heart throbbing in harmony with His. No lengthy formulas or recited acts will be needed or wished for. The soul that ever seeks God knows what to say to Him at all moments and on every occasion, because God, Whom she powerfully attracts by the devotedness of her love, is Himself her teacher.

The soul who by constant struggle strives always to realize that the kingdom of God is within her, finds that sweet silence and repose wherein the Beloved makes His presence felt. " I will . . . lead her into the wilderness " (Osee ii, 14), He says. Persisting in effort to attain this blessed quiet by resolutely combating self, the soul understands the word of her Bridegroom, " and I will speak to her heart " (Osee ii, 14). And this utterance of " things hidden from the foundation of the world " (Matt. xiii, 35) is heard especially during the intimate union between God and His creature in the communication of the breaking of bread. But this sublime act will require detailed discussion in another conference, the continuation of this, for we have just begun the subject.

11. RECEPTION OF, AND THANKSGIVING
AFTER, HOLY COMMUNION

" I will utter things hidden from the foundation of the world "
                                                    (MATT. xiii, 35)

IN OUR last conference we considered the matter of
preparation for Holy Communion, the partaking of the
sacrificial-banquet, essential to the integrity of the Mass
for the one who ministers. And since we all, in virtue of
our lot of " kingly priesthood " (I Peter ii, 9), offer the
Divine Victim to the Father; we all, to render the sacrifice entire and to reap the full harvest of graces it contains, should sit down at the Holy Table and consume
the Immolated Lamb. This is that sacred Gift, His Beloved Son, which the Father gives us in return for our
Infinite Holocaust, and which we are privileged daily to
receive. We saw, too, that the immediate prayer of anticipation depended for its fervor and sincerity on the remote prayer of self-sacrificing action. In unearthing the
troubles that made the remote preparation barren instead of fruitful, we laid bare at the same time the chief
reason for our deriving so little benefit from the visit of
Our Lord during the few moments of actual physical
contact with Him.

You should be able to give the cause yourselves. Yes,
it is self. And this EGO manifests itself particularly in

this way: it talks too much. Conversation is, as you no doubt are aware, an art. And prayer is conversation between the creature and Creator. And it is a truth you all realize from experience that he who talks most, says least. In fact, such a one is a bore, for incessant chattering is monotonous. Why? Because he of the pliant tongue is filled with one subject — himself. The reason we cannot stand others to prattle continually of themselves is because we are being forced into the background, and prevented from doing the very thing we are condemning in our neighbor. That is human nature. It is always the capital " I." But the conversational artist, whether born — a rare mortal — or made, speaks best, for he knows how to listen. It is not what he says, but what he does not say, that counts. And most artists, whatever their field, agree that real art consists in knowing just what to omit; for the perfection of art is to conceal art in the achievement of the exquisitely natural.

And what holds good in the natural, holds equally good in the supernatural. Every day we welcome a Guest, God Himself. And what happens? Before we have barely exchanged the civility of a " good morning " — in our hurry sometimes even forgetting to tell Him we are glad He came — our tongue is unloosed, and we are off with the marathon runners on our favorite topic — self. We want this, that, and a hundred other things, chiefly temporal, for ourselves; we want these, those, and two hundred things for our bosom friends, taking care to cover the entire list by actual count and name; and then? A long list of complaints, claiming forsooth, that we have asked and did not receive. All the while the meek and gentle Lord bears with us, for He knows our weakness; bears with us patiently but sadly, wistfully wondering, " If only that soul would permit Me, what would I not do for her! "

Remember, too, that it requires a great delicacy of attention and a refinement of consideration to be a successful host. The good host makes it a point to study the inclinations of his guest — his business, his chief interests, ambitions, and desires. This knowledge will direct the trend of the conversation. The host aims to become a negligible quantity in the matter of putting himself forward, and yet an essential one in the faculty of being an interested and observant listener. It is the guest who is made the center of interest, and who receives every mark of honor and esteem. Of course, there is in the case of some an affected attention and respect. We do not consider that here. Courtesy, the only courtesy deserving of the name, is born of the heart. It is the external expression of a sympathetic charity.

Again let me remind you that what is true in the natural, is true in the supernatural. But even the supernatural is natural here, and this we too often forget, or act as though we did. That Living Bread Which cometh down from heaven, and is reverently laid on our tongue, is God, the Word made flesh, a living human being, the God-Man. Not only does He come into our heart as our God, our Saviour, our Mediator, but with the additional binding power of our Well-Beloved, our Spouse.

Could we but begin to sense this personal reality of

Jesus Christ in the Holy Eucharist, how differently should we not dispose ourselves toward His reception. He has a human heart that dilates with a human love; a human understanding divinely responsive to our every least mood and thought and desire. And He is God. He could not have made Himself more humble, more approachable. He divested Himself in time of the glory of His Divinity that with It He might invest us in eternity. But we must do our share. He is waiting for us to let Him act freely in our souls, and we, self-absorbed with our petty nothings, let Him wait. We who are His hosts selfishly push our interest always to the fore; we ask and ask but generally for ourselves, or for those to whom we are intimately attached. If only we would ask Him about His affairs, and why He comes to us; and then stop to listen for His answer. But no. We are afraid to ask, afraid to listen, because He will tell us the truth. He would demand some sacrifice, because He would show us the meanness of our real self. We dislike pain, especially self-inflicted pain. And so the lights that should be ours are withheld because we are not receptive; and so the work of our sanctification progresses but haltingly.

Our perfection, remember, is the only reason for our existence. We are created to know God, to love Him, and to serve Him. Service, or activity, depends on knowledge and love. Where can we hope to attain a more luminous knowledge and a more ardent love than in Holy Communion? Knowledge is the power of the intellect; love, of the will. We are, according to our spiritual nature, intellect and will. And God Who gives Himself to us in the Sacred Host is Infinite Intelligence and Infinite Will. Surely He Who created this intellect and will of mine had no other end in view than ultimately to fill them with Himself, exalting them through the instrumentality of grace to union with Him. He who is in the state of grace, as he necessarily must be who approaches to receive His Creator, already possesses Him in His illimitable Divinity. And it is of faith that every Communion well received increases our measure of sanctifying grace, which means that our capacity for enjoying God is enlarged. We possess Him here through faith and love. If our faith is like the grain of mustard seed and our love a flickering ember, our delight in Him will be proportionate. Hence the necessity of His exercising our faith and love by temptations and trials and difficulties, which beset us from the very dawn of life.

But do we accept these caresses of our heavenly Father in the spirit wherein they are bestowed? Or do we by murmurs and complaints and even resentment turn them into additional matter for punishment? Ah, did we but understand our great privilege in being thus marked with the sign of the elect, the saving sign of the cross! It is this very seal that makes us dear to the Heart of Christ, that attracts Him irresistibly to us.

The cross shorn of its precious burden remains in the eyes of the world what it was before Good Friday, a thing of shame and opprobrium. For Christians, the cross is the Crucified. And it is just because men refuse to see the Crucified nailed alive to the tree of odium, that they twist and writhe under the crosses God lays upon them, seeing therein only marks of His displeasure. But that is the wisdom and logic of the world, not of the saints, not of the Saint of saints. How else account for the too-prevalent expressions: " bad fortune "; " hard times "; " What have I done to deserve this? " " Why try to serve God when He sends trouble upon trouble? " " What is the use of trying to do the right thing when you can get along much better by acting otherwise? " Yes, we have already mentally condemned those who act thus. But are we entirely guiltless? Do we always see the Cruci-fied when viewing our apparently insupportable bur-dens? Do we set ourselves to see the Crucified? And when He reveals Himself to our gaze, do we embrace the wounded One, or do we turn away our eyes, because we do not like to admit the significance of His image? And what is it that He says to us, He, the First Beginning and the Last End? " I am the Way " (John xiv, 6). And they crucified Him between two thieves!

It is especially to impress us with His crucified image that Christ Our Lord comes into our heart in Holy Com-munion. How could it be otherwise? Has He not been immolated anew on the Calvary of the altar as a propitia-tion to the Father? Do we not in receiving Him partake of the Sacrificial Lamb? Since He comes in the nature of a holocaust, it is to make us a holocaust with Him; since He comes as the Divine Victim, it is to make us victims like Himself. You see He takes us at our word during the consecration: " Heart of Jesus, Victim of love, make me for Thee a living sacrifice, holy and pleasing to God." (300 *days indulgence for religious.*) He is delighted with our prayer; it is the echo of His own. And He yearns with infinite yearning, and desires with divine desire to communicate Himself to us in the breaking of bread. And then, after looking forward lovingly to that intimate union, He is so disappointed. He discovers we do not mean all that we said. If a sacrifice, a victim, then we have voluntarily given ourselves up to the good pleasure of our Creator. We have agreed to seek only His interests, His will. And our first greeting to Him is so full of self. Truly He has cause to say: " If only, soul that I love, you would permit Me, what wonders would I not work in you! "

But we *are* going to give Him the opportunity He desires. We *are* going to become true artists in heavenly conversation. We *are* going to become faultless hosts. We *are* going to strain every nerve to center our attention on our loving Spouse, giving Him every mark of honor and esteem. And it is not so difficult, for we know His business, His chief interests: His glory, our sanctification, and the salvation of souls. These are the topics that will direct our conversation with Him.

His glory. This is chief and foremost. Our first act, then, in receiving Him should be an interior glance of adoration and praise. He Who has just been laid on our tongue is that Almighty God, before Whom the angels and the ancients and the four living creatures fall down upon their faces, and adore, saying: " Amen. Benediction, and glory, and wisdom, and thanksgiving, honor, and power, and strength to our God for ever and ever. Amen " (Apoc. vii, 12). God, our loving Father; God,

[113]

Christ Jesus, our Saviour, our Beloved, our Spouse; God, the Eternal Life-giving Spirit, our Sanctifier; God, Whom the heaven of heavens cannot contain, is housed in my own heart; God, Who in an instant can destroy the whole world and create countless new ones; this God is waiting on me, is become my servant. He is burning to do anything, everything for me. But I must consent — I have consented: " A living sacrifice, holy, pleasing unto God " (Rom. xii, 1). Jesus, I mean it. Annihilation is the supreme act of worship, the rendering to God of that glory which is His due from creatures. Annihilation! That is what it means to be a victim. No will, no thought, no desire, save His. No resistance to His absolute dominion over me. This is the glory that I can give, the glory He is seeking, for which He is now pleading, as He holds me tightly, His lips against mine, Jesus, Beggar Divine, Jesus-God. The thought is overpowering. Majesty, Omnipotence, Sanctity, Life, Love, . . .

My sanctification. For this He comes. For this He holds audience with me. Of this we shall speak, He, my Guest, talking, and I, His host, listening. The quiet He desires is undisturbed. He has led me into solitude, the solitude of His Heart; and my heart is beating now in unison with His. " Speak, Lord, for thy servant heareth " (I Kings iii, 9). Now He utters things, unspeakable things, heretofore hidden from me — not words, no, but in the palpable silence of peace, the sweetness of His own dear presence. It is the golden wisdom of understanding that is now mine. The light that streams from the Godhead is penetrating the darkness of my intellect, dispelling the clouds of blindness and uncertainty, illuminating truths previously obscure. Looking at Him I love, and yielding without resistance to the ardor of His embrace, I begin to fathom little by little something of His incomprehensible Majesty; something of my own nothingness as His creature. I begin to yearn with vehement longing to lose my nothingness in His immensity, to find my real self in Him, the immutable center toward which my soul naturally gravitates; to possess Him to the fullest extent of my gradually-perfected capacity. Such has been His desire always; such is now mine. Clinging to Him with strengthened faith and love, my whole soul adores, and pleads, " Lord, that I may see " (Luke xviii, 41). Today He reveals to me the hidden springs of selfishness; tomorrow of vanity; now of anger; again of pride. The *hidden springs,* please note. His work is ever thorough; He ever lays bare the roots when we sincerely seek Him. Else the weeds incessantly flourish, the contaminated streams continually flow unchecked — and we become discouraged. But He gives light to see; and strength to do; and courage to dare. We now realize that in very truth we can do nothing without Him. We have thrown away the reedy prop of self and lean strongly through faith and confidence and love on Him, the Holy Strong One.

We have asked and we have received. We shall continue to ask, and we shall continue to receive, until that blessed day, and more intensely thereafter, when we shall experience, if we persevere, the divine truth of these solemn words: " I am thy reward exceeding great "

(Gen. xv, 1). And not until we have found God shall we be at rest and satisfied; and not until we have found God shall we really begin to thirst for Him. And this our delving, deeper and ever more deep, into the abyss of grace goes on with every Communion well made; this is that gravitation toward our soul's center; this is true progress in perfection. And this sublime " oneing " will grow in sweetness and security and intensity until it severs the fragile bonds of the flesh, and vision unending is ours.

The salvation of souls. But little remains to be said, for this follows as a natural consequence from all that has gone before. He, who purely to glorify God strives after his own sanctification, is continually saving souls. Suffering is the only way. Suffering perfects us and sanctifies our neighbor. For we are all members of one mystical body. When we have given up ourselves unreservedly to the purifying unction that comes to us from our Head, our least action is His to do with as He pleases. And He pleases that our works and sufferings and prayers and desires " fill up," as St. Paul says, " those things that are wanting of the sufferings of Christ " (Col. i, 24); and in greater abundance apply to souls the fruits of His redemption, thus furthering the kingdom of God on earth.

This, then, is a little of the meaning of that divine utterance " hidden from the foundation of the world " (Matt. xiii, 35); " receiving the word in much tribulation, with joy of the Holy Ghost; for our gospel hath not been unto you in word only, but in power also, and in the Holy Ghost, and in much fulness " (I Thess. i, 6 and 5).

IV. *Prayer: the third great means of sanctification*

12. DISPOSITIONS NECESSARY FOR PRAYER — ATTENTION AND INTENTION

"To thee, O Lord, have I lifted up my soul" (Ps. xxiv, 1)

OF THE three instruments held out to us by our mother, the Church, for our sanctification, we have already considered two: the Holy Sacrifice and the sacraments. But neither is the Mass, our greatest aid, nor are the sacraments, next in importance, at our disposal every moment of the day. But the third help to the attainment of perfection, prayer, not only is available always, but is binding by the command of our Divine Master to be made use of always, for He says: " We ought always to pray " (Luke xviii, 1).

The graces we shall derive from the first and second instruments will depend chiefly on our use of the third, because, as we have seen, the treasures of the Mass and the sacraments are given to us according to the measure of our good dispositions. And prayer is a disposition of the heart. So that, when by persevering effort we shall have begun to fulfil this word of Our Lord, " pray without ceasing " (I Thess. v, 17), we shall have made our souls most receptive for the impression of the marvelous benefits that flow from the other chief instruments. Having thus been drawn to God, we shall run in the odor of

His ointments. Our progress then shall no longer be that of the snail, but that of the impetuous eagle. You should realize, therefore, how vital a matter is this subject of prayer, since it is the foundation of our whole spiritual life.

Before we begin to treat of this sublime intercourse, let me impress you with one truth of extreme importance: unless you strive *to practise* what you are taught, the mere knowledge *in theory* will avail you nothing except to add to your condemnation. A great many people *think* they know all about prayer, because they have read the greatest masters on the subject. They *think* they know how to pray, and to pray very well, because they can readily recall all that they have perused, and even impart the information to others. So they set themselves up as instructors before they have ever performed any of the drill exercises of beginners. The harm that they do to souls, their own included, will never be known here below. Informative knowledge, truth derived from others, is one thing; experimental knowledge, truth born of experience, another. The difference between them is as vast as the void that separates the earth from heaven, the darkness from the light.

If you wish to derive the full benefit from this conference and the succeeding ones, you must dispose yourself immediately in the proper manner, which means that you must be determined resolutely *to act* in accordance with the light God will give you. To come to the study of prayer with any other motive raises up an insurmountable barrier to grace, and makes a mockery of what is most sacred. Unless you *will* to coöperate with God, God Himself cannot sanctify you.

Our catechism tells us that prayer is the elevation of the mind and heart to God, either to praise Him, or to thank Him, or to beg His grace. This same thought is the initial cry of the Church, borrowed from the holy Psalmist: " To thee, O Lord, have I lifted up my soul " (Ps. 24, 1 — Introit of Mass, First Sunday of Advent). And why? " Shew, O Lord, thy ways to me, and teach me thy paths " (Ps. 24, 4). These words show us at once the meaning of prayer and its purpose. Why does David wish to be shown but to know; and why does he wish to be taught but to do? And why does he wish both to know and to do, except that he may serve? To know, and do (love), and serve, with respect to God, is the only reason for our existence. A life of prayer, then, is essential if we are to " render to God the things that are God's " (Matt. xxii, 21), namely, that perfection of homage which we as creatures owe to God in common with all other created but unintelligent beings.

Notice that the Church, our infallible guide, lays down as the essential condition of prayer the raising up of our minds and hearts to God. Of the mind, the intellect, and of the heart, the will. This last statement may need a word of explanation. Recall for a minute what we learned from the discussion of the sacrament of Baptism: man is created to the image and likeness of God. But this resemblance is in the soul, the spiritual part of man. The animal nature, the body, with all its senses and passions, is material. According to our spiritual nature we are intellect and will, brought forth out of nothingness by an Infinite Intellect and an Infinite Will. Further, it is this intellect and will that is the field of prayer, for it is the soul that is elevated to God in prayer; the soul that seeks to hold intercourse with Him. The body shares to a certain extent in an external manifestation of that interior disposition which is prayer; for example, in posture, kneeling or standing, or in the vocal expression of the soul's communing with God. Since prayer is a spiritual operation, not material, the essence of prayer does not therefore consist in bodily attitudes or in many words, but in the communication of spirit and Spirit.

This communication is twofold: that of attention and that of intention. Attention is the work of the mind, or intellect; intention that of the heart, or will. The heart is commonly regarded as the center of the sensible affections; and because the will is the center, or seat of the spiritual affections — that is, the will loves and hopes and fears and believes — the one term, heart, is often used to designate this radiating power of the soul. So, then, our catechism says that prayer is an elevation of the mind, — attention — and of the will, — intention — to God. In other words, we wait on God as our Sovereign Lord, and we embrace Him as our Supreme Good.

It was mentioned previously that prayer is conversation between the creature and the Creator. This seems apparently at variance with the definition just given, but it is really the self-same thing. Again, we must remember that prayer, intercourse with God, is the function of the soul, of created spirit seeking its Uncreated

Origin. Speech may or may not have anything at all to do in helping to sustain this union; vocal prayers, generally, though good in themselves, are overdone. " When you are praying," says Our Lord, " speak not much, as the heathens. For they think that in their much speaking they may be heard " (Matt. vi, 7). The vocal chords are part of the bodily organism; and God gave us the power of speech to hold intercourse primarily with men, not with Himself. Speech is the oral expression of ideas; and conversation is essentially the exchange of ideas between man and man. The idea is there first. All too often we find that words only very imperfectly express what is in our mind. When there is a striving after intimacy between two persons, the better part of their conversation is left unsaid. The bond of understanding unites them. There is a spiritual contact between them which makes silence more eloquent than speech. But this condition has arisen only because they sought each other's company. Their sympathetic intercourse exists because of the harmony of their minds and wills. Here again it is the attention and intention that count; the attending to each other's considerations, either expressed in words or unuttered; the willingness to give this attention because of the desire for each other's fellowship.

Simply translate this explanation to the spiritual realm, where the question of conversation lies not between man and man, but between created spirit and Uncreated Spirit, between your soul and God. It is finite intelligence and finite will seeking Infinite Intelligence and Infinite Will.

[123]

What is necessary? The desire of the soul to strive after this intimacy with God through conversational contact; and further, harmony of mind and will, achieved through grace by a sustained, resolute struggle against self. " My thoughts are not your thoughts, nor your ways my ways, saith the Lord " (Isaias lv, 8). No. But our work, the aim of prayer, the end of our existence, is to make our ways His very own, as we learn from His command: " Learn of Me " (Matt. xi, 29). Since without God we are absolutely helpless, — " Without me you can do nothing " (John xv, 5) — and since, as the apostle tells us, without His special grace we could neither have a single good thought, nor pronounce His sacred name, it is very evident that it is not we who pray, but God Who prays within us.

Why, then, is not our prayer divine, as God intended it to be? Because He has been denied absolute dominion over our soul — we have refused to renounce self utterly. Only that prayer is well made, is really of God, and not of self, or of the Evil One, which bears its fruit in our lives, which makes the image of the Creator shine forth more resplendently by gradually breaking down the hollow plaster-cast of that superior statue, EGO. Or again, that prayer is well made which helps to destroy the old Adam and so clothe us with Christ; which renders more marked in us the character of victim, making us one with the Sacrificial Lamb; which is the Mass realized in our own lives; for all these expressions mean one and the same thing. The whole of Christian perfection may be summed up thus in the words of the Master: " If any man will come after me, let him deny himself, and take up his cross daily, and follow me" (Luke ix, 23).

At this point it is necessary to make clear that this daily self-denial in little things is absolutely essential for the life of prayer. It is folly to suppose that one can give full liberty to the eyes, and the ears, and the taste, and the touch, and especially to the tongue, outside the appointed periods of prayer, and then expect to make that conversation a thing pleasing to God in the manner and to the degree He has a right to expect and demand. Remember always that the soul is cluttered with the clay of the flesh; that prayer is the communion between spirit and Spirit, and only in so far as this soul of ours subdues the material part of us will its intercourse with the Father become what it should be, what God wills it to be — Godlike. For it is God Who prays in each of us; and the less there is of self to spoil the work by conscious or unconscious interference, the more will God be able to glorify Himself in our hearts, unimpeded by blundering action on our part.

He who for the love of God *tries* perseveringly all day long to overcome self, to do God's will as it is made known to him, is praying all day long, for his will is in union with the will of God. This, in fact, is the one way in which we can execute the command of Jesus Christ: " that we ought always to pray " (Luke xviii, 1). This constitutes the union of the will; the elevation of the heart, that is, the will, to God. This is living in the proper disposition — the desire, expressed in act, to strive after intimacy with God, without which disposition prayer, and hence perfection, is impossible. And it is likewise impossible for anyone who is really trying with earnest effort to overcome self for the love of God, not to think occasionally of Him for Whom he labors, in swift, affectionate remembrance, or short, intense pleas for assistance. Not that these elevations of the mind, whether expressed in mental or vocal aspirations or not, should be forced. On the contrary, everything in the spiritual life should be free and natural. One cannot *think* continually of God, no matter what the nature of one's duties may be; attention must necessarily be given to the work at hand, though it should never be so entirely absorbing as to prevent, now and then, an uplifting of the mind to the Master for Whom it is being accomplished, especially when difficulties present themselves to beg His help; or to thank Him for its comparatively easy achievement; or to glorify and love Him just for being permitted to labor in His service.

Being thus elevated in mind to God by frequent aspirations, and in will, by striving to do all that He has marked out for us as perfectly as we know how, we betray that attention and intention which the Church has designated the essence of prayer; and we are accomplishing the command of Our Lord: " Pray without ceasing " (I Thess. v, 17). Besides, we are then living in very truth the *one* commandment as God desires it to be lived; for, since we are directing all our energy of mind and will to the performance of His adorable will, we are loving the Lord our God with the whole strength of our being. In serving Him we serve our neighbor, who, as a member of the same mystical body, is benefited by our good works; conversely, in serving our neighbor through charity, we serve Him Whose image we see resplendent in every soul.

The importance of living in this habitual disposition of prayer cannot be over-emphasized; this it is which constitutes the real spirit, the state of prayer; this is that fruit which our soul has yielded, and which proves that the time set aside for special communication with God is really well employed. " The fruit of prayer," says St. Teresa, " is good works." And the great Apostle of the Gentiles says the same thing in his epistle to the Romans: " Walk honestly, as in the day; — put ye on the Lord Jesus Christ " (Rom. xiii, 13–14), that is, walk, act, according to the light given you, and strive to accomplish God's designs over your soul as perfectly as you can.

This light to see, which means to know God's will in our regard, in every minor detail, is given us especially during our fixed time of prayer. Unless the understanding, the intellect, comprehends God as the Supreme Good, the will will not efficaciously reach out to embrace the Sovereign Law-giver. Unless we go about praying in the proper fashion, we shall again be guilty of abuse in our use of this third great instrument offered for our sanctification. The discussion of prayer, our conversation with God, has not yet been actually begun; we have only been preparing the soil for the sowing. This preparation must go on daily, persistently, in the manner outlined. There is no need of giving minute rules in this regard, nor is it advisable, for all souls, though alike, are different — none of us has exactly the same weaknesses, the same struggles, the same temptations.

For this conquest of self, the necessary adjunct and partial fruit of prayer, one rule will suffice, and it is practically infallible: Do the thing most repugnant to nature. A word of warning, though. With regard to interior conquests, you may apply it always, without any harm, and the oftener the better; with regard to exterior mortifications, common sense and wisdom are necessary. Since all of us have the most uncommon common sense in the world, and the lion's share of its wisdom, we are by this very superiority incapable of judging for ourselves — hence prudent direction is of supreme necessity. This direction will never be lacking to him who is in good earnest, who is responsive to the invitation of God by the mouth of the prophet: " All you that thirst, come to the waters; seek ye the Lord while He may be found " (Isaias lv, 1 and 6). For he that drinks at the fountain of life shall not thirst forever; " but the water that I will give him shall become in him a fountain of water springing up into life everlasting " (John iv, 14). " For none of them that wait for thee shall be confounded " (Ps. 24, 3), because Thy " words shall not pass away " (Luke xxi, 33).

13. THE MEANING AND AIM OF MEDITATION

"Come, O Lord, visit us in peace" (ANTIPHON AT MAGNIFICAT I VESP.
2. SUNDAY OF ADVENT)

THIS versicle, the antiphon at the Magnificat at Vespers of the second Sunday of Advent, not only indicates the spirit of yearning with which the Church desires the coming of her Redeemer during her Advent preparation, but shows clearly the manner of His visitation to us during the appointed time of prayer. He comes to visit us, laden with graces He desires to pour out upon us in great abundance, always in *peace;* or rather, it is we who visit Him in the peaceful quiet of prayer, for He is ever in our souls, ever laden with an abundance of good gifts, waiting for us so to dispose ourselves for their reception that we may derive the greatest possible fruit from them. Since the Holy Spirit works in our souls in a sanctifying peace — for remember that it is He who prays in us — it is evident that the more earnestly we strive to attain the perfect peace, i.e. control, of the bodily senses and passions, the more readily and understandingly shall we arrive at the knowledge of prayer, for we shall have disposed ourselves resolutely for the teaching of this incomparable Master.

[129]

Besides this habitual disposition of soul, this state, or spirit, of prayer, which we discussed in the last conference, only one thing is necessary for the proper study of prayer and its realization in our lives; one thing, which is really not distinct from the disposition, but is essentially a part of it, and a vital part, too, although often it is not recognized by the soul as of supreme importance, or is even lost sight of altogether. It is simply the frequent repetition from the depths of the heart of this one word: " Lord, teach us to pray " (Luke xi, 1).

Prayer, as you recall, is an elevation of the mind and will to God. The will, in a well-disposed soul, as we have seen, is striving all day long to accomplish the Divine Will and to curb the senses, to quiet them into repose. Seeking peace steadfastly, the soul, when it comes to converse with God at the fixed hours, finds itself more and more free from that spirit of agitation and continual distraction and weariness which characterizes the unmortified. The mind, in its powers of concentration, is left at greater liberty, and aided by grace is directed naturally toward its Uncreated Origin — God. Prayer, after all, is concentration on God.

This concentration of the soul's efforts to find God has been very often catalogued by spiritual writers under three heads, or " states " of prayer: the purgative, illuminative, and unitive. Because of this general classification, many souls, earnestly sincere, are deterred from persevering in their endeavors. Why? Because they argue that since the goal — union with God — is so far above them, they might just as well stop trying, or not even begin, for they will never get beyond the purgative state as long as they live. This is an error which comes from a lack of knowledge of the essence of prayer, and which is greatly augmented by the little knowledge gleaned from the summarizing thought concerning the three states of prayer. What should be remembered is this: All prayer is unitive, for it establishes communication between the soul and the Creator, and hence unites two spiritual beings. If unitive, then it is necessarily illuminative, because God is light, that is, Infinite Knowledge, which is Truth: " and the light shineth in darkness (of human intelligence) and the darkness did not comprehend it " (for it is incapable of so sublime an act) (John i, 5). Therefore is it impossible for finite understanding, coming into contact with Infinite Understanding in the elevation of the human mind and will, not thereby to be enlightened. To the degree in which it is enlightened it is also purged of the old man, since it is rendered more Godlike in its ensuing activity.

What, then, is meant by the three states of prayer? First of all, a sharp and distinct division is not implied. One does not leave the purgative stage to enter the illuminative, as one would pass from one room to another, and close the door after entering. Nor in like manner, from the illuminative to the unitive. No. The mortifications of the purgative way are carried on to the end with increasing intensity; the lights of the illuminative path burn at white heat only in the unitive. And union and enlightenment are not wanting in purgation, as has already been explained. The threefold division simply refers to the predominating movements of grace in the soul in its progress toward perfection; that is, the development of a life of prayer. In the beginning the efforts are bent on mortifying the senses and passions; later, as the *habit* of mortification becomes more and more firmly established, the soul, in the casting off of the old Adam, the stripping of self, begins to see things more clearly from the viewpoint of God: it is enlightened with regard both to God and to itself.

Then this illumination of the mind stimulates the will to embrace with greater intensity of purpose, the one Supreme Good viewed in Himself because of His perfections. The soul in this degree is occupied solely with one concern: " I must be about my Father's business " (Luke ii, 49). Of course, it must be remembered that in both the illuminative and unitive states, God does most of the work. Not that He does not do it everywhere; but the soul's consent to His operations is here ever so much freer, because it has been disburdening itself of the weight of the flesh. Once a soul is completely dead to self, it is all-powerful, because it is God Who wills and works alone in it.

This, then, is the goal of prayer. This is that perfect development of the life of grace whose germ we received in Baptism, and which the Church, the Bride of the Word, the dispenser of His gifts, makes possible for every willing soul to achieve. This is the fulfilment of the Saviour's promise: " We will come to him and will make our abode with him " (John xiv, 23). This is not a barren promise, but one to be hoped for, since, as St. Paul says:

" What things soever were written, were written for our learning; that through patience and the comfort of the Scriptures, we might have hope " (Rom. xv, 4). Our hope is in the Lord Who " shall come with strength " (Is. xl, 10), in the peace of His visitation, to enlighten the eyes of His servants. Rejoicing at the things that our Mother the Church has said to us, let us go into the house of the Lord, the temple of our soul, where the Lord shall make the glory of His voice to be heard, and " the God of hope fill you with all joy and peace in believing " (Rom. xv, 13).

What does it mean to enter into ourselves, to go into the house of the Lord, our soul, that we may converse with Him Who dwells there? It means that we strive to direct our minds, that is, our thoughts, to Him Whose companionship we wish to cultivate, for the sake of better knowing His likes and dislikes, that we may satiate the one and avoid the other. The only way to acquire this knowledge is to set ourselves systematically to study that Beloved Being, our God, to Whom we wish to conform ourselves. God for us means Christ. Since Christ came on earth to teach men both how to live and how to pray, or rather simply how to live, for prayer is the only true life, we must ponder on that Divine Life as the Church makes it known to us in her teachings and in the gospel narrative. And this pondering, or reflection, or thinking, we as religious are bound to do for a certain period each day.

Why do we meditate? Because we " must learn to leave ourselves and all other things for the love of God "

(Abbot Blosius, *Spiritual Instruction*). Mark well: the reason for meditation is not to employ ourselves in pleasing reflections, however spiritual and holy they may be, nor to be gratified by feelings of sensible fervor and devotion; for example, to be moved to tears in considering the agony of Our Lord, or the sorrows of His Mother, and thereby to imagine ourselves very good and indeed quite holy because of our apparently deep affliction. No, indeed. The only reason why the mind thinks is that the will may subsequently act. Were we to spend the whole day in thinking on spiritual things, and never once, as a result, do an act of virtue, whether of self-denial, self-control, faith, confidence, love — our reflecting would have been valueless, our time wasted. Thought such as this is not meditation — it is day-dreaming. True prayer is activity, for life is expressed in works. It is essential, then, to understand at the very beginning why it is that we wish to converse with God, to draw near to Him in prayer: that we may overcome ourselves daily as our faults are made known to us, in order to become like Him we love. In order to do this we study His life, reflecting purposely on it.

Now, before we find out how to go about our thinking in an orderly fashion, one important truth must be grasped. It is this: *mere* meditation is not prayer. It is simply a *means* (thinking) to an *end* (doing). The *doing* is prayer. All this will soon be explained. Neither should we torment ourselves because we cannot follow the method which divides the meditation into two or three points. The subject is thus presented for the sake of

[134]

uniformity, and it is a mistake to force ourselves from one idea to cover the points presented. The one thing necessary is to grasp *one* truth, and make certain that it strikes home by bringing forth fruit in our lives.

I said a moment ago that *mere* meditation is not prayer. Then why bother about it? Because it is one of the very best means to help us to talk with God. Notice I have said " *with God*," not " *to God*." When we talk *to* another, the one we are addressing is a silent listener; when we talk *with* another, there is an exchange of ideas. And prayer is conversation *with* God. Progress in prayer or advance in perfection simply means that we learn more and more graciously to play the part of an attentive and courteous host, who eliminates himself as far as possible, in order that the beloved and honored guest may be at full liberty to express himself freely with regard to the interests dearest to his heart.

Do you remember what was said some time ago in the conference on Communion? He talks best who listens best; and meditation disposes us to listen. To whom? To God. We pray best when we listen best to the Holy Ghost, Who talks to us only in peace, in holy desires, good thoughts, inspirations of grace, inclinations of the will to embrace what the understanding proposes as tending toward the one Supreme Good; and gives strength to carry out the resolution formed. Remember always: it is God the Holy Ghost Who prays in us. The less we interfere with His work, the more He can accomplish. Meditation — presupposing always the life of daily mortification as previously declared absolutely necessary —

by directing the attention to God, and keeping out as far as possible all distracting ideas, puts the soul in a favorable disposition for converse with God by giving the Holy Ghost an opportunity to enlighten the mind and inflame the will. Self is the one thing that interferes with the operations of God in our soul; and meditation helps us to the point where we begin to pray when we forget ourselves in God, ignoring our selfish interests and beginning to remember only His, which are: His honor and glory, our sanctification, the salvation and sanctification of souls. In the peace of a quiet and orderly meditation will the blind begin to see, the lame to walk, the lepers to be cleansed, the deaf to hear, the dead to rise again, the poor to have the Gospel preached to them.

Meditation, then, is the angel of God who prepares His way before Him in each individual soul, to the end that He will turn and bring us to life. It is the orderly and carefully planned preparation one makes for receiving an expected guest. The more earnestly this preparation, in the form of self-conquest, is carried on outside of the time of prayer, the less trouble shall we experience in setting the room of our minds to right at the hour of this holy exercise, and the more successfully shall we entertain the Divine Guest of our souls, Who dwells in us continually.

Perhaps some of you are beginning to feel a trifle impatient because of all these preliminaries. But a clear understanding of the meaning and aim of meditation is vital before we discuss the manner of going about it.

One erroneous idea would be sufficient to spoil the work of a hundred conferences. This is a splendid opportunity to practise some of that patience St. Paul recommended to us in the early part of this discussion. Never be in a hurry where spiritual things are concerned. Hurry is born of the devil, and is one of his choicest tools for injuring souls. God is never in a hurry. He works only in peace and quiet. We cannot perfect ourselves — God's grace understood — overnight; we have the whole day of life to achieve this end. Precipitation has been the ruin of many a possible saint. It arises from secret self-love, and causes disgust and discouragement and ultimately a positive distaste for spiritual exercises; all because of an uncontrolled disquietude over one's spiritual advancement. As long as we *try* we need never fear or worry, for we *are* advancing. Only when we give up trying have we cause for real anxiety about our progress, but that is just the time when none is evident, for we feel secure. But it is a false security, in which a proud self and a prouder devil have steeped us.

Peace, then, poise or control of the mind, is necessary if we wish to meditate at all. If we find ourselves disquieted at the beginning of this exercise, let us pause and question ourselves as to the reason, before attempting anything else. If we find the cause is a fault of our own making, let us tell God we are sorry, ask Him to help us to avoid it, and put the matter out of our heads — forget it, for He has already done so. If it is a trick of the devil, tell him to go about his business and take himself home where he belongs, with the word of our Master and

Model: " Begone, Satan " (Matt. iv, 10). Then let us ask Our Lord to keep him there, and to help us with the exercise. The method of this mental and spiritual exercise we shall consider in our next conference, remembering for the present that God visits us in peace.

14. THE METHOD OF MEDITATION

"Enlighten O Lord, the darkness of our minds by the grace of Thy visitation" (ORATION IN MASS OF 3 SUNDAY OF ADVENT)

DURING the closing days of the time of Advent, the spirit of the Church is one of increasing joy in the expectation of the coming Redeemer. The self-same spirit should animate us at every moment, but especially at the precious moments consecrated to prayer, for " behold the joy that cometh to thee from God " (Baruch iv, 36). When should we be most joyful if not at the hour when we are engaged in intimate conversation with the Well-Beloved of our soul? Our disposition for prayer should be one of anticipated eagerness, a joy established in peace and tranquillity of mind and will. This yearning with desire after the things of God, and after God Himself, can be manifested in spite of great natural repugnance and disgust. Look at the Son of Man in the garden. " My Father, if it be possible " — and who better than Jesus knew that to the Father all things are possible — " let this chalice pass from Me " (Matt. xxvi, 39). Humanity rebels but Divinity conquers. For at once is uttered the sublime FIAT: " Nevertheless, not as I will but as thou wilt " (Matt. xxvi, 39). The ' nevertheless ' speaks volumes: what concerns Me personally is entirely beyond

[139]

the need of consideration: Thy interests, Thy desire, Thy will, O Father, are also supremely Mine.

So too with us at the time of prayer. The will should be above the feelings, no matter what these may be — disgust, irritability, hatred, despair. The deeper the misery, the greater the joy, the real, lasting, spiritual joy of the soul in prayer. Easter Sunday was so divinely glorious precisely because of Good Friday; and the greatest sorrow that can ever happen — sin — gave rise to the greatest good the world has ever seen or will perceive — the Saviour, Jesus Christ, true God and true Man. It is on just such occasions as this, when we experience great loathing for our conversation with God that we should " be nothing solicitous: the Lord is nigh " (Phil. iv, 6 and 5). The Lord is verily nigh unto them that call upon Him in spirit and in truth, which is prayer. And prayer in its initial form — meditation — is what we shall now consider.

Recall that meditation is only a means, i.e. thinking, to an end, i.e. doing. The doing is prayer. The reflection is the work of the understanding — it attends to God. The action is the work of the will — it embraces God. To the degree that my mind grasps an object as a true good, my will reaches out toward that object in desire. This desire may be affective or effective. It is *affective* when I perceive within me dispositions of love, hope, joy, admiration, sorrow, fear; *effective,* when I set out to accomplish what these dispositions have suggested, that they may bear fruit in my life. But the power of the intellect is light, i.e. knowledge, and the power of the will is love, i.e. activity. Ordinarily, when there is little light, there is little love, because in general my love for my friend increases the better I know him.

It sometimes happens, however, that with great knowledge there is but little love. This disproves nothing. It serves but to show that the knowledge of information — book-learning, and this too in spiritual matters — is enjoyed in theory only, not in practice. A good will is lacking. And without a good will we cannot be saved, much less sanctified. It is not sufficient to know. Mere learning in the most extensive quantity will never save any person, or make him really happy. The devil is much more intelligent than the greatest genius the world has produced; but the devil is hardly happy. No. Theoretical knowledge alone is not so much valueless as dangerous; it is dangerous because one knows what is required, and yet acts unconformably to that knowledge. It serves only to increase guilt. The very fact that the will is inactive in a case such as is being considered, proves indisputably that self and not God is the mainspring of that knowledge. Or again, it may be self and the devil. God does not bless with productive grace that learning which has been acquired from a motive of vanity, or accomplishment, or curiosity. " Never read anything," says the author of the *Imitation of Christ*, " in order that thou mayest appear more learned or more wise — for the kingdom of God consisteth not in speech but in virtue " (III, 43). This virtue is acquired from Him and in Him and through Him Who " teacheth men knowledge and Who giveth a more clear understanding to little ones than can be taught by man" (*Idem*). This understanding is the light of the Holy Spirit, Who by the grace of His visitation enlightens the darkness of the minds of all that are born in this world, who earnestly seek and beg for His guidance.

Resolved then to apply ourselves humbly to prayer, because of Him we love, let us say in all sincerity, " Rabboni, that I may see " (Mark x, 51). What is it that we wish to see? (Remember that to see spiritually means to understand. This is obvious. For instance, I may not grasp the method of solving a problem in arithmetic. When it has been clearly explained to me, I say, " Oh, I see," meaning, " I understand "). What is it, in other words, we wish to understand? God and ourselves, in so far as we are able; our relations with God; our conduct toward Him; His goodness to us. How shall we set about it? By looking at God, and then at ourselves. God is the one true Mirror in which all creation is accurately reflected. God for us means the Man-God, Christ Jesus, Whom the Father has given us for this very purpose, to be our very perfect model. To this end we shall study His life — an incident of it — the prayer in the garden, let us say, to which allusion has previously been made.

We have already composed ourselves for prayer, and begged the help of the Holy Spirit. To keep our imagination from roving about the countryside and parts distant, we shall bridle it like an impulsive horse, by checking its spirit of wanderlust. By anticipating its demands we shall forestall this fretful steed. It may wander; yes, we shall permit it to, but our will must direct its movements. It may travel as far as the garden to a thicket of olive trees, blanketed by an obscure night. We feel our way forward, urged on by the sound of heavy breathing — rather, of a sob and a moan. We peer into the gloom, and straining, suddenly stumble. We have fallen over a prostrate form. The body is quivering. The clothing is dank with — is it the dew of the night? Rather a peculiar dankness this, — warmishly sticky. A growing suspicion runs a shiver up our spines. Our hands move tenderly over the now motionless figure. Our fingers touch hair — matted, cloying hair. Again a shiver, stronger than before. It is we who are breathing hard now. Our finger-tips smooth an aching forehead wet with perspiration. — And the perspiration is blood. — As we realize the truth, an agonized cry is wrenched from the heart of the Oppressed One: " My Father — " (Matt. xxvi, 39).

My Father. It is as Man that the afflicted Saviour calls upon His heavenly Father. He is now the representative sinner, standing before the bar of God's eternal justice, loaded down with the sins of countless Adams and Cains; of innumerable Sodoms and Romes; of Neros and Julians without end; with secret sins more leprous than these, of multitudes upon multitudes. In the sight of the Father He is the iniquity of the world from its creation to its destruction. What wonder that He recoils and trembles at the crushing, permeating foulness. What wonder that the rivers of blood, whipped into mad torrents by the hammering pulsations of a heart dilated with divine love and human fear, rise higher and ever higher until they break all bounds and saturate the hard, sin-crusted earth with the expiating laver of the God-Man.

In the darkness we tenderly lift the unresisting head, and wipe away the blood and dust. But the handkerchief is soaked, and the face, dry only for an instant, is again bathed with blood and perspiration and tears. Our own tears are falling, and the only consolation we can offer is that of a silent, love-inflamed heart. Our finger-tips continue to caress the pain-racked temples. Jesus is grateful. He loosens His grasp from the earth and gravel, into which His right hand had furrowed, and placing it over our own, directs us to where the hurt is most piercing. Again, as though the act of gratitude had inspired new anguish of spirit, bursts from the fevered lips the cry, " My Father, if it be possible — if it be possible " (Matt. xxvi, 39).

But the heavens are as brass, and the night grows more ominous. The Father refuses to hear. How can this be? How can the kind, merciful, loving Father, Whom the Son, now truly a worm of the earth, came to reveal to man, be apparently so harsh, so unyielding, so cruel? Is it then not possible? Ah, no. The cry for mercy for this afflicted Man, half-dead in our arms, goes up to heaven in an intense plea from the depths of our soul: " Father, if it be possible." Immediately comes back the reply in a swift enlightenment of our understanding: " It is not possible. It is for you. It is you who in justice should suffer this agony of body and mind and spirit, but you cannot. You can sin, but God Himself, He the prostrate, bleeding One, must make reparation, for only He can.

Look now, you whom He has espoused, look at the work of your hands. This is your God and Spouse, and you do nothing to lighten His burden. Aye, you but help to make it heavier. More than the blasphemies of His enemies, more than the slights of His friends, does the coldness, indifference, languor of His chosen ones, His spouses, afflict Him deeply. " I have chosen you," He says to each of us, to help Me in the work of redemption. My sufferings are all-sufficient for you; they will wipe away all your debt. But I have called you to Me, that you might suffer for others, not to the degree that I have done, but according to your weakness. Oh, did you but understand the sublime charity, the divine virtue of this reparation, how would you not embrace it! How would you not seek after it! And yet you are bound to seek, because you are bound to grow in resemblance to Me your Spouse. You profess to follow Me, your Master and Guide. I have said, and now prove by the agony of this moment: " Greater love than this no man hath: that a man lay down his life for his friends " (John xv, 13). A spouse should find her only happiness and glory in sharing the condition of the Well-Beloved of her soul. You seek comfort and ease and, yes, luxury, and your own will; and I, bitterness of soul and body, the will of my Father, the will of men, your will. How then can it be possible that the " chalice pass from Me? " (Matt. xxvi, 39).

" If it be possible " (Matt. xxvi, 39). The moan is ours. Remorse and shame, contrition and love, gratitude and adoration sweep over our soul in purifying moments of accepted grace. Enlightened by the Life-giving Spirit, and strengthened by the vigor that flows into our hearts through the out-pouring blood, which is fast weakening the Lamb prepared for slaughter, we raise our heads to heaven, our resolution made. " My Father," — a struggling moon has cleared the sky, and in its light we see the face of Jesus, now calm but inexpressibly fatigued — " My Father, it shall be possible. Let this chalice pass — into our hands. With Thy help we shall drain it to the dregs, together with Jesus, Thy Son and our Saviour."

But we must be definite. If we mean what we have just promised the Father, we shall begin now, today, to make good our share in the redemption of man. Therefore, we must avoid mere generalities, and frame a resolution that will strike home effectively today. The thought that God wished us to realize, the truth He desired to be fruitful in good works is simply this: Our sufferings, patiently borne for our neighbor's sake, give more glory to God, and work us greater spiritual benefit than those same sufferings endured for ourselves, as a penance for our sins. To put this truth into practice, we generously resolve, out of love for God and souls, to offer for our neighbor — and let God determine who that neighbor may be — five acts of mortification — three this morning and two this afternoon — mortifications, however, not of our own choosing, but those sent by God in corrections, reproofs, public humiliations, unkind words, passing indispositions, uncongenial companions.

By meditating in this manner, day after day, and bravely determining to keep our resolutions, even though we fail time and again in the effort, we cannot but advance in perfection. In proportion as we are really sincere and whole-hearted in our desire to please God, shall we be given light to see our defects, and grace to overcome them one by one. Our failings are not a hindrance to holiness; they are positive helps, if we employ them to our advantage. It is only in the conquest of these faults that we are sanctified; and the fight must of necessity continue until we are no more. This is what constitutes to " make straight the way of the Lord " (John i, 23). This is the work we must perseveringly persist in, lest the reproach brought against the Jews be also ours: " There hath stood one in the midst of you whom you know not " (John i, 26). But striving with determination, we have reason to rejoice, because as long as we attempt, " the Lord is nigh " (Phil. iv. 5).

This reflection has been made with you to serve as an illustration from which we are going to infer very definite principles in our next conference. We shall analyze our actions and discover what may be dispensed with without positive detriment to our reflections, and what is absolutely essential for a well-ordered meditation. Nor can the opposition be raised that a single instance will not suffice adequately for so important an induction; the instance might be multiplied indefinitely and always with the same general results.

Nothing, then, can deter you from advancing in holiness except a lack of good will. Possessed of this indispensable requisite, you need " be nothing solicitous " (Phil. iv, 6) as the apostle advises; but in everything by

prayer " let your petitions be made known to God "
(Phil. iv, 6) " Who will come and will not tarry "
(Antiphon at Lauds of third Sunday in Advent) and
" will bring to light the hidden things of darkness, and
will make manifest the counsels of the hearts " (I Cor.
iv, 5).

"The Lord is nigh unto all them that call upon Him: to all that call upon Him in truth" (Ps. 144, 18)

THE near approach of Christmas is marked, during Advent, in the liturgy of the Church by a more and more intense exultation of spirit. It would seem as though the Bride of the Word can no longer contain herself in the jubilation wherewith she cries aloud to the world her joy at His long-anticipated coming. " Drop down dew, ye heavens, from above, and let the clouds rain the Just: let the earth be opened and bud forth a Saviour " (Isaias xlv, 8 — Introit for the fourth Sunday of Advent). " Stir up Thy might, O Lord, and come: and succor us with great favor " (Oration for the fourth Sunday of Advent). This appearance of the Eternal Son in time, for which our Mother the Church so lovingly and rapturously prepares, is not only a matter of salvation for all mankind in general; it is a delivery which delivers each individual soul, you and me, from the bondage of self, which is death, unto the freedom of death, which is life. And the attainment of this life, which is none other than Jesus Christ Himself, the Word Incarnate, is available to " all that call upon Him in truth " (Ps. 144, 18). Neither is the end of our intercourse with God, our calling upon Him in truth, a vague and indefinite act, for we are given its reason immediately: " My mouth shall speak the praise of the Lord: and let all flesh bless His holy name " (Ps. 144, 21 — Gradual for the fourth Sunday of Advent).

In these few words the Church emphasizes a truth she is continually teaching the year round: that Christ reveals Himself (" the Lord is nigh " — Ps. 144, 18) to the well-disposed soul in prayer (" to all that call upon Him in truth " — Ps. 144, 18). Prayer, remember, is an elevation, a raising up, of the mind and will to God, for the purpose of adoring Him, thanking Him (" My mouth shall speak the praise of the Lord " — Ps. 144, 21) and supplicating Him (" let all flesh bless His holy name "; — Ps. 144, 21: which equals ' Thy will be done ').

As you further recall, ordinarily the first step to prayer is meditation, for in our last conference we saw that purposeful reflection enables us to hear the " voice of one (the Holy Ghost) crying in the wilderness (the desert, the barren waste of our lives): Prepare ye the way of the Lord: make straight His paths: every valley shall be filled: and every mountain and hill shall be brought low: and the crooked shall be made straight, and the rough ways plain " (Luke iii, 4–5). These mountains and hills that need to be brought low are our sins and imperfections; these valleys that require filling are all virtues that need constant attention in order that they may thrive properly and arrive at maturity and these are the very things we clearly perceive in a meditation well made. As vices are one by one uprooted, and virtues one by one become more flourishing, we advance steadily — though to ourselves it often may be imperceptibly — toward that end for which we have been created, that end which a life of prayer accelerates — God. In testimony of this truth we have the word of the prophet, who says that when this work, the preparation of the way of the Lord, shall have been accomplished, " all flesh shall see the salvation of God " (Luke iii, 6). And who is the salvation of God? Christ Jesus, the Word made flesh, our Mediator with the Father. So it is clear, then, that meditation as a means (thinking) to an end (doing — which finds its perfection of activity in sharing the very life of the Godhead) is of prime importance in helping us to arrive at the port to which we are steering — union with God.

All necessary grace has been purchased for us by our Divine Redeemer, Who wills to pour it out upon our souls through the ministering action of the Holy Spirit, in the measure to which we dispose ourselves for its reception. Since a good meditation so disposes us, we must study to discover what are its essentials, that we may not be robbed of the fruit of graces through ignorance or misunderstanding or false ideas. To this end we shall revert to the scene in the Garden, wherewith our Saviour began His dolorous passion, and we to respire again supernaturally. This was our consideration in the last conference. We now shall examine our actions which formulated that consideration, and from them infer certain fixed principles, which will guide us hereafter in all our reflections, so that we may know when we really begin to pray, and how long our prayer really lasts.

In the first place, we begged the light and help of the Holy Spirit: " Lord, that we may see." This is essential, for remember always, it is God Who prays within us. It matters not, however, whether this prayer be vocal or mental; but if it be vocal, the mind must attend either to the words uttered or to the Person addressed — preferably to Him to Whom we speak. Nor is it necessary that the form given here, " Lord, that we may see," be the word spoken. Any plea for light may be employed, or a simple inclination of the mind towards God — but the prayer must be *short*. The briefer it is, the more intense will it be in its earnestness and sincerity. God judgeth the heart. He looks at our intention — the reason why we do things — and at our attention — the care with which we perform all our acts, whether physical, mental, or spiritual. But the prayer of the poor blind man is excellent, because we are all blind to a certain degree spiritually; that is, our understanding is darkened and requires illumination. Only some are blind and some are blinder; some wilfully, some through carelessness or ignorance.

Having invoked the Holy Ghost, we next curbed our wandering imagination by forcing it to picture the scene we willed — Our Lord, bathed in sweat, in His agony in the dark garden. Is this picture necessary? By no means. Meditation is reflection, and thinking is not conjuring up beautiful images, however holy they may be in themselves. Is it, then, useful to so employ the imagi-

nation? Yes, in the event that we possess an active imagination; and with certain provisions. The imagination
may be a help, and it may be a hindrance; it may be a
hindrance in the very act of being a help. What does this
mean? Simply this: The imagination is a help when it
stimulates our thoughts by fixing our interior gaze on
an object worthy of our attention and admiration. It
may be a hindrance because, as a general rule, the imagination is a very fickle lady, and refuses to be satisfied
long in any one place, but fidgets over the face of the
earth, the seven seas, the moon, and the stars, so that it
will often supply us with almost endless distractions. This
is where the mortification of our eyes avails much. We
ourselves, in a good many instances, are directly responsible for any amount of distractions during our spiritual
exercises. We see too much; we desire to see even more
than too much; and curiosity has never been a virtue,
neither will it ever become one. Curiosity in spiritual
things is especially deplorable and a positive wrong. But
distractions that arise despite our best efforts all day long
to control our wayward eyes are not of our making;
they are a test of our determination to fight on.

How is the imagination a hindrance in the very act of
being a help? It may cause us to day-dream instead of
assisting to pray. The imagination is of value only in so
far as it serves to arouse a series of reflective thoughts.
The danger for those whose imagination looms large and
is in excellent working order is this: Unless they are very
watchful, they will employ their time in unreeling a
splendid assortment of pictures, beginning with the

sacred drama and ending with the martyr's stake, a hooting, jeering mob on one side, a praying, admiring flock on the other; the martyr in the sublime act of gracefully lowering his head to receive the slightly less graceful stroke of the executioner's sword. And who is the victim of this eloquent sermon in pantomime? It is the very soul whose imagination is working overtime. This is day-dreaming. It is evident, then, that an imagination in itself is an excellent thing, but here again it is a question of use or abuse. And this fickle lady — or fickle colt, what is the difference — is apt to be very elusive, unless one has a good, strong, directing grip and maintains it.

More than half the trouble would be eliminated if we should only persist in using the blinkers. Blinkers, as you know, are the blinders put on a horse to keep his gaze straight ahead. If we want to keep looking straight ahead spiritually — and we must, for our vows bind us to do so — we must look down. To look ahead, look down physically. Only please use common sense, and do not walk into the first lamp-post you have been too mortified to see. It might result disastrously — for the lamp-post, of course. It is strange, though, as you will find out for yourselves. The more you look down to look ahead, the more you will look up — to others. Why? Because the restraint of the eyes will gradually bring about a contempt of self — a looking down on self, and that is what we are aiming at. The more we sink in our own esteem, the more esteem we have left to give to our neighbor. Mortification, then, will invariably lead to humility, and

humility to charity, which is love. And when our mortification gets to the point where we in truth love our
neighbor as ourselves, we shall also love God with our
whole heart and mind and soul, as He commands. We
shall have then begun to keep the *one* commandment
perfectly.

It seems as though we had traveled a long way from
our analysis, but we have not. There are so many things
to be made clear, and the best place to explain them is
where they feel perfectly at home. So we shall continue
again.

I hope you now understand that if you have a microscopic imagination there is nothing about which to
worry. It does not mean that you cannot meditate, that
is, think reflectively. We begin to think of Our Lord's
sufferings and the meaning of it all, after we had looked
at His blood-stained garments in the chill, grim darkness. Whether this picture was vivid or vague is immaterial; the important thing is we began to *think*. What
really started our mental machinery in motion? The cry
of the Lamb " My Father . . . if it be possible " (Matt.
xxvi, 39).

It was a thought, then, that caused us to think. In this
case a thought that Our Saviour uttered, and which he
recalled. At other times, it may be one of our own, or
more frequently, perhaps, one that we hear read. What
I am going to mention now is so very important that I
wish you would learn it until you can say it backwards
and forwards: Meditation *does not* consist in remembering thoughts (sentences) read. Meditation consists in *de-*

veloping our own thoughts with regard to certain truths which command the attention of our understanding by force of reasonable appeal. Here is Our Lord in the garden. Why is He suffering? What does it all mean? For all mankind? No. What does it all mean for me personally? Forget your neighbor at this point; look at yourself, or rather I should say, into yourself. This is where many go astray. If they do anything at all, it is in favor of some other person to his disfavor. It is the case of seeing the mote in their brother's eye and failing to see the beam in their own. Some person certainly was responsible for that terrible anguish that manifested itself in blood; and we bemoan the Judases and Peters and Pilates and Herods of yesterday and today. But just how much did we contribute? Oh, no, we could not think of that! Why, we never did anything so terrible that it would make the Master suffer so. Really, we are good — in our own estimation, yes. We acknowledge our sins and confess their share in Christ's expiation, but only in a vague, general way. We are really not honestly sincere. We say, " mea culpa," but rather from a sense that it is the proper thing to do at certain times, than from a realization of our guilt. We are simply being polite with God. We do not get at the core of the matter — we do our meditating superficially, if we do it at all. When God wants to show us our real selves by bringing the truth home to our own door where it belongs, we will not open to allow it admittance. Why? Because of one of two things: either we are too lazy to exert ourselves and really *think* about the truth that has been brought to our attention, or else, acknowledging the truth, we are too much the coward to face it, and make it play the vital part in our lives which God intended it should. " This applies to my neighbor, not to me," and we immediately proceed to forget.

But how did we manage to bring the truth home to us in the meditation which served as a model? We looked at Our Lord and considered Who He is and why He suffered so, and who was responsible for His agony. But we did not leave the blame for it with our neighbor. We were sincere, and Our Lord through His Life-giving Spirit gave us light to see wherein we had failed, and just how far our conduct needed to be reformed. And what was the light? Understanding — realization of our misery and God's goodness. This was " the voice of one crying in the wilderness: Prepare ye the way of the Lord " (Luke iii, 4). Only in the silence of our close companionship with our agonizing Saviour were we given grace to see. If you remember, we looked again and again at Him during our reflections. We felt the murky blood and the quivering body; we heard the sobs and the prayer; we thrilled to the touch of His dusty fingers, as they guided our hands over the throbbing temples. This was simply the work of our imagination which helped to keep us near to the Beloved of our soul. Whenever we find our imagination roving abroad during meditation, all we need to do is to quietly bring it back again to the desired object. We never have far to go. Christ, our God, is always within us. We must look for Him only in our hearts. There we can re-create His whole life under His supervision. This is not impossible, for He dwells in our soul's center always in His divinity. But since we find it rather difficult to realize the nearness of a pure spirit, we allow our imagination to reclothe God with that Sacred Humanity He Himself assumed when the Word was made flesh. Nor should this call forth any difficulty. His body is now in a glorified state, and hence can pass through matter. And if we have little or no imagination? It is not necessary. The imagination serves just to aid, if it does not prove a hindrance, as was explained before. A simple thought of Christ within us is the one essential to re-collect our wandering thoughts.

Up to this point all the talk has been about the thinking. What about the doing, which is prayer? Have we as yet done no praying whatever? We have. Continually? No. Mere reflection is not prayer; it leads to prayer by moving the will to express itself in acts which are the logical consequence to the workings of the understanding. Our considerations of Christ's suffering in the heartbroken plea, " My Father," left us silent with the silence of sympathetic companionship. Was this prayer? It was. It was the far-reaching cry of a soul moved with love and tenderness and compassionating pity. Our mind and will were in harmony with the mind and will of Christ in His anguish. It was our limited intelligence and will reaching out toward the Infinite Intelligence and Will clothed in agonizing humanity. Prayer, remember, is an elevation of the mind and will to God. Our prayer was of short duration, however, and we immediately began to think further. Again we looked at Our Saviour to bring back our imagination that had begun to wander. We saw the movements of grateful love which repaid us for our sympathy, and we began to realize something of His excessive misery. We forgot self in the urgent necessity of procuring divine assistance for a fellow-being, and we earnestly implored the Father, the words of the Son beating against our brain: " My Father, if it be possible, let this chalice pass " (Matt. xxvi, 39). How long did we pray? Only while the words formed themselves mentally? No. We prayed as long as the disposition lasted. But our prayer was heard, for the answer came back immediately in the illumination of our understanding. We were given grace clearly to see why Christ had need to suffer so, and wherein we had been wanting in offering ourselves to carry on the work of redemption hand in hand with Christ. What happened? Remorse and shame, contrition and love, thanksgiving and adoration, swept through our soul in spontaneous movements of an inflamed and invigorated will. These were the *affective* acts which were produced by the will, as the rapid result of a mind enlightened by grace. This was prayer, although we may not have formulated one word even mentally. God does not need our words; He needs only our dispositions, for these constitute prayer. If the words, for example, which mentally expressed our act of sorrow, let us say, came naturally and spontaneously to our mind, and perhaps even to our lips, together with the movement of the will, which was the essence of the act of sorrow, very well and very good.

To *force* ourselves so to frame an act even mentally is wrong. We are spoiling a perfectly excellent prayer by taking our mind from God and fixing it on an exercise in literary composition of which He has no need. Neither have we; only we are so bound up with the material realities of life that we act much the same with the spiritual. Unless we at least mentally think the words, " My God, I am sorry," or " My God, I love You," we imagine we have not produced an act of sorrow or of love. If all this happens freely and easily, very well. But when we have to force ourselves to compose this mental address, we make a great mistake, for we are only trying to convince ourselves of the reality of our dispositions. Our dispositions lie too deep for adequate speech. So that if we experience only our inability to understand the successive, or very often the confused, movements of soul, all the better. This is excellent prayer. This is the reason for our meditation. This is the real *doing* of the will, for which the thinking of the mind prepared us. This is when we experience that " the Lord is nigh " (Ps. 144, 18), for we have called upon Him in truth, which is humility of heart, or a sense of justice.

But we did not rest with *affective* prayer. Since this was real prayer, of the will, and not a sentiment of the emotions, it was followed by *effective* desires. We resolved with determination to make our prayer bear fruit in our lives for that particular day. We framed our resolution accordingly. Striving with deliberate effort to make good our morning promise, we continued to pray all through the day, for the dispositions wherewith we concluded our meditation were sustained by the very fact of the effort. And the disposition is prayer.

Now let us sum up the essentials of a well-ordered meditation: 1. The aspiration which brings the help of the Holy Spirit. 2. The sustained reflection on the truth proposed, which is the attention of the mind to subject-matter, and includes the fight to recall wandering thoughts (picture). 3. The movements of will, the dispositions which are the end of meditation, the only purpose of reflection, which constitute prayer in affective and effective desires. This last is the most essential and necessary part, for there the soul finds God and relishes Him. Having called upon Him in truth, we then " speak the praise of the Lord: — and bless His Holy Name " (Ps. 144, 21).

16. THE FACULTIES EMPLOYED IN MEDITATION

"Having different gifts according to the grace that is given us"
(ROMANS xii, 6)

WHO of us has not been thrilled, when, as little children, we saw the Nativity scene re-enacted, in figure, each succeeding Christmastide? The straw, the oxen, the shepherds, St. Joseph, the Blessed Virgin, the Infant, seemed so real to us! How anxiously did we not await the arrival of the Wise Men, bringing their gifts of gold, frankincense, and myrrh? We realize now that they came in response to divine inspiration; in truth, they came, as others since they have come, to the throne of the Eternal Son of God, to study in order to imitate. " Learn of me " (Matt. xi, 29) says Our Lord. And what better aim could we have, since it is the aim God wants us to have, than to master that sublime study, Christ Jesus, the Eternal Prayer of the Father, uttered so that all men can hear and understand? The Magi heard and understood from the beginning; they followed the star of grace until it brought them to the feet and to the heart of their God. Having found Him they sought — Him they sought because they loved — they offered Him a perfect prayer: gold, frankincense, and myrrh — symbol of perfect union. Nor was their prayer momentary; these gifts

[162]

of theirs lasted as long as they lived. They never re-tracted from their offerings; they gave once and for all; they gave — themselves.

And we are the Magi. Do we come to adore the Child empty-handed, or do we bear the gifts He desires from us — the only gifts He wants: gold, frankincense, and myrrh? These only will suffice, for these alone represent a true holocaust — the annihilation of self. "He that saveth his life," says this remarkable Babe, "he that saveth his life, shall lose it; and he that loseth his life, for my sake, shall save it" (Matt. x, 39).

We have been studying how to lose our lives for His sake. We know how to lay before Him gifts, gold (our will) and myrrh (the bitterness of life, the conquest of self). But the fragrant odor of frankincense (prayerful thoughts of the mind) is not so easy to direct, for cross-currents of rebellious winds may waft it whither we will not. It requires absolute quiet and calm for the incense to go straight up without any deviation.

In general, all of us have the same currents to combat: the strong, tempestuous winds that arise from the seeth-ing ocean of self; the slow-gathering, soul-destructive whirlwinds of passion; the noxious, choking fumes that belch forth from the pool of temptation; the tantalizing, fitful breezes of disgust and tribulation; the icy, fear-whipping gales of dread and unknown horror; the mel-low, delicious breath of holily-disguised evil. These and countless others. But mortification is the "Peace, be still" (Mark iv, 39), that will quiet these furies, and, faithfully followed, will gradually lull them to rest.

[163]

But up in the rare atmosphere the eddies of unsought and unexpected distractions will undoubtedly always encircle the fragrant and clear-rising incense of our thoughts; encircle but never distress them. No, none of these things can harm the soul that is faithful and watchful, faithful because it is watchful. Why? The Lord " sent His word and healed them," sings the Psalmist, " and delivered them from their destructions " (Ps. 106, 20 — Gradual of second Sunday after Epiphany).

The Lord sent His Word, Christ Jesus, Who heals faithful souls by the ministering power of His Holy Spirit, and Who delivers them from the possible destruction wrought by the world, the flesh, and the devil. " For that which we believe from Thy revelation concerning Thy glory, that same we believe of Thy Son, that same of the Holy Ghost, without difference or distinction " (Preface of the Trinity). The revelation of God is the Word made flesh, born to make known to man the Eternal Love of the Father for the Son, and of the Son for the Father, which is the Holy Spirit. The healing power of the Lord and Word is in that same Holy Spirit, in the bonds of love, for it is Love that sanctifies, that deifies man. This is accomplished by the Spirit of Infinite Love Who inspires each of us with good thoughts, and holy desires, and right counsels; Who shows us our real self mirrored in God, the one Eternal Good; Who gives strength to die to self and live to Christ; Who does everything — if we will but ask Him. It is for this we pray, to this end that we meditate.

But our meditation may be cast in different molds,

for we have " different gifts, according to the grace that
is given us " (Romans xii, 6). This is an important point
to remember, for here the individual processes of thinking cannot be mapped out in any cut-and-dried-and-
buried fashion, because the directing influence of grace
must be reckoned with. So that it is not how much of a
prepared meditation we remember, point for point, that
counts; it is how much truth we ourselves, by our own
powers of reasoning, have drawn from any given subject,
and have forcefully applied to ourselves, that is of value.
If, then, fifty of you were reflecting on the agony in the
garden, mentally digesting the ideas proposed in the previous conference, and drawing therefrom food for further *individual* thought (the real part of *your* meditation), there should have been (if the thinking were going
on in the right way) fifty different viewpoints or attitudes of mind with regard to the person of Our Lord and
His sufferings; fifty different applications to self of different aspects of the same truth, and hence fifty personally different resolutions. It does not matter a particle
that certain concrete resolves were suggested in the reading; these were merely suggested and might probably fit
one case out of a hundred. But — and this is the essence
of the meditation, the only cause for its being — there
should have been fifty differing prayers.

Note that I have said *differing* prayers, not *different*
prayers. All prayer is essentially the same, being an elevation of the mind and will to God, for the purpose of
adoring Him, thanking Him, and begging His grace.
Only in the considered circumstances, the dispositions of

individuals will vary according as the thoughts move the will to adoration, wonder, astonishment, awe, humility, sorrow, fear, love, joy, hope, faith. With some, humility will be the predominant disposition of heart; with others, sorrow, or patience, or love. Nor is it to be assumed that this humility or sorrow experienced by the soul, and under whose impulse it makes earnest promises to do better, is the only act of homage rendered to the Creator. Hardly. The soul may be penetrated with a sense of humility, and at the same time, almost unknown to itself, call forth accompanying acts of thanksgiving, and glory, and hope, and joy, and love. So that the essence of prayer, then, consists in these acts, or movements, or dispositions of the will. This is that doing (prayer) which is the immediate result of deliberate reflection or meditation; that doing (action) which is the end of meditation and the first sparks of that fire which, provided the soul be found faithful, will ultimately enkindle it into a vibrant flame of life, of that life which is the true beginning of true life, unending, limitless, unfathomable.

It is well to bear in mind always that meditation is, as already so often has been mentioned, only a means to an end, and that end is prayer, conversation with the Author of our being. The means to attain this end may vary, for we all have " different gifts according to the grace that is given us " (Rom. xii, 6). It is to our good that we discover the gifts which we have received, so that we may not abuse them, but use them properly in conjunction with the sanctifying action of the Holy Spirit poured out upon us through the untold merits of the

Word made flesh; for unless we consent, God Himself cannot sanctify us.

First, there is the gift of imagination — normal, over-fed, under-nourished. Which is mine? If I have the ordinary amount, or something less than the ordinary amount, there is little to worry about. It will be the too active imagination which will prove the biggest hindrance to orderly reflection and prayer. This kind will be apt to run away with itself on the smallest provocation, or no provocation at all. This is the type we previously discussed, which leads to day-dreaming and the building of spiritual castles in the air. Such a restive horse must be held in constant check. " Blinkers," in this case, are very necessary, though they are necessary always. Neither should the pigmy imagination be disturbed because it cannot create a striking picture. It is not essential to meditation; thinking is essential.

This brings us to the second gift, the gift of reason. What kind of reasoning power have I? What type of mind is mine? I may possess an intellect that is not satisfied until it unearths the roots of things; or one that travels with a hop-skip-and-jump from subject to subject. Again, mental laziness may mar the normal working order of an average intelligence, one that is neither too quick nor too slow; that grasps an idea after an earnest amount of honest effort, and retains it in the grasping; that does not weary of a task before devoting to it conscious and sincere endeavor; that is always open to conviction and ready to learn.

If my mind is of the scholarly type which must needs

dig down to foundations, and this holds true though there be little or no book-learning, this very aptitude will avail much in concentration on God. Simply employ on spiritual subjects the attention given to ordinary duties and interests. The danger is here not so much the failure to persist in earnest reflection, once meditation has been begun, but not to begin at all, because of the variety of interests in which the mind naturally delights, and the consequent negligence in attending to the one Supreme Good. The remedy in this case is to curb all unnecessary mental pleasures, for these may prove of even greater hindrance than sensual ones, since they tend to pervert the very faculty which alone can begin to fathom God just a tiny bit.

But suppose my mind is of the skipping variety, always eager to taste of the new before the old has really even been one-quarter absorbed. The bee that gathers the juice sets himself to work to absorb the flowery nectar, before it can be transformed into honey. To flit aimlessly from rose to tulip and from hollyhock to carnation will not suffice. A stern fight will be needed to force myself to persevere in the labor at hand — to persist in my efforts at self-conquest, and therefore to persist in determined reflection that actually digests truth.

Or perhaps I may have only an ordinary mind, which the majority of people do possess. That is well, for there is safety in numbers. This assures me of the fact that I am capable of normal thoughts on any subject whatever; and if that, then, also of ordinary decision and action. I stand as good a chance of getting 100% in my meditation as anybody else around me, provided, of course, that I put into the task a 100% effort. Effort and result go hand in hand, because the result, which is the work of grace, depends on my effort, that is, my coöperation with God the Holy Ghost, Who wills to perfect me if I so choose. Effort 50% — result 50%. Effort zero — result zero. Aye, and worse than zero, for we have abused, thrown away precious favors that God held out to us. We must become specialists, and all specialists, using their one talent, strive to become 100% perfect. Specialists are not extraordinary men; they are ordinary people who have developed their one talent extraordinarily well. We have been given the *one* talent beyond excellence: the supernatural life — Emmanuel — God with us and within us. It is up to us to develop this gift extraordinarily well. We can do it; it is not impossible for anyone. Only we must *concentrate* on this one thing; we must direct all our energies towards its achievement, subordinating all other work to this one work of supreme importance, for which we have been loaned this hour of life. This labor on which we must concentrate all our days is, as you have just seen, the development of the supernatural life of grace, or the advance in perfection, or progress in prayer, for all these terms mean the same thing.

To those of ordinary ability, who think and act in an ordinary fashion, the danger in spiritual reflection will be this: " I'm only an ordinary person. God does not expect great goodness from me. That's all well enough for the saints. I'm no saint, and never shall be. It is presumption on my part to aspire so high — it is ridiculous." Reasoning thus, his spiritual exercises are performed in a very ordinary way, which means in a commonplace, monotonous, indifferent sort of way, which produces no fruit but rather increases guilt. As we have already seen some time ago, it is a general truth that the day is no better than the morning meditation. Because the ordinary attention given to usual duties is lacking, the meditation is poor. It is the drudgery, the monotony, the drill exercises of beginners in the spiritual life that tell on the vast majority, who find the drudgery, the monotony, the drill exercises of temporal affairs so irksome.

Why is this so?

The spiritual life of the vast majority is *minus* because their ideal is low. Their mind is down to earthly levels. One must look up, lift up one's head to see the stars. So, too, with the stars of grace. One must rise to them. One must exert oneself, coöperate, consent, act. After all, choice is now made for eternity. Once death rips away the false mask of the flesh, we stand revealed in our true character — clothed with the glory of sanctity that streams from the image of the Crucified with which our soul is sealed, or blotched with the hideousness of evil that has been tenderly nourished, until the leprous scar has wormed out the heart of our soul, and our very reason damns us forever. If we aspire to be saints in heaven, we must strive to be saints on earth; and if we wish to be devils hereafter, no effort is needed on earth.

Effort recalls the third gift, the will. There are only

two kinds: resolute and irresolute. The resolute kind will get there; the other kind will not. To the degree that our will has been resolute will be the degree of glory to come. That is the only degree we can carry to heaven with us — our degree of glory. We must have it, because without it we do not exist in the college of the blessed. Heaven is the post-graduate course; death the commencement. This degree is given for one course only — a science course. It is a Master's degree in the science of the Master. The signature which marks it valid is written in the blood of the Lamb, on the living substance of our soul, and the seal is a gory cross. These are the credentials we must present to the Father Who directs and *is* the life of the blessed. Otherwise we shall be denied admittance. Only *one* entrance examination is allowed. Only one *can* be. That is obvious. What about our credits? What about our demerits?

An irresolute will is its own curse, but it can be redeemed. But how? " Ask and it shall be given you " (Luke xi, 9). Of ourselves, we can do nothing; God is our sole strength and support. If we have not made progress, it is because we have relied on self. We are not to rely on self; we are to *conquer self*. Grace alone can do it. But we are ashamed to beg. Beggars are the cast-offs of society. The trouble is, we are spiritually big, and we must become spiritually little. We must become beggars spiritually. Are we not really cast-offs of the Father? Was it not the Son Who purchased for us re-admission into the society of the élite — the chosen ones, the elect of God? Really, we are not so much after all, when we come to think of it. Only we do not think of it — that is the sad part — at least, not as often as we should.

And this recalls the gift of memory. " Remember thy last end and thou shalt never sin," says Ecclesiasticus (Eccl. vii, 40). How often do we remember our Last End, Who is also our First Beginning? Our memory may be poor in this respect, or it may be good. If it be poor, one thing is certain: we have been feeding it improper food. The memory evokes that with which it has been fed. Give the eyes and ears and taste and tongue full liberty, and the memory tells the story — when we would not. Supply it with spiritual nourishment, and at the right time it will aid. Or we have a memory retentive with regard to temporal affairs but very deficient in the matters of the spirit. This condition is of our own choosing. " Seek ye *first* the kingdom of God and His justice (does not the Babe of Bethlehem teach this by His example?) and all these things (health, talents, success, friends) shall be added unto you " (Luke xii, 31); that is, according to the measure in which you have need of them.

The Babe, who is the Light of the world, remembered one thing only in coming to dwell among us: " Behold, I come to do Thy will, O God " (Heb. x, 9). He Himself testified in death to its accomplishment: " It is consummated " (John xix, 30).

The Magi who came to adore the Babe, who sought Him they loved for Love's sake, remembered one thing only in their wanderings after Truth: " Where is He? " With the bride in the canticle they complained: " I sought Him whom my soul loveth " (Cant. iii, 1). And with her in the canticle they exult: " I held Him and I will not let Him go " (Cant. iii, 4).

We are the Magi. We seek that we may find. And meditation will help to reveal Him to us. Let us look over these gifts we employ in meditating — imagination, memory, will, and understanding — and see wherein we are deficient, wherein we are gifted. Our aim here is to make the poor good, and the good better. Then shall we be resolutely consenting to that healing which the Lord wills us to possess by means of His Word.

17. THE TIME OF PRAYER

"But thou, when thou shalt pray, enter into thy chamber, and having shut the door, pray to thy Father in secret: and thy Father Who seeth in secret will repay thee" (MATT. vi, 6)

WHAT is it to pray? To pray is to hold communication. The creature, in prayer, communes with its Creator. Such is the essence of life, for he alone who prays really lives. "Now this is eternal life: That they may know thee, the only true God, and Jesus Christ, Whom Thou hast sent" (John xvii, 3).

Why do we pray? That we may know; and knowing, love; and loving, serve; and so possess life in its fulness. I say in its fulness, because just as in the order of nature various states of health, or existence, make themselves manifest, so also in the spiritual. Only he has perfect bodily health in whom all the organs function perfectly. The like is true of the soul. Some people feel well even when sick; others " enjoy " ill health at all times, regardless of their true physical condition; but the worst sufferers are they who always " simply exist " — a dragging, monotonous, unconsciously-stinted (and so, nearly incurable) existence.

Yet in all conditions of well-being, in the midst of ailments real or imaginary, one thing is absolutely indispensable, for without it the higher type of animal life would cease to be — and that is breath. This statement in itself is so obvious as to appear ridiculous; no one, short of an insane person, would attempt to contradict it. And what applies in the order of nature, applies equally in the order of grace; nor is the analogy quite so strained as might offhand appear, for both spheres find their origin in the same Author, and are governed by fixed principles, similar in their scope and application. God Himself makes use of this comparison most frequently. " Unless a man be born again of water and the Holy Ghost, he cannot enter into the kingdom of heaven " (John iii, 5). " I am the living bread which came down from heaven; that if any man eat of it, he may not die. If any man eat of this bread he shall live forever; and the bread that I will give, is my flesh, for the life of the world. For my flesh is meat indeed; and my blood is drink indeed. This is the bread that came down from heaven. Not as your fathers did eat manna, and are dead. He that eateth this bread shall live forever " (John vi. 51–59). Physically, man is born; and he grows to manhood by assimilating food: spiritually, the same development may be traced. This parallel having been established, I revert to what has been said previously, namely, that that which applies in the order of nature, applies equally in the order of grace.

No matter what the ailment, real or imaginary, may be, one thing is absolutely essential to all conditions of spiritual well-being — breath. And prayer is a breathing of the soul. I said a moment ago that prayer is a communication between the creature and the Creator; now that it is a breath of the soul. How can a communication be a breath? If the statement can be shown to hold true in the natural, we may find its counterpart in the supernatural, which, though beyond comprehension, is not therefore at variance with reason. Respiration is the process of inhaling air and expelling it. To breathe is to live. While a man breathes, he is; when he ceases to respire, he is no more. Respiration, then, is the communication of bodily life. Prayer is the breathing in of the soul in the Life-giving Ether, God, whereby are communicated to it those necessary pulsations which are the mainspring of its being. Prayer is respiration. The soul breathes in God, and exhales the sweet odor of Jesus Christ. As the soul is the breath of God, " And the Lord God formed man of the slime of the earth: and breathed into his face the breath of life, and man became a living soul " (Gen. ii, 7), so prayer is the breath of the soul. As the breath of the body in a relatively perfect physical organism is easy, free, natural, unconscious, and continuous, so also is prayer in a relatively perfect spiritual being, the soul. It should be as natural for us to pray as to breathe. Respiration in soul and body should be a simultaneous action. This is not at all impossible. God gives no commands or counsels incapable of achievement, and He has said: " Pray without ceasing " (I Thess. v. 17), which again reads: " We ought always to pray " (Luke xviii, 1).

But how is this continuous spiritual breathing, prayer, to be accomplished when one has so many occupations to divert the mind? Theoretically, it sounds perfect and may be that for — well, possibly contemplatives; and even then there might be some slight exaggeration, pardonable, of course, yet none the less just a slim stretching of actuality. Surely God cannot expect me to pray always when He himself is responsible for the assignment of my round of duties — in the kitchen, the classroom, the office, the laundry; at the switchboard, the paying-teller's desk, the forge; as the manager of any group for whose turn-out I am responsible; or in whatever position I may find myself. Rank nonsense! No person can pray *always*. Why, anyone with a single grain of sense knows that there are a thousand and one things any man or woman, religious or lay, must attend to in the course of the day. Absurd!

But at the risk of being catalogued among those who want the very last grain of common sense, I politely disagree. The root of the whole trouble was unearthed in the sentence that came before " absurd." We do *not* have a thousand and one things to look after; God never intended that we should. There is but one God, one Truth, one life, one ego, one soul; there is but *one* duty, *one* aim, *one* business, designated by the One God to occupy that *one* ego, that *one* life, that *one* soul. What is it? Listen to the words of Eternal Truth: " Be . . . perfect, as also your heavenly Father is perfect " (Matt. v. 48).

But what does it mean to be perfect? Simply to keep the commandments perfectly. Which commandment? That *one* on which " dependeth the whole law and the prophets " (Matt. xxii, 40). " Thou shalt love the Lord thy God with thy whole heart, and with thy whole soul, and with all thy strength, and with all thy mind: and thy neighbor as thyself " (Luke x, 27). One God, one life, one soul, one duty imposed by *one* commandment. Nothing could be clearer than these words of Our Lord, and yet how often and how sadly are they misconstrued. Christ does not say to us: " Thou shalt love the Lord thy God with one-half of thy heart, and one-fifth of thy soul, and the one-one thousandth and first part of thy mind " (heart and soul and mind are here identical in meaning) ; but He states most emphatically " with thy *whole* heart." And He repeats the command thrice in order to imprint the lesson upon our, at times, all-too-wilfully-obtuse intellects. " With thy whole heart " — the heart, in common parlance, the center of the sensible affections; " with thy whole soul " — the soul, the spirit that animates every action; " with all thy strength " — strength, the plenitude of the power of a mature will; " with all thy mind " — the mind, the spiritual faculty by means of which knowledge is acquired.

The essence, then, of God's command is simply this: " Subordinate all your interests to the one only interest I had in mind when creating you — that you apply yourself with singleness of purpose, which involves determination of effort, to the acquisition of one only lesson: that you love Me *whole-heartedly*. The affections of the heart must be centered in Me; every action must be performed with a view to My good pleasure; all knowledge that does not have Me for its ultimate objective, is vain; the will, by painstaking development, like the muscles of an athlete, must be toughened in the exercise of combating and conquering its rebellious movements until,

[178]

through generous and constant submission to Me, it finds its true home in the measureless depths of Divine Power, a child at rest in the bosom of its Father, by dissolution in My adorable Will. Life is love, " for I," the Author of life, " am love " (I Epistle of St. John, iv, 8).

To live is to love; to love is to will; and by willing, as perfectly as we can, to keep the *one* commandment, as perfectly as we can, we keep all the commandments, which is all that God requires of us; though the obligation of perfecting or developing the will to maturity is not thereby foregone. This doctrine is not mine, but Christ's Who said: " If you love Me, keep my commandments. He that hath my commandments and keepeth them, he it is that loveth Me. And he that loveth Me, shall be loved of my Father; and I will love him, and will manifest myself to him " (John xiv, 15, 21).

Again on the same night, His last night on earth, and at the same meal, His last meal with His friends, He solemnly and lovingly repeated, as the parting instructions of an Infallible Guide to which they might appeal after His physical presence among them should be withdrawn: " If any one love Me, he will keep my word, and my Father will love him, and we will come to him, and will make our abode with him " (John xiv, 23). This is simply another manner of saying that " thou shalt pray to thy Father in secret, and thy Father Who seeth in secret will repay thee " (Matt. vi. 6); for mark well: living is loving; loving is willing; and willing is praying. Which can conclude only thus: living is praying — praying is living. Prayer is the breath of the soul. Prayer is spiritual respiration by which we inhale deep draughts of God, and exhale the sweet odor of Christ.

Such is prayer in a relatively perfect soul — the unceasing operation of a mature will which is dissolved in God's. One difference should be carefully noted between physical and spiritual respiration. Ordinarily, man from his birth respires in easy, free, natural, unconscious, continuous movements. Spiritually this is attained only after a hard struggle with a perversely selfish and rebellious will. Originally it was not so, and God did not will it so. But in Adam we have all sinned, and we bear the effects of that fall in body and soul. Despite man's rebellion, God's ordinance was not to be set aside; Christ purchased for us our primal inheritance by His Blood. We are redeemed. It remains for us to coöperate with Him in order that the work of redemption in us may not be impeded, but that His designs may be fully executed in our lives. We must live as He lived; will as He wills; pray as He prayed and desires us to pray — always — without ceasing. To achieve this condition is our only end in life. To achieve it we need only to will it. Longing for it, desiring it, wanting it, no matter how fervent in our estimation is the yearning, is *not* willing it. Will with determined effort. Willing means fighting, not looking on while another does the work, wondering meanwhile if we ever will become like that ourselves. In the vernacular of the day " Be yourself." *Be* what God wills you to be. Oh, if we would only permit God to act, what wonders would He not operate in us and for us. God holds out the gift with an excessive love, for He tells us " I have loved

thee with an everlasting love " (Jeremias xxxi, 3). We
must do something on our part — we must stretch out
our hand for it, which action involves an effort. This
stretching out of the hand is the reaching forth of the
will to embrace the Divine Will.

How is this Divine Will made manifest to us? Chiefly
by prayer, * which consists in *willing* to inhale God so
that we may exhale the sweet odor of Christ. My memory
may go back to yesteryear; my imagination may con-
jure up unwanted fancies; my understanding may consider the bitterness of this morning's failure, or the joy
of yesterday's success; it is the *will alone* that brings back
these prodigals to the feet of the Father. It is the will that
persists in breathing, however imperfectly. We may be
spiritually long-winded or short-winded; we may have
spiritual asthma or bronchitis, or anything else which
may more seriously affect our breathing apparatus — all
these are not hindrances but aids to the attainment of
perfect functioning in our spiritual life, because the very
attempt to overcome these obstacles is the cure. Progress
in correct spiritual respiration, the scientific development of the will, consists in persevering attempts, which
necessarily imply failures, repeated failures it very often
may be. Success in the striving depends solely upon our

* The sacraments are the channels of grace *par excellence*. Though
they are efficaciously operative in themselves by virtue of the dispensive
power of Our Lord, still, He has ordained that their effects be proportionate to the dispositions of the recipient. Prayer aims to cast these
dispositions into perfect alignment with the divine ordinances by anni-
hilating in the creature the very last minutiae of self-interest (*Sister*
MIRIAM TERESA).

use or abuse of divine grace, never wanting, and showered in superabundance on them of good will. If we are steadfastly determined to please Him, and, in spite of our best resolutions, fail, very miserably perhaps, He is none the less pleased and glorified, provided the kernel of the fall, humility, be thoroughly digested. In His own good time, and according to the dispensations of His All-wise Providence, He will take pity on our feeble, faithful efforts, and the Father Who seeth our secret prayer will repay us; He Who loves us will come to us and make His abode with us, for His delight is to be with the children of men.

But before this shall come to pass, since our breathing apparatus is more or less disordered, and our will flabby and relaxed, we must get to work and practise proper breathing exercises, and tone up the undeveloped muscles of the wavering will to the end that our communications with our Creator may be direct, forceful, fruitful; that we may learn to keep His *one* commandment perfectly; that prayer, the breath of life in the soul, the breath of God, may be the peaceful continuous inflowing of His vivifying Spirit. Only then shall we observe the whole law and the prophets; only then shall we keep the commandments perfectly, for He Himself will observe them in us; only then shall His prayer and ours, repeated daily, be a living, actual fact, " Thy will be done on earth as it is in heaven " (Matt. vi, 10); only then shall we diffuse, in all its magnificent splendor, the sweet odor of Jesus Christ.

18. THE PLACE OF PRAYER

"But thou, when thou shalt pray, enter into thy chamber" (MATT. vi, 6)

WE HAVE seen that Christ Our Lord in the first part of this word " when thou shalt pray " means unceasing, continuous prayer; normal spiritual respiration, the uninterrupted communication between the creature and the Creator. Having established the time, always, we have now to fix the place. " Enter into thy chamber." A definite locality, then, . . . " thy chamber," yet not quite clear, perhaps, without some explanation of the term. " To enter " means ' to go in,' certainly. But where? That is the vital point.

Ordinarily, the first definition of the idea which comes to mind with regard to the word under consideration is: a private room. This definition does not seem sufficient, since we are to pray always, and it stands to reason that no human being in whatever sphere of life, can enter, or be within his room at every minute of the day. The same holds true if we interpret the word as ' church ' or ' oratory.' Still, this is the saying of Eternal Truth, Who never gives a command, counsel, or precept incapable of fulfilment. What are we to conclude? Simply this: " Chamber " is not to be taken merely in its literal meaning,* since turn it about as we may, it presents a seeming

* We find that St. Augustine and St. Ambrose incline to the literal meaning of the passage in question. ED.

[183]

absurdity. If the words of a man, taken solely in their restricted, literal meaning appear inadequate, and we have every reason to respect their originator as a person of sound mind, accurate judgment, and unimpeachable moral integrity — and where do we find these attributes in their fullest perfection other than in Christ Jesus — we may correctly interpret them in a mystical or figurative application. So also now. To adhere solely to the material, literal use of " chamber " may appear unreasonable; therefore we may, logically, and rightly, too, look at it in a deeper, more hidden sense — consider it a figure of speech.

But the excellence of any figure of speech depends upon its aptness, its peculiar fitness to convey under the impression of one image an idea or form to which it is readily analogous or similar. What might require a paragraph of abstract explanation is forcefully compressed in a single concrete figure. Let us examine, then, in what manner this applies to the case at hand.

The restriction of the notion of a chamber external to man, or existing in the material world, has been dispensed with; therefore, the figure which implies comparison between objects of unlike classes should refer, in this instance, to the interior man or the spiritual world — therefore the heart, the soul. " But thou when thou shalt pray, enter into thy chamber " (Matt. vi, 6), that is, enter into thy soul. What? *Enter* into my soul? This sounds even more obscure. How can I enter, go in, into that part of me which is essentially " I "? Enter into myself? Just so.

[184]

theless, for no act can be absolutely aimless; if it were it would cease to be an act.

You know that if you are engaged by a man to help him build a house, you are neither going to draw a salary nor keep your position by failing, day after day, to report for duty. Your daily action in going to work is a very deliberate one, for you realize that on it depends your sole means of subsistence. You have in this instance both a determined end, and an end which is very definite in your mind.

Again, you may be at home after your day's labor, immersed in a favorite section of the newspaper, or listening to a ' jazz ' concert over the radio — perhaps both together, and an inquiring mosquito, without any salutation other than that of a pointed caress, makes free with your head. Instinctively you act. Your killing that mosquito was a purposeful act, — it had a definite end in view, although at the moment of operation that goal was not clearly defined. You did not stop to reflect in this fashion: Something is annoying me at the top of my head. That something has just stung me. Ordinary things which sting are called mosquitoes. This thing must be a mosquito. Mosquitoes are nuisances which should be exterminated. Therefore, I shall kill this one. As a matter of fact, you did not know whether it was a June-bug, a fly, or just an insect. All you knew was that your quiet (if you insist on calling it such) was being disturbed, so you wished the cause removed, and instinctively you raised your hand. It really made little difference to you whether the pest were killed or simply made to seek a new place of settlement; you were interested in the diversions you had selected, and your attention was fixed on them. You acted, quite unconscious of your real motive.

This latter type of acting will not do at all in order to enter properly into ourselves at the time of prayer, although it is, unfortunately, the only kind of good many people pursue. At prayer, their minds are filled with a thousand distractions which they make little or no effort to dispel, and the thought of God, or the fact of their supposed conversation with Him is vague, fleeting, and as little disturbs what is uppermost in their heads as the movement of the hand that shifted the mosquito drew their attention from the paper and radio. No, indeed, this type of acting will never do for prayer.

To pray well requires as much, if not more, determined effort than that shown by the man, who engaged to help build a house, and who knows that his livelihood depends on the way he performs his work, does all he can to acquit himself in the best possible manner of the duties entrusted to his charge. He cannot look about him haphazardly while trying to drive a nail, neither can he do calisthenics on the top of a two-by-four scaffold, and at the same time try to shingle the roof properly and preserve his balance. Why reason things differently just because it is prayer that we are trying to build up? You cannot drive home the nail of your petition in the approved fashion while at the same moment you are occupied with cannon to the right of you, cannon to the left of you, cannon before, behind,

above, below and all around you. Neither can you properly shingle the roof of your house of prayer (without
the roof, a building is not complete or habitable, and the
shingles secure the interior from extremes of heat and
cold, snow, rain, wind, storm, débris of all kinds) while
you perform mental gymnastics, and, at the same time,
hope to preserve your spiritual balance on the two-by-
four scaffold of indifferent devotion you may have
hauled up, even to a considerable height. No. Prayer is
not a ' Fourth-of-July ' celebration. It is rather the kind
of an affair every one of us is called upon to perform
daily — it is hard work, and a great deal of it, achieved
only " by the sweat of thy face " (Gen. iii, 19).

We shall now weld the links of what I have just said to
what preceded. It was remarked that to enter into myself, I had but to be alone with my thoughts, to *will* to
establish a solitude in my heart. What I have attempted
to prove to you was the fact that to be alone with your
thoughts was not to day-dream, nor to build castles in
the air, nor to let your imagination stray where it pleases
— different types of distractions — because all these
things are merely vague wanderings of the mind which
while away the hours more or less pleasantly, but arrive
nowhere and accomplish nothing. Since they arrive nowhere and accomplish nothing, being of the nature of
reveries, vain dreams, they are valueless; they are not
purposeful acts. Prayer is, above everything else, an act
having a deliberate end in view — an end clearly defined in the mind. So that to enter into myself, to
go into that secret chamber which is my soul, — and

[189]

remember that Our Lord demands this as an indispensable prelude to prayer — requires on my part a *determined effort,* namely a movement, an act of the will.

But in what does this movement, this act of the will consist? In the analogy drawn between the chamber and the soul, I said that the door in the one case represents the will in the other, while the key is our faith. I also mentioned that the normal way of entering a room is by way of the door, the key of which we take an ordinary amount of precaution not to lose. Very well. If a door and a key, then also there must be a keyhole. Given the first two without the last will get me no more inside the room than if I had no key at all, and were a thousand miles removed from the door.

What is this spiritual keyhole? The desire, the disposition to pray. I may have faith, stronger or less firm, I always have a will, but unless the desire be present to combine the two, it will avail me nothing in my intercourse with God. By desire I do not mean that emotion or feeling, exuberant in some people, which at one time can recite all the litanies in existence (to the annoyance, it very often may be, of neighboring worshipers); can say two or three thousand *Aves* a day for some special intention; burn out half a gross or so of votive lights; hear two or three Masses, — and let slip some duty of state — sing loudly and long in processions; love Benediction on account of the soothing effect of music and incense and candlelight — and not perceive this fundamental cause in self — and on another occasion omits Mass even on

Sunday for the flimsiest excuse; has no time for morning
and evening prayers; cannot see the value of reciting the
rosary; — ' prayers are never answered, so why bother '
— and the only procession indulged in is that which ac-
cumulates in front of a theater.

All this is not devotion but sentiment, tossed about by
every wind that sweeps through the taut chords of passion. The right disposition consists in the knowledge,
more or less vivid, that the act is one of duty or counsel
plus the deliberate resolution to do what that knowledge
tells me should be done. Feelings, as such, have nothing
whatever to do with the matter. Frequently, they are the
principal reason why a great many really good people fail
to advance. We are so constituted that we are prone to
approve as eminently truthful and correct what we see,
or hear, or touch, or taste, or smell, in other words, what
our senses convey to us. Still, the sooner we learn that in
our spiritual life, the animal nature, because of original
sin, is often a hindrance, which must be cast aside, the
better it will be for us, and the more rapid will be our
progress.

After all, what is this struggle which each of us must
go through if we wish to be saved, but the hourly combat between the flesh and the spirit, the subduing and
conquering of the animal life, corrupted by sin, by the
power of the spirit that is supernaturally ours by grace?
We are too apt to forget one important thing: We are
reasoning *animals*. The body is from the earth, earthy,
and in our fallen state tends towards things of the earth.
So also, the flesh, taken from below, finds relish in the

things which are below, and desires them. Because we do not stop to consider this fact, or forget it at times, is the reason why we are so surprised and hurt when some unexpected occurrence makes painfully clear to us that we are, well — yes, we hate to confess it — selfish, and greedy, and envious, and jealous, and conceited, and proud, and — finish the list for yourself, it will do you good; when all the time we thought what the majority of our neighbors thought of us — that we were generous, and charitable, and self-sacrificing, and humble, and refined, and everything else.

On the other hand, the spirit, enlivened by grace, which is from above, also seeks its own environment and tries to draw us toward heights far removed from the miserable delights of the flesh, with which it is clothed. Made to the image and likeness of God, a pure Spirit, the soul, a spirit, seeks to rid itself of the encumbrances which the lower element at times presents so utterly alien to its needs and yearnings, and so absolutely out of harmony with that life which is itself. You know what happens when two opposite forces, both powerful in themselves, meet. There is certainly going to be a terrific collision. Of course, there is going to be a fight, and a mighty hard one at that, for St. Paul tells us that " the flesh lusteth against the spirit, and the spirit against the flesh " (Gal. v, 17). Then, why be surprised to discover in ourselves desires and wants eternally at variance with each other? The thing to realize is this: one of these forces is going to win out in the end. It is for *me* to decide which one that will be. Am I going to let the flesh with its lusts drag me down, or am I going to let the spirit, with its heavenly aspirations, lift me on high? You think, perhaps, that the struggle is an uneven one? Not in the least. Left to ourselves, of course, we could accomplish nothing. "Without me," says Christ Jesus, "you can do nothing" (John xv, 5). But grace, that marvelously divine gift which He purchased for us, is ours for the asking. "Ask, and you shall receive" (John xvi, 24). "You shall," He says, and His word is His bond. Realizing this truth, we can cry out with St. Paul, not fearing the conflict, nor be anxious as to the outcome: "I can do all things in Him Who strengtheneth me" (Phil. iv, 13). "God and I are a majority," says St. Teresa. "God and I are a majority," let us sincerely repeat.

But let us see in what way the feelings, the emotions, the passionate desires of the body are an obstacle, for they are also an aid. The senses are a hindrance, an obstacle, only in so far as we gauge our spiritual devotion by them. The senses are also, and let this be remembered, positive helps given us by God to draw nearer to Him. It is in fighting these inclinations of the flesh, this animal nature, that we advance toward God. Do not be deceived. Perfection does not consist in having nothing to overcome, but in *overcoming*. To become perfect means to be *determined* to persevere in fighting, cost what it may. God tested the angels, before He rewarded them, and He tests us, but in another manner. He gives us a body and says: "Before I can reward you for your fidelity, prove that fidelity to Me by bringing under the control of the

[193]

spirit, which is made to My own image, the animal nature with which I have vested your soul."

A soldier cannot fight unless he is strong, and he will never be physically strong unless he has been properly nourished. The soul, the soldier fighting under Christ's standard, cannot carry on the warfare without strength from above, and this spirtual nourishment is obtained chiefly through prayer, and prayer made in the manner taught by Christ Himself. To pray properly, says our Divine Master, we must enter into ourselves. " But thou when thou shalt pray, enter into thy chamber." " Enter thy chamber, thy soul, made to My likeness, where I reside. Enter to find Me by finding thyself. I have given thee the key, faith. The keyhole is now uncovered to thee. The more shining and bright the key, the purer and more free from rust and cloggings of dirt the keyhole, the more perfectly will the door swing on its hinges — easily, naturally, freely, without groanings and squeakings. Hast trouble, child, in unlocking? Patience, little one. I am here, within. I will, I desire to help thee, but thou hast forgotten to ask. Ah — thy pardon is the open door. Enter."

19. THE MANNER OF PRAYER

"But thou, when thou shalt pray, enter into thy chamber, and having closed the door, pray" (Matt. vi, 6)

W E HAVE already fixed the time of prayer, always; and the place, the chamber of our soul, our interior. Before considering how we are to pray, we need first to understand by what means we are to keep ourselves in the established place during the prescribed time; for though it is not an easy matter to enter this spiritual dwelling, it is only all too easy to slip out. If we are to pray in our interior, we have to find out how to stay there, before the manner of our prayer is explained. Otherwise, not remaining within ourselves as Our Lord commanded, we shall understand nothing of what He would say to us, for speaking of the soul He tells us, " I will allure her, and will lead her into the wilderness, and I will speak to her heart " (Osee ii, 14).

This solitude is our interior chamber, the soul which we enter by applying the key of faith — our unconditional belief in His veracity — to the keyhole of a proper disposition, that is, the knowledge of what He wants done together with the determination to do it; and by turning the knob — an act of the will by which, come what may, we are going to remain alone with our thoughts, with our real self, to find ourselves and Him. We have entered now, with His help, but are we going to stay? Perhaps we will not like the disclosures that may be made — that is, the furniture and hangings. They may be faded and worn, or in some instances lacking, and the light may be too strong or too dim. But never mind the apprehensions. This is not the moment nor the place to falter. As you know, the very worst troubles we have to endure are the anticipated ones, which rarely come to pass. Besides, curiosity is not a virtue, so put it away in moth-balls and then forget where you placed it. Standing on the threshold, we desire to consider what it is the room contains, but our Master warns us that one thing still remains to be done. " Enter . . . and having closed the door, pray " (Matt. vi, 6). The door then must be shut, and shut tightly, so that none may intrude and violate our privacy.

A closed door is a barrier, a wall which excludes the external. This door which leads to the chamber of the soul, is, as was remarked before, the faculty of the will — that is, the power we have within us of doing; the most highly prized possession we own, in the use of which man either ennobles or degrades himself, rendering himself Godlike or like to the brute creation. This is truly tremendous power, God-given, whereby man is a magnificently independent, responsible being, capable of employing that very liberty, received from the Creator, to thwart His plans and violate His commands if he so choose and dare, for being free, he is not constrained to act other than as he pleases. We cannot conceive of a force more supremely potent than this door of our will, at once invigorating or devastating, according to the manner of its application. This faculty, this power of willing, is the door to our interior. But to enter, as we have seen, the door needed to be opened, and to remain in seclusion it is just as vital to close that door, and see that it stays so. To open or to shut simply means this: the power of the will expresses itself in an action, which in the first case involved the resolute effort to turn our mental searchlight upon ourselves, and in the second, to keep our finger on the lever to prevent the light from flickering. Hence, it depends on an individual act of the will to close the door; to bid distractions of all kinds remain outside.

What a simple thing to close the door! I will to leave all cares outside, and immediately it is accomplished? No. The door was shut by an act of the will, yes. But at times, and very frequently, too, perhaps, it will rattle and creak and actually blow open. What is the matter? Ah, we forgot to look after the windows. They are un-latched, and the north wind of the world is whistling in, overturning the furniture, flapping the hangings madly, and really almost tearing the door off its hinges. Is it any wonder that the door flies open? Not a bit. We wonder how we ever managed to shut it in the first place. We will have to get those windows fastened, and the blinds pulled down before a regular ' nor'wester ' is upon us. It will take some time, too, I fear, and more than time only — it means a struggle, and a very hard struggle at that. Do you recall what was mentioned some time ago? The windows of this interior dwelling are the bodily senses. Do you now understand clearly?

Only one conclusion can be drawn from the fore-
going, and it is the right one. If during the time of
prayer we wish to be in a condition suitable for communication with our Maker, it is absolutely necessary,
outside of the actual periods given to prayer, to curb
the bodily senses, that is, to practise mortification. As
will be shown presently, mortification is only another
name for recollection. Should this not be done, what
happens? We come to prayer with a thousand and one
worldly ideas dashing around wildly in a mad marathon
to break the championship record; a million and one
pictures are thrust upon our imagination. Is it any wonder, then, that there is difficulty in keeping the door
closed?

If we wish to pray well during our fixed time for
prayer, we must, and this is of cardinal importance,
preserve during the day the *spirit* of prayer, a spirit of
mortification, or recollection. Yes, I realize that I am repeating, quite frequently, too, but this cannot be said
too often. Please let it penetrate — deeply. Grasp it with
all the power at your command, just like the tired
laborer in the subway who holds on to the strap in a
deathlike grip, trying to keep his balance while the car
swerves around within the curve of a 45° angle. This
much, then, is settled.

But why am I so insistent on this point? Because, as
you recall, we saw that Christ Our Lord told us to pray
always, and it is only by preserving a spirit of prayer,
continually, that we can and must keep His commandment. In other words, it is magnifying the keyhole of

the disposition for prayer until the door of the will is one immense keyhole, the key of faith enlarging itself in proportion. When this has been achieved, there is no trouble. This is only relatively true, not absolutely, for no matter how high the degree of prayer which God, in His mercy, may have helped us to attain, at times, there will be minor occasions of annoyance, though they will not be able to disturb either our prayer or our peace. Heaven is the one place where we will be free of all care and tribulation and sorrow.

But, by coöperating with His grace we can achieve even in this life — and how ardently God yearns to see it accomplished in every soul that He has created — that degree of union with Him through prayer which He has been pleased to ordain. He Himself tells us what He longs for so much: " If any one love me he will keep my word, and my Father will love him, and we will come to him and make our abode with him " (John xiv, 23). And He says this more than once. " We will make our abode with him," that is, dwell in him, live in him continually, become the very life of his life and the sole and principal source of all his activity. What a promise! One that only God could make and fulfil literally; one as wonderful as the promise made on the shores of the lake: " the bread that I will give is my flesh for the life of the world " (John vi, 52), and fulfilled at the Last Supper: " Take ye and eat: This is My Body " (Matt. xxvi, 26).

God wants to accomplish this in me? God wants to take up His abode with me? He does, but you do not want him to. Why? Because you do not love Him. " If any one love me " (John xiv, 23) — that is the sole condition. We think we love Him, but in reality we love only ourselves, for the most part. Why do friends communicate with each other? Because they love. Friendship grows cold and dies through lack of intercourse. The same holds true in our relations with God. Why do we communicate with God, that is, why do we pray? Because we love. And we can measure our love by the frequency and fervor, though not sensible fervor, of our prayers, our communications. If we really loved God as we should we would love Him always, twenty-four hours in the day. If we loved Him always, we would want to communicate, hold intercourse, converse with Him always. And this would be to pray always. By preserving the disposition for prayer during the entire day, and the night, too, we are praying always, and consequently proving our love for Him continually. Do you begin to see the necessity for the spirit of prayer, the spirit of recollection, the spirit of mortification?

Mortification! Even the very sound of the word is rather disagreeable. It brings up memories, perhaps, of bitter medicine and the like. But God can do all things. He turns bitter things into sweetness, and into sweetness such as the compressed delights of all this world could not begin by the fraction of a drop to distil. But — pain? No person likes pain. No, no one. One Man did though, Who said, "I am the Way" (John xiv, 6). And they called Him a fool. He says to each of us, because He is the Eternal Now, " I am the Way." We say to Him, not so much in words — that were hard enough to bear —

but in act, which is infinitely worse and a thousand times more painful, " Thou art a fool. Why dost Thou tell us this word? We know better than Thou." Yes, we think we do. We are like the householder who with his gran-aries filled to overflowing said to himself, thinking to have no further care for the morrow, " Soul — take thy rest, eat, drink, make good cheer " (Luke xii, 19). What happened? And the Lord God said to him that night, " Thou fool, this night do they require thy soul of thee " (Luke xii, 20).

But please follow. I know that I am alive. Yes. I know that I can do or not do, as I please. Yes. I know that things do not always turn out the way I had planned, in fact, more often not. Yes. I have lived long enough to be absolutely sure that in this life I can be absolutely cer-tain of only one thing: one thing that will not fail me: one thing that every person must face. Some day,* and very soon, no matter how far distant, time for me will cease, and eternity begin. I shall die. Some day, and very soon, curious eyes will pause before a little gravestone in God's acre and read:

HERE LIES

YOURS TRULY

BORN: IT MATTERS NOT WHEN.

DIED: YESTERDAY, IN THE LORD.

WHILE IN THE WORLD HE FILLED A

PLACE, NOW FILLED A LITTLE BETTER

THAN JUST AS WELL, BY ANOTHER.

R. I. P.

---

* Written June 25, 1926. ED.

I am traveling, and traveling fast, toward eternity. This truth I cannot deny, although I might like to. The proofs of it are only too frequent and evident. Independent creature that I am, I cannot control my growth, nor the length of my days. Only He Who gave life has the right to take it away. Action here on my part would be mortally sinful. (And I know whereof I speak, because even this temptation was not spared me while for three weeks I lived in the hell of the atheist's unbelief. Oh, if those souls so cruelly tempted to despair could only fathom something of the everlasting and fatherly love with which God in His mercy and pitying forgiveness reaches out toward them. The poet sings of mother's love, and this mother's love, this totality of all mother love is only a filmy shadow of the love God holds out to me who am so tortured to despair!) If I cannot bear with myself now, for a few brief hours, how do I expect to bear with my miserable self hereafter, forever, always? That is devilish wisdom. The sad thing is that there are only too many souls devilishly wise because they refuse to become divinely foolish. "For the wisdom of this world is foolishness with God" (I Cor. iii, 19). Christ said, "I am the Way" (John xiv, 6). And they crucified Him between two thieves.

I am hurrying toward eternity. Whether I like it or not, I shall live forever. I must. My soul is immortal. After I stop breathing, I will be judged, weighed in the balance. My past record will be looked up; I will be examined on my merits and demerits, and classified accordingly. Then I will be put where I belong. I will be in

[202]

the same class with the saints — or with the devils. Do not think for a minute that one, the minute he dies, somehow or other is transformed miraculously into a cherub with shining-bright wings, and a gold crown, and a harp, and all that; or foully disfigured into a horrid creature with hoofs and horns, and wings like a bat. Oh, no. These are the ways artists try to convey to our human nature the essential qualities of good and bad spirits, aye, of the men and women who have gone on before. Here on earth we are very particular about the company we select, the companions with whom we mingle. None of us likes to be seen together with one frowned on by public opinion, even if that ostracism be undeserved. Then why show such precautions here below and never give a thought to the friends you will have up above? You choose right now, freely, deliberately, whether you are going to be in the same class with the saints or the devils. Once time for you is no more you receive judgment, not mercy. When the records in the Book of Life are referred to in the presence of witnesses (the devil is his own advocate there) you receive just what you deserve — nothing more, not a hair less. God is Infinite Justice. And just what that decision will be depends upon your own self at this minute, and for every remaining minute of your life.

You realize now a little more deeply that this life after all does not amount to much more than a row of nine-pins waiting for the smashing death-ball to be shot down the alley of Time. There is no danger that the ball will roll down the gutter or that some of the pins will

be left standing. The aim is too accurate, and the outcome too certain. For us, Eternity is the only reality, the
only reason for 'what is to each one a most important
Present.

The essential point of this vital Present is that we make
a good selection of the friends with whom we shall converse forever. Of course, none of us desires to be seen together with those frowned on by the élite — the elect
ones of God who chose Him as their everlasting portion
while they lived here below. It is a very select club — this
class of the saints, more select even than the Phi Beta
Kappa's or the Delta Gamma's or whatever else they may
call themselves. The fraternity of the saints is the Alpha
Omega fraternity — the first and the last in point of
excellence and endurance. It has its own kind of initiation and meetings. And a " frat pin," too. A little different from the ordinary " frat pin " which, made of
gold and precious stones and a chain and a guard, lasts in
its primal beauty for a while, and then the gold tarnishes
and the jewels drop out or the ornament is lost altogether.
No. This emblem of the saints is worn by all being in-
itiated here on earth: this " frat pin," a cross, shaped of
a sprig of thorn, becomes only in eternity an ornament
revealed in its true splendor, formed of the gold of
charity, encrusted with the diamond of faith, the em-
erald of hope, the pearl of purity, the amethyst of sorrow and mortification, the ruby of courage, the blood-
stone of desire, the turquoise of watchfulness. Such is
the " frat pin " of the Great Founder Who was nailed
to the wood of a tree.

But perhaps I am just a trifle confused? I thought I started to talk about " having closed the door " and here I am in the midst of a discussion on organizations and memberships and by-laws. But no. Just walk along with me, and do not attempt any by-paths. I only am trying to answer your questions before you ask them to save myself disjointed interruptions. This is quite boring to you, no doubt, for we all like the sound of our own voices, even though that sound may be an echo.

You are, of course, among those who are undergoing the process of initiation into the Alpha Omega society. You would not think for a minute of joining the other persons with their boisterous talk, uncouth manners, evil desires and actions, and their rather unpleasantly odoriferous perfume. Our whole life is the period of initiation into this congregation of the saints. Death is the crucial test, the final examination for admittance therein. Only by passing through the valley of the shadow of death shall we gain the glorious summit of the mountain of full-fledged membership. A concourse of this nature and size must have its means of communication if the members are to live in harmony and union. This communication among the blessed is prayer. Prayer is the language of eternity, the language of the saints.

If we aspire to share the life of the blessed hereafter, how can we hope to do so understandingly, if during our period of initiation, the hour appointed for this one special purpose, we fail to acquire at least a working knowledge of their language?

' But,' you object, ' if all this prayer business be necessary for the life to come, it is rather hard. It is a little too much to demand for salvation! ' No. What is absolutely essential for salvation is simply this: baptism, and at death the state of grace. ' Then why all this trouble about prayer and the proper disposition and mortification and everything else? ' Recall that a tree is known by its fruit, for " do men gather grapes of thorns, or figs of thistles " (Matt. vii, 16). And as the tree falls, so shall it lie. It shall fall only in the direction toward which it inclined from its youth. Prayer is the one means open to all mankind to obtain the graces necessary for salvation, that the tree of their life may fall in the right path, and may not be cast into the fire to be consumed.

Besides, when anyone prepares to embark for a distant land, curiosity at least compels him to take a look at a book containing the elemental knowledge of its tongue, if he knows nothing about it. Not that we should set ourselves to prayer out of curiosity. That would be very wrong, and God would punish the fault severely. But the point I wish to bring out is that a person likes to be familiar with the sound and meaning of at least a few words of the language he is going to hear for the next year or two or five. Then why not become acquainted with the language you are going to hear spoken for all eternity? Certainly it will be sufficient to be able to say ' Good morning ' — it will never be anything else; ' Yes, Father,' those that say *no* are in the other place; ' Thank You ' — eternity will be all too short in which to be properly grateful; and ' I love You,' for even in heaven love expresses itself, and this is the action we are going to perform forever: love continual, incessant, the perfection of prayer which, nevertheless, admits of degrees of intensity.

But yet this vocabulary is very limited, though it is sufficient for valid membership. Knowledge only of these ranks us within the category of the ignoramuses. And no one wants to be considered an ignoramus, even in heaven. To be sure, the Father dearly loves his 'ignoramus' son, but He can hardly be proud of him when He knows his knowledge is so very limited because the son himself wanted it thus, and actually refused the Father's offer to teach him. The Father offered to more than teach. He promised to do nine-tenths of the work. The one-tenth required of the son was to coöperate, to consent. He certainly must have been a slothful and ungrateful boy! Are you not that ungrateful son?

Indeed, you are not. Perhaps you may have been up to the present, but it will not be so any longer. Do not hang your head in shame. Look into the face of the Father, and, seeing what you see — love, infinite yearning love, cast yourself into His outstretched arms, and clinging to His neck, kiss Him in sorrow and purpose of amendment. He does not remember the past. He is the Eternal Now. Your desires which He views with delighted complacency please Him more than you think. In His sight — how different from that of men — the desire, if incapable of accomplishment, is as good as the act.

'My Father, for your wonderful mercy and goodness

to me, a miserable and ungrateful child, I thank You.
And Father, I love You. Really, I do. I mean it, Father.
To prove that I do, Father, please teach me to pray. To
pray as You want me to, not as I would like for myself, because I love You, my Father, my Own.'

Since you no longer question the necessity of closing
the door tightly, we may proceed with learning how this
is to be accomplished. Yet one other superlatively important idea I would like to emphasize before we continue. The idea is this: I am talking to *you*. *You* means
' yourself,' John Doe, Tom Jones, old or young, thin or
stout, anemic or robust, whether you sleep soundly at
night or suffer from insomnia, whether your nerves are
on edge or on a pair of rubber heels. *You* are the one in
mind, whether butcher or baker, rich man or poor man,
beggar-man or thief. The list excludes no one. But you
do not like being classified with a thief. Pardon me, but
do not become excited. Or insulted, either. We are all
thieves of a kind, as a matter of fact. Unless we are trying to keep *all* the commandments, that is, the *one* commandment, perfectly, and all the time, we are robbing
ourselves of the merit we might have gained, of the
proper development of our real life; we are stinting our
spiritual growth, and robbing God of the glory that is
His due, and our neighbor of good. He who dares to say
he fulfils the requirement may cast the first stone.

But yet, a thief has a soul that needs attention. He is
not entirely bad, for there is some good in every one.
Perhaps the good in him did not have an opportunity to
develop. Why not be generous and give it to him now?

If a man be almost submerged in quicksand, he needs a pull, a strong pull, and a coördinated pull to prevent his going under. Does it matter to him if he be saved by the roots of his hair? Even if he be only knee-deep, he requires a helping hand in order to extricate himself. Who of us has not been at least ankle-deep? And Somebody turned to the thief at His right and said to him, *because he showed the proper dispositions:* " This day thou shalt be with Me in Paradise " (Luke xxiii, 43), proving what He had so often taught: " I came not to call the just, but sinners " (Mark ii, 17).

Yes, I fear, we are all in the thieving business, but we do not like to admit it. The trouble is the truth hurts. Because the truth is squeezed, generally, within a non-adjustable boot of a brain many sizes too small. Then the shoe pinches and the truth hurts. If we, in the past, have not kept the *one* commandment perfectly, should we not realize that we have been stealing? I think so. Now that we are all on the same level, we can dispense with our pride, put it into our pocket, fasten the flap, and then leave it there until it evaporates. If we do this, we will have no further annoyance with the pest.

Again I seem to be wandering. Here I am talking about everything under the sun when I promised to show how to keep the door shut. But nevertheless, my child, although you may not have been conscious of it, we actually have been pushing that door of your will a little bit closer to the door-jamb by fumbling with the casement windows. You do not see how? You have been broadening your spiritual outlook by taking a bird's-eye view of your portion of this earth's sphere, and discovering to your discomfort that " you " does not stand out prominently in the foreground of the photograph as you secretly expected. In fact, you are only a tiny dot among a million other similar dots, and some of them are a trifle larger than yourself. Now we possess the grain of humility which like the mustard seed is going to blossom into a hardy tree with sturdy branches and dense foliage wherein the birds of the air can build their nests. Possessing this grain, we may proceed cautiously; without it, it were folly even to think of getting to work.

Once more I am going to repeat. If I wish to pray well, if I desire to keep that door of my will closed tightly, I must attend first to the windows of my senses to prevent the entrance of disturbing drafts. Which means that outside of the time actually set aside for prayer, I must try to keep myself disposed for prayer by resolutely doing what I know God wants me to do, because He desires it. I now realize the necessity of prayer: God wishes it always, and I must practise it continually if I am to arrive at the goal of my existence according to His designs. I further confess that I am not quite as important as I thought I was. 1 am only an ant, in truth. But an ant is also an incessant toiler, a prodigious laborer. This is unearthing the foundations of self-knowledge upon which we are to build.

The fastening of the windows to which I have made frequent reference is nothing else than the subduing of our animal nature, the conquest of a titanic giant, EGO, (myself). This extraction of self, the decayed tooth in a sound mouth, is very painful. You will need courage for the operation *because there is no painless method* which possibly can be used; at least, I never heard of any. It is an instance, too, where pulling is the only cure. There is no use in filling the cavity with astringent-soaked absorbent cotton. That may dull the hurt for a while, but the chugging thump-thumpety ache will soon make itself felt all the more intensely. No, that will not do. *It must come out.* That is the only safe and certain way of knowing that the exposed nerve of self-love, which is causing all the trouble, is *absolutely dead* because removed. If it must go, then, it must.

But who is to be the dentist? Ah, there is the hard part. You are the dentist yourself. But is there no help? Yes, there is a mirror, God, adjusted at exactly the proper angle, into which you must look while at the task, to be certain you are undertaking it in the orthodox — scientific — manner. God, too, will supply the surgical instruments and medicine — the light to see our defects, the helps of His sacraments and actual graces, the soothing novocaine of His love, poured in to quiet the pain in proportion as we correspond to His inspirations. Besides, His Hand will be gripping ours to guide the fingers in their duty, which duty is not as easy as you think, because this tooth does not come out with one pull. It is an affair that comes out piecemeal, in splinters. And the tooth is all out only when the roots have been extracted completely. Even then one has to probe around in the wound to discover any possible chips that may have lodged there and escaped notice. But once the tooth is out, oh, what relief! And when the wound is entirely healed, what peace and contentment!

But let us get to work. Here is the tooth, self, which has to be extracted. The large cavity is my pet sin or sins, the smaller ones my occasional faults and imperfections. The nerve, penetrating the roots, that gives life to the tooth, is self-love. It is the thing that makes me whimper, and perhaps storm and stamp, when someone says or does anything to violate the sacredness of this EGO (myself). What is it that leads me to do all this, to commit these sins and faults? If you think for a moment you will agree that transgression comes into the soul chiefly through the avenues of the senses. A glance, a taste, a touch, a word spoken, and the passions are aroused; but instead of keeping them down where they belong, and mastering them with a resolute will, we give in because our dignity has been offended, our self-respect has been wounded, *our pride has been hurt.* And we fall. Nothing hurts so much as wounded pride. But remember — humility is born of pride smashed to a pulp, and pride smashed so finely that when it is strained through the cheesecloth of hard knocks, no traces of any kind are left, not even a stain, but only the lingering fragrant odor of virtue. Prayer without humility is not real.

We all are interested in getting those windows, that insist just now on banging to and fro persistently, fastened tightly, are we not? Maybe at present they do not even bang — that is something — because they have been kept open so long in all kinds of weather that the hinges and hooks are rusted and refuse to work. We not only wish to close those windows of the interior chamber firmly, but we also want to do it in the most efficient manner possible. The cry of the age is efficiency. The cry of the Church, the voice of God, is at all times and in every age — efficiency, spiritual efficiency. The Efficient Cause of all efficiency is God. And prayer, since it seeks God and leads to Him, must be above everything else efficient. We want, then, to know the most efficient way of closing those windows of the senses and keeping them closed. I will tell you, but I do not promise that you are going naturally to rejoice in the knowledge. The most efficient way to close the windows of the senses — and do not forget, this is the *only* way of making certain that the door of the will is going to remain secure — is to humble them. What do I mean? To humble them means to mortify them, for the words here mean the same.

I told you that real prayer, sincere, earnest, determined, efficacious prayer is based on humility. We overcome the animal in us by humbling the senses, by killing the pride of the eyes, and of the ears, and of the touch, and of the tongue. Pride, as you know, is the root of all evil, the root of all sin. Just look over your own past, and analyze your sins to the last degree, and what is the result? Pride. You do not need a magnifying glass to see it, either. It makes itself manifest, provided you are willing to face it. Pride is another name for self-love, that quivering, quicksilver nerve we are trying to extract — to root out. By stamping out self, that is, pride, we by that very act advance in humility, and humility is the root of all virtue. And prayer is virtue. After all, prayer is the sincere, determined effort to attain to God, Virtue Itself, and if our prayer is of the right kind, made rightly, there must be visible necessarily in our conduct some degree of increase in virtue, however slight.

Here is an infallible test: if there be no advance in virtue, although we were to spend hours and hours in what we or others might consider the most exalted type of prayer, *that prayer is not of God*. So that in humbling, which means mortifying, the senses, we are really praying because we are advancing in virtue, and so rendering our soul more pleasing to God. This is the method of acquiring the *spirit* of prayer, the disposition of prayer to which I previously referred. By the mortification, the humiliation of the senses, we dispose ourselves during the entire day in a manner becoming a child of God who would commune, converse with Him, and, as it were, predispose Him, at the actual time of prayer, to shower on us the plenitude of His graces.

In addition to the mortification of the senses, there is another mortification that is most excellent and will most speedily, most efficiently bring us to God; a mortification that goes hand in hand with the humbling of the animal in us, although in itself it is superior to it. This is the mortification of the will, the finest kind of humiliation we can practise. If we add thereto the mortification of our legitimate desires, we have the quickest, the safest, the most certain, but the most painful road to God.

Here again I seem to be off on a tangent. I thought I told you that if we attended to the casement windows, the senses, we would thereby safeguard the secure fastening of the door of the will. So I did, and so it is. Every time the eye or the ear or the tongue says " I will " and your will says " You will not," you are strengthening and developing your highest faculty, and helping to get your spiritual breathing apparatus in order. It means that, repeating these efforts daily, persistently, you will have acquired such control over these avenues of distraction and dissipation that when you compose yourself for prayer you will be able to say to them, with the facility born of long practice, " You shall not disturb and distract me because I *will* otherwise."

So with comparative ease, you will cast out of your mind vain imaginings, and idle day-dreams, and useless thoughts. As a matter of fact, you will discover, if you are faithful in applying the remedy, that, closing the window of the eye to curious and unnecessary gazing and reading, and the window of the ear to useless and frivolous conversation and gossip, there will be less and less to distract the imagination and memory and understanding when you come to prayer, because you refuse to introduce these gnats into your mind outside the time of prayer. Not that distractions are going to cease the minute you begin the practice of mortification, or even when you have acquired great self-control and have advanced in prayer. No. You will have to fight as long as you live, but you *can* master these nuisances and that is what you are aiming to do. If you are persevering, they will in time prove no more annoying than the mosquito that settled on your head when you were occupied with the paper and radio, and which did not divert your attention from your amusements but was banished with practically unconscious effort. So by locking the windows of the interior chamber you will secure also the door, because you will have the spirit of prayer continually; and being properly disposed, a single act of the will should ordinarily keep the door locked.

Why, then, must the will be mortified? The reason is not far to seek. Have you ever seen a locked door that would not stay locked? There was something the matter, perhaps, with the lock. Now it is very possible for a person to mortify the sensual appetites and gain a fairly commendable control over them, and in the doing proportionately achieve an excessive complacency in the performance, and an exaggerated opinion of oneself. It simply means that in subduing the pride of the flesh we have fed the pride of the will, forgetting in our poor foolish human fashion — man is so inconsistent — that man waters, but only " God gave the increase " (I Cor. iii, 6). A proud will, a will that is spiritually proud, is a secret worm that eats away the very core of the apple of spiritual progress. It is doubly dangerous because it is generally unperceived by the one so afflicted, and leads to self-deception, and illusion, and unconscious deceit.

So it is that the very finest mortification is the mortification of the will, the submitting of our freedom of action, in so far as it is compatible with the duties of our state, to the liberty of another in even indifferent matters. This does not mean that I am not permitted to have an opinion nor to make use of the common sense and good judgment that God has given me. It does mean that in an instance where there is no question of obligation to perform the will of another, I freely do his will instead of my own, granted that the ordinary result of either action would be of equal importance, and that others dependent on my time or convenience would not suffer thereby. In other words, all the consequences of the surrendering of my will affects me alone and no one else. Such a mortification is all the more advantageous in that it can never be carried to excess, nor is there any suspicion of spiritual pride aroused. On the contrary, this strikes at the very root of all trouble — the will.

It is a point to be remembered in passing that the end of mortifying the animal man is *not* literally to kill the body — that would be sinful — but to subdue it, that is, to kill it figuratively. The warning is needful because an excess of any kind, a tending to any extreme, is dangerous and incompatible with sound judgment.

It was remarked that if we added to the mortification of the will the mortification or humiliation of our legitimate desires, we would have found the quickest, the safest, the most certain, but the most painful way to God. Our will is the very soul of our being and dearer to us than life itself. Our will feeds on desire; we reach out, strive to gain that which we want. If I permit my desires to rest in perishable things, my will is going to acquire perishable things and rest in them also. If I will to attain to God through prayer, I must be particularly careful to curb the natural inclinations of the heart and direct them to God. I am not speaking now only of inordinate affection for creatures, using " creatures " in the limited sense of human beings. I mean even the ordinate, the perfectly lawful affection or inclination which we may have for our own ease and comfort; for appreciation, esteem, the honor of our good name, the companionship of friends, of books, and pleasure of legitimate amusements, the quest for knowledge — in brief, all creatures — using the term in its widest extension or meaning. All creatures must be made use of only in the manner God intended they should be employed by man — to help him to attain his last end, his Creator. Everything in my life must be made subservient to the will of the Creator; and no object either material or intellectual, should it be either consciously or unconsciously sought after, must be permitted to become the goal of my existence. The greater, the more intense the purity of the love wherewith we seek God, the more quickly shall we find Him. And purity of love means integrity of will. It is the will that ultimately shall be united with God.

That the acts of that will may be swift, certain, devoid of self-interest and conformable to the Divine Will, it is essential, for the sure attainment of this end, to detach the heart from all created things, for desires of any kind are a magnet that draws the will in their wake. If we wish our will to attain to God, we first must desire this end, sincerely and earnestly; we must beseech God for it, certainly, but at the same time, we must do all in our power, persistently and patiently, to subject our will and wishes to His, which implies the killing of self, the extracting of the decayed tooth, the closing of the windows, and the fastening of the door.

v. *The "Word made flesh" for our sanctification*

20. ON THE MYSTERY OF THE INCARNATION

" And the Word was made flesh and dwelt among us " (John i, 14)

A CHILD is born to us, and a son is given to us "
(Isaias ix, 6); let us rejoice. " Sing ye to the Lord a new
canticle, because He hath done wonderful things " (Ps.
97, 1). " A sanctified day hath shone upon us: come
(let us) adore the Lord: for this day a great light hath descended upon the earth." (Gradual, Third Mass of Nativity of Our Lord). And what is this light? The brightness of Divinity veiled with the garment of humanity,
for the Lord " hath sent redemption to His people " (Ps.
110, 9). But to what purpose? " To the righteous a light
has risen up in darkness " (Ps. 111, 4), so that " all the
ends of the earth have seen the salvation of our God "
(Ps. 97, 3). And what is this light? What is this salvation? This light is life, the only true life of the soul,
Christ Jesus, the glory of the Father in the person of the
Incarnate Word, for such is the sublime utterance of St.
John in the wonderful opening passages of the Gospel:
" In Him was life, and the life was the light of men "
(John i, 4). Our holy mother, the Church, tells us in the
power of her authority that this Life and Light is " true
God of true God; begotten not made; consubstantial
with the Father; by Whom all things are made. Who for

[221]

us men and for our salvation came down from heaven and was incarnate by the Holy Ghost, of the Virgin Mary, and was made man " (Nicene Creed).

" And was made man." What words more moving, more divine, more joyful than these? God became man. " He Who is Life, our Life, has come down amongst us," says St. Augustine. And why? " That we might become God " (St. Augustine). This is the mystery of the Incarnation.

Let us look into this stupendous mystery with the eye of faith, that we may be " bathed in the new light of the Word, made flesh," and thus, our understanding illuminated, " show forth in our actions that which by faith shineth in our minds " (Oration, Second Mass of the Nativity).

" And the Word was made flesh " (John i, 4). These are the simple words in which St. John records the giving by God to man of the most marvelous gift He could possibly bestow — the Word. Who is this Word? Recall from the conference on Baptism what was then said concerning the work, the activity of God. God from all eternity has been occupied with Himself — only God is capable of understanding God. Only He can fathom His perfections perfectly. And God, remember, is Infinite Intelligence and Infinite Will. God comprehends His Being, the Substance of His nature, to the limit of His power of understanding, which is without limit. This perfect comprehension of Himself, this limitless understanding, is an Infinite Idea, an Infinite Thought. This Infinite Idea, this Infinite Understanding, is the divine

utterance, the Word. With us a word is an utterance, the
expression of an idea. With God, the Infinite comprehension *is* the Word. For we must not imagine that God
communicates Himself, or, in other words, makes Himself known to Himself, through the power of speech.
God is a pure Spirit. On us, who are intelligent animals,
He has bestowed the gift of speech for the purpose of
communication with our fellow-men. That is, we make
ourselves, which means our thoughts, or ideas, known to
others through the expression of certain sounds, which
constitute words and stand for an idea. With God, Who
is a pure Spirit, the perfect comprehension is the infinite
communication; and the communication is the understanding.

This perfect communication, this infinite understanding, is the expression of God — the Word, Who is also
called the Son, and the Second Person of the Blessed
Trinity, of Whom the Lord hath said: " Thou art My
Son, this day (the span of eternity) have I begotten
Thee " (Ps. 2, 7). To beget means to engender, to bring
forth, to produce fruit. This productivity, this action on
the part of God, has been going on from all eternity, for
this infinite comprehension of Himself, from which flows
an ineffable love for Himself — the Holy Ghost, the Life-
giving Spirit, and the Third Person of the Blessed Trinity — is eternal Life, eternal Activity, God. With God,
remember, this ineffable love, the Sanctifying Spirit, is
the embrace of the Infinite Will with that Infinite Good,
Himself, which His Infinite Understanding reveals as
alone worthy of Himself. But the understanding and

[223]

embrace are simultaneous actions, or operations — one. So that in all truth, the Son proceeds from the Father and is co-eternal with Him, " The brightness of His glory and the figure of His substance " (Hebrews i, 3); the Holy Ghost, from the Father and the Son, and is co-equal and co-eternal with them, the ineffable communication of the unifying spirit of love. And yet the nature and the substance of the three, as we have seen, are one. Wonderful God — one in His divinity; threefold in His activity. And this unfathomable Being " was made flesh " (John i, 14), became Man, not from all eternity, but in time.

Our mother, the Church, teaches us that it is the Second Person of the Blessed Trinity Who became man. It was the Word, the Wisdom of the Father, Who, in comprehending God, Himself, comprehends perfectly all things that are or that might be; and Who saw with infinite understanding the absolute necessity of descending upon earth to expiate with infinite atonement, which God alone could do, the horrible outrage which man had committed against His Majesty and Power, and for which His Justice demanded reparation; and thereby to restore man to his original inheritance — participation in the very life of the Godhead. For " God became man that man might become God " (St. Augustine).

But how was this clothing of the Deity with the clay of humanity, this descent of God upon earth, accomplished? In the first place, before we try to understand how this union between the divine and human natures was effected, we must try to realize what this union, this descent of the Godhead upon earth, implies. When we say that God descended upon earth, we mean simply this: The Eternal Wisdom, the Son of God, realized with divine clearness of understanding the need of God's revealing Himself to man under a form which man could comprehend most readily — his own human nature; not only that the Word might by this action render eternal satisfaction to His Father's justice, but especially that He might, as it were, render Himself more accessible to man, in order to win him back to Himself; to bridge over the chasm which sin had made between the Creator and creature — between the Father and His beloved child. It was the Word, then, Who descended upon earth, " Who gave Himself for us, that He might redeem us from all iniquity, and might cleanse to Himself a people acceptable, a pursuer of good works " (Titus, ii, 14).

But in what did this descent consist? Does not God fill all space by His immensity, and sustain all creation by His power, and govern all the earth by His providence?

He does. But He Who is " called Wonderful, Counsellor, God the Mighty, the Father of the world to come, the Prince of Peace " (Isaias ix, 6), Whom the heavens cannot contain, lowered Himself, out of exquisite love for man, unto the very dust of the earth; emptied Himself, so to speak, of His grandeur, His glory, His greatness. He Who is Everything abased Himself unto nothingness. This was the price of the revelation of God's love for man. But God is humility; and this unheard-of humiliation alone could effectively batter down man's inordinate pride, which is the cause of all revolt. Who, dimly realizing the humility of God, can suffer himself to remain proud?

The Incarnation, then, is the Eternal Wisdom submitting to the decree of divine authority, which is the judgment of God the Father; submitting, moreover, through the quickening power of love, which is the Holy Spirit. This submission is at once the visible expression of the Divinity in time, the Word made flesh, for with God to will is also at the same time to accomplish.

Yet this revelation of God to man, this visible appearance of the Uncreated Spirit as true man is supernaturally natural.

The God-Man did not manifest Himself on earth as a mature human being, although He could have done so. This would have been, in a sense, too startling. Man might possibly have cause to question the reality of that human nature for which there could be no natural explanation. Besides, God is humility, and there is an abasement greater even than this. The Eternal Wisdom, because He is the Eternal Wisdom, saw fit to be born of a human mother, according to the decrees established by Himself for the propagation of the human family, of which He was to be born the Elder Brother. By appearing upon earth as a little babe, He would preclude any doubt man might bring up as to the reality of His humanity: to deny here is to doubt the evidence of the senses; and the subsequent activity of the Godhead, while inhabiting that body, would certainly dispel the fears of any thinking man as to the veracity of the divinity.

In the natural order of things, a child is the fruit of

the union of two loves. What brought the Eternal Word into the world in time? Love. God created for Himself a virginal heart free from all stain, wherein He might dwell for the few months before His birth — and that heart was Mary. Mary loved God with the most perfect love a creature can render Him. Mary loved God purely for His sake alone. There was nothing of self in her love — it was absolutely disinterested. Mary yearned with ardent yearning for the coming of the promised Messiah, the revelation of God. And God rested in Mary as in a garden of delights. She was absolutely His own. There was nothing in her to hinder the operations of the Holy Spirit. From the first instant of her Immaculate Conception she had been unreservedly His.

God wills to become man. God wills to become man in a natural way — to be born of a human mother. God inclines toward Mary with infinite love, for He beholds in her a reflection of His splendor, as perfect as it is possible for a creature to achieve. Her body is pure-spiritualized. God sends His messenger to Mary to announce to her that she is to be the mother of the Word. " How shall this be done," she questions, " because I know not man? " (Luke i, 34). The angel reassures her: " The Holy Ghost shall come upon thee, and the power of the Most High shall overshadow thee. And therefore also the Holy which shall be born of thee shall be called the Son of God " (Luke i, 35). God, in the person of His messenger, waits for Mary's reply.

God, Who is Sanctity, in willing to reveal Himself to man as the Incarnate Word, must needs will to appear clothed in the holiest material substance He has ever created. And that substance is Mary's body. Therefore He asks her consent to its use. What humility! But all humility is represented in Mary. God is really begging for admittance into the family of man. God in creating man, took a handful of clay and breathed into it an immortal spirit. Now God, the Uncreated Spirit, is asking man, in the person of Mary, for a handful of clay wherewith to make Himself visibly known. What a beggar! God cannot become man unless man consents to acknowledge the kinship. God wants man, but does man want God?

Mary, who is the concentration of all the good in all mankind, without the evil; who is the accumulated love of all the loves that ever did inflame or might inflame the hearts of men for God; Mary who is more truly the purified essence of these loves, in breathing forth her FIAT, consented for all humanity — anticipated your consent, and mine — to the lawful and rightful place the Son of God made Man should hold as the new and redeeming Head of the human family. It was love divine that impelled the Word to manifest Himself among the nations; it was divine love on the part of man, in the form of Mary, that provided Him with the garment of flesh wherewith He could make the manifestation possible.

" The Holy Ghost shall come upon thee and the power of the Most High shall overshadow thee " (Luke i, 35). Mankind in Mary has willed to claim the Word as the Elder Brother. God cannot save man and thereby raise him to a participation of the very life of God, unless man so desires, since man had deliberately rejected the gift, which is life, which is God. But Mary in our name said: " Be it done " (Luke i, 38). " And the Word was made flesh " (John i, 14). The Incarnate Word is the union of the divine nature and the human nature in the person of Jesus Christ. Mary, at the moment of her consent, was engulfed in God. She who is full of grace was filled with the Holy Spirit of God, the Spirit of Infinite Love, Who miraculously engendered in her the Incarnate Word by the power of the Most High. It was Mary, then, who really consented for the Word, the Divine Utterance of the Father spoken from all eternity. Such is the abasement, the humility of God.

After she had relinquished her right over the material substance of her body, God, Who filled her being to overflowing, was free to use that holiest of substances as He chose and desired. And He chose, because He desired to inhabit that substance which He Himself had made — to enter into it, the garment of the flesh; to limit, if I dare say it, His Immensity, within the compass of a few grains of sand of that earth which He Himself had founded in the beginning. Thus was the Word made flesh.

But the consideration of His dwelling among us we shall leave for the next conference.

21. THE REASON FOR THE INCARNATION

"And the Word was made flesh and dwelt among us" (JOHN i. 14)

IN OUR last conference we penetrated a little into the meaning of the mystery of Christmas, when the " Word was made flesh " (John i, 14). We viewed the generation of the Son of God from all eternity in the bosom of the Father, and saw how unfathomably reasonable it was that the Eternal Wisdom should manifest Himself upon earth. We understood in what a supernaturally natural manner the Word was conceived in time. That Infinite Love with which the Father and the Son communicate themselves each in each other, from eternity to eternity, and which is the Holy Spirit, produced fruit in time also, for Love is infinite activity, life. The love of the human race for God, which was in Mary's heart, attracted to itself with magnetic attraction that Infinite Love which exists between the Father and the Son — the Eternal Spirit. I say " magnetic " because the love that filled Mary's heart was born of God, was implanted there by that same Eternal Spirit; and it was God in Mary that attracted God. It was the Omnipotent Creator Who saw Himself reflected in Mary's soul with that total degree of perfection which a creature could possibly render.

It was this Godlike purity of soul that made Mary's body unspeakably holy; which caused that which was

of the earth, earthy, to become exquisitely refined, purified, exalted, until matter was something almost immaterial. It was with the holiest of substances, then, that
God chose to vest Himself, for He had created it with
this end in view. And the Holy Ghost, the Eternal Love
of the Father for the Son, and the Son for the Father, in
His overshadowing of Mary, immersed her in that ocean
of Infinite Charity, which is Himself, until she was completely lost in the Divinity. In that exaltation of spirit,
when God poured Himself out on Mary, Mary was permeated with the power of the Godhead. At that moment,
the Eternal God inhabiting Mary, willed to create. And
the will was the Word Incarnate. The Eternal Spirit,
by the power of the Father, His own power, formed for
the Eternal Wisdom a body from Mary's substance.
" And the Word dwelt among us " (John i, 14).

The Eternal Wisdom of the Father, spoken in a manner man can hear and understand, is the Person of the
Word, Jesus Christ, the Infinite Utterance. " In the beginning was the Word, and the Word was with God, and
the Word was God " (John i, 1). The revelation of
God to God, of God Himself and in Himself, is He Who
is born of the Father before all ages. The revelation of
God to man is the selfsame Word, but in human form —
the Man-God, Christ Jesus. With us a word is the revelation of an idea. The Word uttered by God to reveal, to
make known to man an Infinite Idea, and Infinite Understanding, Himself, is the First-born of Mary, the Babe of
Bethlehem, Who now dwells among us.

Behold Him lying on the straw — fragrant, dimpled,

wonder-eyed, smiling. Fragile as a rose-petal, beautiful as an opening bud, almighty with the omnipotence of God. " A child is born to us, and a son is given to us " (Isaias ix, 6), let us rejoice. " Sing ye to the Lord a new canticle, because He hath done wonderful things " (Ps. 97, 1). " Glory to God in the highest, and on earth peace to men of good will " (Luke ii, 14). " The root of Jesse hath budded forth: the star is risen out of Jacob: a Virgin hath brought forth the Saviour " (4 Antiphon II Vespers of Feast of Circumcision). " We praise Thee, we bless Thee, we adore Thee, we glorify Thee. We give Thee thanks for Thy great glory. O Lord God, heavenly King, God the Father Almighty. O Lord Jesus Christ, the Only-begotten Son — For Thou only art holy, Thou only art Lord. Thou only, O Jesus Christ, art most high, together with the Holy Ghost in the glory of God the Father " (Gloria of the Mass).

But where is this glory of which the Church exults in her adoration of the Trinity? Nowhere is it manifest. Not in the cave — dark, damp, cold, ill-smelling. Not in the sleepy-faced oxen, nor in the braying ass. Not in the poor, tumble-down manger, nor in the coarse, sharp straw. Not even in the lovely girl who kneels, unmindful of the damp and cold, in ecstatic motherhood, at the head of the crib, her mantle wrapped around her Treasure, now pillowed in her arms. Not even in her Treasure itself — a chubby delectable Infant, a baby boy. Ah, but " His name was called Jesus, which was called by the angel, before He was conceived in the womb " (Luke ii, 21). " For His exceeding charity wherewith He loved

us " (Eph. ii, 4) God sent " His own Son, in the likeness
of sinful flesh " (Rom. viii, 3). This is He Who came
" down like rain upon the fleece " (Ps. 71, 6) to save the
human race. Now has " the grace of God our Saviour
appeared to all men " (Titus ii, 11) in a wondrous fellowship. The Creator of the human race, taking unto Himself a living body, deigns to be born of a virgin; and
becoming man from no human generation, hath bestowed upon us His divinity.

Here again, in her hymns of rejoicing, the Church
keeps ever before us the one amazing thought: " God
became man that man might become God " (St. Augustine). This was the only reason why " the Word was
made flesh and dwelt among us " (John i, 14). This is
the only reason why the Word Whom we behold in the
helplessness of infancy at Bethlehem continues still to
dwell among us in the even greater helplessness of the
Eucharistic Crib.

The Nativity! Kneeling before the manger, which the
Church, the wisest of mothers, re-creates for us each
year, how have we not been softened and ennobled and
inflamed. Who could feel otherwise in the presence of a
baby just born, a wonder ever old and yet new, a fresh
revelation of the mystery of life. God is very near —
both at birth and at death, for death, after all, is but the
entrance into life. We do not need to be told — we
realize His presence. But when the babe is the God-Man?
When we can see and touch and handle and embrace the
divinity? What wonder that those delicate, curling fingers have an eternal hold on the heart of the world; that

the spirit which He came to reveal, and revealing to instil in the souls of men, the Spirit of God's ineffable Love, the Holy Spirit, moves mankind with a purifying force that will not cease until the Christ-Child finds a crib in every human heart.

What wonder that the unction of this sanctifying grace, especially at the season when the greatest of birthdays is being kept, should manifest itself in heartfelt expressions of " peace on earth to men of good will " (Luke ii, 14). For such is the mystery and miracle of Christmas; of Christ-Mass, when joy was born into the world — eternal joy, the glory of the Father poured out on sinful man in the Person of the Word made flesh.

But is the love of man for God, and of brother for brother, to cease with the dying echoes of the angels' GLORIA? Is Christ to be born for one generation only? Is the story of Bethlehem to be recounted always in the past tense? Is there to be only one day of the unifying bond of universal good-fellowship which inclines men to men, as brothers of Christ, and through Christ? Is the Babe to be laid there in the manger once and forever?

No, indeed. Every day is Christmas day, but we do not seem to remember. Every day is Christmas day — not symbolically, but really and truly. Christmas! The very word tells all: Christmas, the *Christ-Mass*. Every day the Church is another Bethlehem, the altar another manger, on which is laid the new-born King, the Eternal Son of the Eternal Father; not in the dazzling radiance of the divinity; not even in the dignified beauty of His sacred humanity; but in the lowly, unspeakably lowly, appearance of common food. Yet this bread is no ordinary bread — it is the Bread of Angels; the Bread that is at once our Oblation and our Repast. We know the Holy Sacrifice is our greatest means of sanctification; and Holy Communion, a powerful second. 'For this am I come into the world,' says the Divine Child, " that they (you and I) may have life, and may have it more abundantly " (John x, 10). The abundance of this promised and proffered life is contained in the Mass, the second Bethlehem, as well as the second Calvary, and in the sacraments. Thus did the Father will that man should become God, partake of the very life of the Creator, after God had become man.

In the divine plan of redemption, Bethlehem was a means to an end. And that end was Calvary. But it also was the tabernacle and the " Ecce Agnus Dei " " Behold the Lamb of God " of the prayer before Communion. The annihilation of the Divinity under the veil of the flesh was the necessary prelude to the annihilation of both divinty and humanity under the veil of bread. It needed the God-Man to prepare men's minds for the stupendous miracle. " Amen, amen, I say unto you, except you eat the flesh of the Son of Man, and drink His blood, you shall not have life in you " (John vi, 54). Is this, then, the nature of the life — that abundant life He came on earth to bestow? It is. Yet there are hearts incredulous even to truth uttered by Infinite Truth; incredulous because they are enmeshed in the snares of the world, the flesh, and the devil. To such as these the *Sursum Corda* — *the lift up your hearts* — of the Redeemer was rank nonsense, was ridiculous. " The saying is hard and who can hear it " (John vi, 61). And they " walked no more with Him " (John vi, 67). But we, with the believing disciples, kneel at the foot of the crib, at the foot of the altar, and in response to His plaintive appeal, with hearts full of faith, and love, say loyally to atone for the neglect of obdurate wills: " Lord, to whom shall we go? Thou hast the words of eternal life " (John vi, 69).

What is eternal life? Again the Christ-Child answers: " Now this is eternal life; that they may know Thee, the only true God, and Jesus Christ, Whom Thou hast sent " (John xvii, 3). It is through Jesus Christ alone that we know the Father. " No man cometh to the Father, but by me. If you had known me, you would without doubt have known my Father also " (John xiv, 6–7). " The words that I speak to you, I speak not of myself. But the Father who abideth in me, He doth the works " (John xiv, 10).

True. It is the Father Who " doth the works," the Father Who is the power and creative force of the unfathomable Trinity. By His might are all things accomplished, for, says the God-Man: " The Father is greater than I " (John xiv, 28). It is through the merits of Jesus Christ, by the power of the Father, that Divine Love, the Eternal Spirit, effects these " works," our sanctification. In the Mass and in the sacraments, which are the source and fountain-head of grace, the infinite merits of the Redeemer are applied to our souls to sanctify them. Only God could give us a sacrifice of infinite value; only God could impart to an outward sign a secret divine power and unction. And Jesus Christ has done this by His own power and in His own right, for " I," He says, " and the Father are one " (John x, 30). Such is the manner in which the Word still dwells among us in the Mass, the drama of His life from Bethlehem to Calvary; in the Blessed Eucharist, possible only because of the Mass, wherein we have always " the Child (who) is born to us and the son (who) is given us " (Isaias ix, 6); in the other sacraments also, through which He imparts Himself according to the measure of the good dispositions He finds in the souls He has created. Since, " from the rising of the sun even to the going down, my name is great among the Gentiles, and in every place there is sacrifice, and there is offered to my name a clean oblation " (Mal. i, 11), cannot the Church in very truth make her own the cry of the Psalmist, " All the ends of the earth have seen the salvation of our God; sing joyfully to God, all the earth; the Lord hath made known his salvation; he hath revealed his justice in the sight of the Gentiles " (Ps. 97, 3–4–2), whereby the mystery of the Word made flesh, the light of His Glory, hath shone anew upon the eyes of our mind. Then, " sing ye to the Lord a new canticle, because He hath done wonderful things " (Ps. 97, 1). *Venite adoremus.* Come, let us adore.

22. THE MANIFESTATION OF THE INCARNATE WORD

"This is the sign of the great King"
(ANTIPHON AT MAGNIFICAT OF I VESPERS OF EPIPHANY)

THE considerations on the mystery of the Nativity brought home to us a little more clearly the manner and meaning of the revelation of God to man in the person of the Word made flesh. The feast of the Epiphany marks the manifestation of the Saviour to the Gentiles, that is, to the souls of all mankind. The four corners of the earth are gathered together in the figures of the three kings who kneel in humble, loving submission at the feet of a tiny Babe, Whom by faith they recognize as " the Lord, the Ruler (Who) is come "; nevertheless, " the kingdom is in His hand, and power, and domin- ion " (Introit of Epiphany). These forms, prostrate be- fore the manger, prove conclusively that this Child is no ordinary baby, but a mighty Sovereign, Who clearly has come into His dominion, the kingdom of the hearts of men. For the Magi represent humanity — in the past, and now, and in the ages to come — who gladly and freely accept Him as their liege-lord. This is so because " He came unto His own," His chosen people, " and His own received Him not " (John i, 11). " But as many as received Him," — and St. John says this of us,

— " He gave them power to be made the sons of God; to them that believe in His name; who are born, not of blood, nor of the will of the flesh, nor of the will of man, but of God " (John i, 12–13).

Therefore the Epiphany, being the revelation of Christ to the Gentiles and their acceptance of His royalty, is the symbol of the manifestation of the Incarnate Word to the souls He came to save — to your soul and to mine. Therefore, the Church sings: " Begotten before the day star and before the ages (in the bosom of the Father) the Lord our Saviour was this day made manifest to the world " (1 Antiphon at II Vespers of Epiphany). Let us see how this manifestation was accomplished, and seeing, learn what it implies.

" When the Wise Men saw the star they said one to another: This is the sign of the great King. Let us go and search for Him, and offer Him gifts, gold, frankincense, and myrrh " (Antiphon at Magnificat of 1 Vespers of Epiphany).

Notice, first, that these wanderers are called " Wise Men." Why are they so called? And in what does their wisdom consist?

Holy Scripture designates them " the Wise Men " simply because they are learned in the ways of God — which is true wisdom. All else is folly. They were thinking men, and they rose above the fallacies of their fellow-creatures in so far as they set to work with determination to discover the answer to that question which every reasoning being faces some time or other during his life; that question which Pilate proposed to the divine Pris-

oner standing, in silence for the most part, before him:
" What is truth? " (John xviii, 38). Pilate immediately
turned away from the True Light which would have
enlightened him had he but waited for a reply. The
Magi acted otherwise. They were not curious; they were
in earnest. In other words, they were well disposed to
receive that which they sought, namely, knowledge of
the truth. God is the one only real Truth. The Magi,
unlike Pilate, *turned toward Him,* " the true light which
enlighteneth every man that cometh into this world "
(John i, 9). Since they willed to face the light squarely,
they were illuminated to their utmost capacity, and received the penetration of faith, the strength of courage,
the longing of desire, and the vehemence of love.

We, too, if we willed to face the Truth squarely,
would see with intensity of vision, and be satisfied to the
fulness of our measure.

Each of the Wise Men, then, faithful to the graces
vouchsafed him, faithful to the purifying movements
of the Holy Spirit, to Whom he submitted with total
submission of freedom, was privileged to see the star.

What is this star?

What is this — this sign of the great King?

Is it a real star? So it would seem, for it was a light
seen by each of them severally, and, as history relates,
by the ancients of lands other than their own. It was the
testimony of the empyrean heavens to the light that is
come upon the earth. The courts of the Father were
emptied that night when Wisdom Eternal was veiled
here below; choir upon choir of angels and archangels,

of thrones and dominations, of powers and principalities, of virtues, of cherubim and seraphim chorused and re-chorused their celestial hymn of welcome to witness His verity: " *Gloria in excelsis Deo, et in terra pax hominibus bonae voluntatis.*" " *Glory to God in the highest; and on earth peace to men of good will* " (Luke ii, 14). That was the invisible rendering itself visible; the inaudible, audible. And the star shone on in the midnight stretch of sky. That was the created, admitting the power of the Uncreated, the symbol of the light that is risen up in darkness. Only the earth was silent, steeped in utter oblivion. One baby more or less — what did it matter?

But the earth was silent, because it was tumultuous, and in oblivion, because in remembrance. Ribaldry, wine, song, and caricatures of dance; gluttonous feasting, unseemly jests, blasphemies, curses, murderous threats, suicides, fratricides! So the silence of finer emotions in the fury of unleashed passions! As for any regard to the soul — the world has no soul. By that I mean, such is the hypothesis on which it then acted and now still continues to act. It is as material as the matter of which it is composed. Thus now, and thus when Christ came into the world. That was the material which greeted the advent of the Immaterial by ignoring His existence. The eyes of the world were turned toward the star, the symbol of Life, but the eyes were vacant pools that reflected nothing, for the principle of vision was not in them.

We, too, shall see the star in the brightness of its glory, but only after tearing off, unflinchingly, the darkening

[241]

filament which obscures the perfect operation of our principle of spiritual vision.

" When the Wise Men saw the star they said one to another: This is the sign of the great King " (Antiphon at Magnificat of 1 Vespers of Epiphany).

How does it happen that they knew the star immediately? How do they all, and each for himself, know at once that this is not an ordinary star, but " the sign of the great King? "

Only because in itself the star was in the nature of a sacramental — it brought grace to those who beheld it, not with curious, but with believing hearts. Perhaps, though, the figure is a bit mixed? Do men view a star *with their hearts?* Ordinary stars, no; but this is no ordinary star. The brilliant, scintillating substance that radiated in the blackness of sky was seen with the eyes of the body, yes; but its symbolism, the truth which it proclaimed, its mystic meaning, was revealed only to the clean, the pure of heart, for these only shall see God. So the Magi saw, and understood the symbolism of the star. The light of grace made it clear to their intellects, and moved their wills to embrace the proposed good.

And what was the proposed good? What did the star mean for them? It meant the cross. They were the very first to leave all and follow Jesus, Whom they knew, in the security of faith, only by the inspiration of the Holy Spirit. This faith was the reward of their search after truth. Their fidelity to the promptings of conscience is vouched for by Divine Truth Himself, their infallible Master, in the oneness of their enlightenment and the unity of their journeys and meeting. Meeting one another and recognizing anew the power and wisdom and goodness of God, in the unfathomable workings of Divine Providence, what did they do? " Let us go and search for Him " they said, " and offer Him gifts, gold, frankincense, and myrrh " (Antiphon at Magnificat, 1 Vespers of Epiphany).

We, too, in all our meetings, no matter where, or with whom, or at what time, if we would glorify Him as it is our business to do, must always, in all things, in every place, " go and search for Him."

But what aided the Wise Men in their search? Holy Scripture tells us: " And behold the star which they had seen in the East went before them until it came and stood over where the Child was " (Matt. ii, 9). The star was for the Magi the physical symbol of the presence and guidance of God. These Gentiles, the chosen people of the New Law, were directed over the desert wastes to the Promised Land by the star, their pillar of cloud by day and by night of fire. They followed unswervingly, and without mishap they found the Child, the Uncreated Truth, Incarnate in the person of the Word.

We have the brilliant star of grace, and star after star of grace upon grace. Have we also found the Child; have we really *found* Him?

Why, after all, did the Wise Men go and search for Him? Was it to satisfy a natural longing to look upon the face of the promised Messiah, the Redeemer Who was to come? Was it to satiate the craving of their souls for the consolations of His nearness, the unspeakable pleasures of His divinity? Ah, no. Both motives would have been imperfect, and the first more naturally so than the second. Both would have been selfish, and the Wise Men, because they were in very truth wise, did not seek self. The Wise Men, because they were in very truth wise, sought God, and God alone. They themselves tell us why they went to search for Him: " Let us go — that we may offer Him gifts, gold, frankincense, and myrrh " (Antiphon at Magnificat 1 Vespers of Epiphany).

The intention of the Wise Men was pure — the true essence of generosity.

And we? Why do we seek God? Can we readily and sincerely say with these enlightened Gentiles: " We have seen His star (the light of grace) in the East, and are come (with gifts) to adore Him "? (Matt. ii, 2).

They came with gifts *to adore*. That is the annihilation of worship, the humility of love. Nothing for self; all for the beloved. Nothing through self; all through the beloved. Nothing in self; all in the beloved.

Having seen the star which " went before them until it came and stood over where the Child was," the Magi " rejoiced with exceeding great joy. And entering into the house, they found the Child with Mary His Mother, and falling down they adored Him; and opening their treasures, they offered Him gifts; gold, frankincense, and myrrh " (Matt. ii, 9–11).

They offered Him gold.

What is gold? Gold is one of the most precious of minerals, the dearest treasure after which man yearns, the wealth he desires to possess in complete abundance.

Gold — the peak of material happiness! Is that all they had to offer the Child? He was poor, yes, — the stable told everything — but He had no need of such a gift. He had created all the wealth that was being extended; it was already His by right of absolute ownership. Neither did it involve any sacrifice on the part of the givers, for they had a superabundance. And the gift, you know, without the giver is bare — a mockery of a sacred relationship. Then the gold must have been a symbol of something, must it not, even as had been the star? But of what was it the symbol? Of man's dearest treasure, of that wealth he desires to possess in complete abundance — without ever becoming satiated — his will.

Gold is of pure value when it is pure and refined. What is the carat-value of our gold — our will?

They offered Him frankincense.

What is frankincense? It is an aromatic gum that gives forth in the process of combustion a sweet-smelling perfume. But what could have been the purpose of such an offering? Was it simply to render the stable agreeable? The place was foul-smelling, yes. But He could have been born in a palace permeated with all the scents of Araby, only He did not so will. Who gives a person a gift which he knows has been deliberately and designedly rejected beforehand? No, that was not the reason. Since the frankincense serves that one only end, it too must have symbolized something. What is there in man that gives forth a sweet-smelling perfume while undergoing the process of combustion? It is one thing only — the intellect. But how is this? The sweet-smelling perfume is the beautiful thought that is engendered in the fire of an intensely-directed and inflamed will. All beauty is of God, the Eternal and Infinite Beauty. This intellect of mine, according as I choose, which means according as I *will*, can become a garden of delights or a pool of fetid water. The frankincense, that is, the intellect, is made by God and offered to Him by His creature on whom it has been freely bestowed. But the object of that intelligence is God Himself for Whom it was created, and it is the will, the principle of the natural life or power or heat of the soul, which guides that intelligence to its ultimate end, by directing its operations toward its Creator, so that by the fire of an ardent will the aromatic gum of the mind undergoes combustion, namely, right thinking, and gives forth that delicious perfume so pleasing to the Creator — God-given thoughts, prayer.

How much incense do we daily offer to God? The greater the fire, remember, the more abundant and dense will be the aromatic vapor, for there is no danger here of the original substance being consumed into ashes. The intellect and will are made by God to be filled with Himself, and therefore their capacity is, in a measure, unlimited.

They offered Him myrrh.

What is myrrh? Myrrh is a bitter resin. What is the intrinsic value of resin to a new-born baby? Its value is great to this Babe, because of that which it symbolizes. Myrrh is the bitterness of life offered to Him that it may be sweetened and purified in His acceptance and use of it. Only we must have a clear understanding of what the true bitterness of life really is. Most of us have a false notion on this point. We consider it to consist in trials, and difficulties, and misunderstandings, and sicknesses, and tribulations, and sufferings. The only bitterness in these things is our viewpoint. We are wearing spectacles with distorted lenses. All these crosses are willed or permitted by God, and He wills and permits only that which is good for us. The cross is a caress. And caresses are sweet. Then what is the bitterness of life? The bitterness of life is the pain of exile. In what does the pain of exile consist? It consists in being debarred from union with Him for Whom we were created. And that which debars us is — SELF. So the bitterness of life consists in the conquest of self, and this necessarily must go hand in hand with the offerings of gold and frankincense, because we already have seen that *there is no true elevation of the mind and will to God without mortification.* Gifts: gold, frankincense, and myrrh constitute a perfect prayer, a symbol of perfect union. The Magi were the Wise Men, very wise men, men wise with the wisdom of God. Are we?

23. THE INCARNATE WORD THE LIGHT OF THE WORLD

"Thou hast prepared . . . a light to the revelation of the Gentiles"
(LUKE ii. 31-32)

THE first manifestation of the blessed Infant to those outside the pale of the chosen people, was made, as we have seen, to the Magi, the glorious Wise Men of the East. Their submission of faith and their perfect offering were commemorated fittingly by the Church. But in the Feast of the Purification of Our Blessed Lady, the Church forcibly reminds us, in whose name the three Kings lay prostrate before the crib, of our inestimable heritage as the chosen people of the New Covenant. It is the presentation of Christ in the temple — not the purification of our Blessed Lady — that the Church emphasizes. Why? Because in the person of Simeon, the Mosaic Law admits the right of the New Dispensation to take precedence over it, and acknowledges the future spiritual primacy of the Gentiles in the service of the heavenly Father.

" And behold there was a man in Jerusalem named Simeon, and this man was just and devout, waiting for the consolation of Israel; and the Holy Ghost was in him. And he had received an answer from the Holy Ghost, that he should not see death, before he had seen the Christ of the Lord. And he came by the Spirit into the temple. And when his parents brought in the Child Jesus, to do for Him according to the custom of the law, he also took Him into his arms, and blessed God, and said: Now Thou dost dismiss Thy servant, O Lord, according to Thy word in peace; because my eyes have seen Thy salvation, which Thou has prepared before the face of all peoples; a light to the revelation of the Gentiles, and the glory of Thy people Israel " (Luke ii, 25–32).

In the words of St. Augustine, " the old man carried the Child: but the Child governed the old man."

We, too, carry the Child. Does the Child govern us? Does the Child govern us completely?

And Who is this Child? Who is this Light of the Gentiles?

" This Child," the same holy man is speaking, " this Child (is He Who) is set for the fall, and for the resurrection of many in Israel and for a sign which shall be contradicted " (Luke ii, 34).

A fall — a resurrection! This Light is not then an ordinary light. It will illuminate some and blind others. It will blind them with the dazzling radiance of holiness and truth; it will blind them because this Light is too pure for sin-diseased eyes. A fall, a stumbling, a sticking in the mire of doubt and error and unbelief! A resurrection — new life, new vision, the understanding of Him Who appearing among men in the substance of our flesh — and the Mystery is still very new — was presented by His parents in the temple!

A sign which shall be contradicted! A Light, and also

a sign! Why speak of contradiction, when there is concern only of a Babe, a very, very young Babe? Contradiction: that means diversity of opinion, and misunderstanding, and quarrel, and persecution. Is this He of Whom the angels sang such a short time ago: " Glory to God in the highest; and on earth peace to men of good will "? (Luke ii, 14). What a strange Babe! Ah, but this is He of Whom the prophet has foretold: " the Lord, Whom you seek, and the Angel of the testament, whom you desire, shall come to His temple, . . . and who shall be able to think of the day of His coming? and who shall stand to see Him? for He is like a refining fire, and like the fuller's herb; and He shall sit refining and cleansing the silver " (Mal. iii, 1–3). This is He Who Himself will say when He is grown to manhood and utters the wisdom of the Father not by the lips of prophets but by His own dread lips: " Think ye, that I am come to give peace on earth? I tell you, no; but separation. For there shall be from henceforth five in one house divided: three against two, and two against three. The father shall be divided against the son, and the son against the father, the mother against the daughter, and the daughter against the mother " (Luke xii, 51–53). Why shall these things come to pass? Because " my thoughts are not your thoughts, nor your ways my ways, saith the Lord " (Isaias lv, 8).

Verily, His ways are not the ways of the world, not even our ways, though they should be. How could they be! " My kingdom is not of this world " (John xviii, 36), this thorn-crowned Babe Who escaped the murderous hands of Herod will, thorn-crowned again, say to Pilate. The amazed monarch will question: "Art thou a king then?" (John xviii, 37). To which the Eternal Truth will respond: "Thou sayest, that I am a king. For this was I born, and for this came I into the world; that I should give testimony to the truth. Every one that is of the truth, heareth my voice" (John xviii, 37).

He had to be born. Only *He* could give adequate testimony to the truth that is the Father and Himself and the Holy Ghost. The offerings of man were not and could never be wholly sufficient, entirely reparatory. "Sacrifice and oblation, thou wouldst not" (what a strange cry — the first cry of life — from this strange, strange Babe) "but a body Thou hast fitted Me" (Heb. x, 5).

It is this Body, this tiny, fragile Body that houses Immensity, which is now being offered to the Father in the temple. The sacrifice had been made to the Father long ago, in the eternal ages. It had been renewed at the moment of the Incarnation, and again with the first indrawing of the dank midnight air, the stuffy, animal-scented air. But all of these oblations, this one selfsame oblation, had been secret, hidden, known only to the Father and the Spirit of His Love. This holocaust is public, an act of religion, and accepted as such by the hierarchy of the Old Covenant. It has to be, for it is the fulfilment of a divine decree.

"After the days of her purification, according to the law of Moses, were accomplished, they carried Him to Jerusalem, to present Him to the Lord: as it is writ-

[251]

ten in the law of the Lord: every male opening the womb shall be called holy to the Lord " (Luke ii, 22–23).

This is the first time that God Incarnate has appeared in the temple erected to His honor. He is come to take possession of it forever. " Do not think that I am come to destroy the law " (Matt. v, 17) — does not the temple house the tablets of the Law, and itself symbolize their mystic meaning? — " I am not come to destroy, but to fulfil " (Matt. v, 17). To fulfil, in this sense, to perfect. Yet one day the veil of this temple will be rent, and on another the building itself will be in ruins. What is more evident than its destruction? But the destruction is necessary for the fulfilment; the utter destruction, first, of the body of this Child, Who has just now entered His dwelling, carried in the arms of His mother; and after that, and because of that, the utter destruction of the glory of Solomon. Only when the body of this Child, grown to the beauty of perfect manhood, will have been suspended, disfigured and bleeding on the shameful tree of the cross, and bleeding, will have been bled white in the sickening marble pallor of death, only when His naked side will have been pierced and will have oozed large drops of purple blood and murky water, only then will the people that sit in darkness see a great light, for the Light of the world will have gone out. And when Light and Life are gone, the darkness and death will testify with terrifying evidence to the Illumination and Power that had been and apparently are no more. Yet these very witnesses will make known to all men the truth of Him Who is divine veracity; will make known the splendor of His might, and the glory of His substance. Then it no longer will be the humble submission of the Man-God: " The Father is greater than I " (John xiv, 28), but the tremendous canticle of eternal equality: " I and the Father are one " (John x, 30), because, having judged the infernal princes of this world unto destruction, He will have come into absolute possession of His kingdom. And of His kingdom there will be no end. For they who constitute this heavenly kingdom will not be of the earth, earthy; neither will their doctrine and worship bear the least stamp of sordidness or materialistic profession. They who constitute the kingdom of this unfathomable Child, Who in His own name declares Himself a King, will adore the Father in spirit and in truth, with a selfless adoration akin to the flawless and superabundant oblation made, in the rite of the purification of the Blessed Virgin, to the God of Jacob and of Israel.

Simeon is still uttering in transports of joy and hope of redemption: " My eyes have seen thy salvation, which thou hast prepared before the face of all peoples " (Luke ii, 30–31).

We, too, have seen the salvation of the Lord; we have not only seen, but have tasted the sweetness of the consolation of Israel. Simeon saw but once, and was satisfied, and was content to die, according to the word of the Lord, his God. We see daily, and are never satisfied, and refuse to die, according to the word of the Lord our God, " If any man will come after Me, let him deny himself "

[253]

(Matt. xvi, 24), — "Father . . . not my will but Thine be done" (Luke xxii, 42).

But Simeon really saw because the Truth Which he held in his arms illuminated him perfectly, and that was why he was content, and ready to do only the will of his God.

We do not *really* see, because the Truth which we hold in our hearts illuminates us but imperfectly, and that is why we are not content, and are not ready to do *only* the will of our God.

Yet Truth is *one*, and Truth is Light, "the Light (that) shineth in darkness" (John i, 5) — the Light that is the glory of Israel and the revelation to the Gentiles.

And the Child that is smiling up at Simeon in winning benediction is set for the fall and for the resurrection of many in Israel — truly He is the resurrection and the life of this old, old saint — but a *light* to the Gentiles. And we are the Gentiles. Our forbears, the Magi, saw, and were glad. Simeon, a Jew, saw, and was glad. We see — but how much? We are glad — but how? Not nearly as much as Simeon, not nearly as much as the Magi. Why? Because we take the Light which is Truth too much for granted.

The Magi separated themselves from their companions, their home, their country, *from themselves* in their search for the truth.

We have separated ourselves from our companions, our home, some of us perhaps from our country, in our search of the truth. Why then do we not see as clearly as the Magi? Why are we not nearly so whole-heartedly glad? Why? *Because we have not separated ourselves from ourselves.* That is the reason. But there is a little bit of separation, no doubt. With some, there is a larger little bit; with others, a smaller, but not a total and complete separation. Therefore the Light, which is Truth, does not illuminate us perfectly; the vessel through which its beams must penetrate is flecked with the soil of self which obscures and blights all that we say and think and do. Therefore we are not content to stay at home and enjoy the brilliancy of the divine illumination which we carry about with us; we go abroad seeking lesser lights as though they were the greatest, the one only Light. We are perfect moths — dazzled by the false radiance that emanates from these false luminaries. Being dazzled, we are blinded, blinded to the knowledge of real Light and Truth. Our wings get singed, and still we persist. Then some of us, penitent, return to the invigorating splendor of the one only Light, and some of us, some of us persist alas, until we get a fatal burn.

Am I flitting around a false light? Am I?

But why is it so necessary for us to admit the full glory of the Divine Presence to shine forth undimmed? For this reason: He Who is now lying asleep in Simeon's arms, Whom the old priest in prophetic utterance has just called " a Light to the revelation of the Gentiles " (Luke ii, 32) will say later on, when He is disputing with blinded intellects and obdurate wills, " I am the Light of the world " (John viii, 12). Again, later on, He will say to His disciples: " You are the light of the world.

[255]

A city seated upon a mountain cannot be hid. Neither do men light a candle and place it under a bushel, but upon a candlestick that it may shine to all that are in the house. So let your light shine before men that they may see your good works and glorify your Father Who is in heaven " (Matt. v, 14–15).

" I am the Light of the world," I, Jesus Christ, the Wisdom of the Eternal Father, Who illuminate men by the penetrating power of My Life-giving Spirit.

" You are the light of the world " (Matt. v, 14). He, God the Son, has said this to each of us whom He has chosen to be His disciples, to be " a light to the revelation of the Gentiles " (Luke ii, 32). " I am the Light of the world: you are the light of the world." Therefore I am you; *therefore we are one*. One and the same light; one and the same life, one and the same love.

We, then, are that city, that new Jerusalem, the temple of God, that eternal kingdom, seated upon the mountain of this world. We are that candle which must shine to all that live in the house of this world. We are that light, Christ, which must shine before men that they may glorify the Father Who is in heaven, even as He Himself, the incomparable Son, glorified Him upon earth.

How much of the Light, Christ, that dwells within us, do we permit to shine forth? The radiance, remember, should be constant, steady, even, and full. It will be so when the vessel is crystal-clear. But how much energy do we put into the cleansing? How much of the fruit of good works — the end of prayer — do we bring forth in our lives? " In this is my Father glorified," says the Son Who best knows the Father, " in this is my Father glorified: that you bring forth very much fruit " (John xv, 8). It is for this very purpose that He has chosen us. " You have not chosen Me, but I have chosen you; and have appointed you that you should go, *and should bring forth fruit; and your fruit should remain:* that whatsoever you shall ask of the Father in My name, He may give it you " (John xv, 16). " If you abide in Me, and my words abide in you, *you shall ask whatever you will, and it shall be done unto you* " (John xv, 7).

" If you abide in Me: " that is, if you live My life, think My thoughts, say My words, do My work, desire My desires, hate My hate, love My love, " you shall ask *whatever you will* " — anything, everything — " *and it shall be done.*"

If we *thought over* this remarkable utterance — and who if not the disciples should *study* the words of the Master? — we would be stunned with the incomprehensible magnitude of it all.

When shall this thing be? When we are not *two* candles but *one* — Christ — one light — *Lumen Christi.*

This is why the saints are so powerful. They no longer live, God lives within them. They no longer ask, God asks in their name. They no longer do, God does for them: *God in them answers His own prayer.*

How did these faithful disciples of Christ become one light with Him? Simply by living His words. Listen now to Eternal Truth in His wonderful prayer for us, His disciples: " I have given them Thy word, and the world

[257]

hath hated them, *because they are not of the world;* as I also am not of the world " (John xvii, 14).

Can we say in all sincerity that we are not " of the world "; not even a particle " of the world "? Does the world, aye, our own little world, hate us or flatter us?

And the Wisdom of the Father continues: " Sanctify them in truth. Thy word is truth " (John xvii, 17). Sanctify them, O Father, in Me, Thy Eternal Word, Thy Incarnate Word, Thy Eternal Truth. " And for them do I sanctify Myself, that they also may be sanctified in truth " (John xvii, 19). " That they also may be sanctified in truth," in Me!

Christ sanctified Himself for us, according to His own word *that we might be sanctified in Him.* Again He says: " Remember my word that I said to you: The servant is not greater than his lord " (John xiii, 16). What is the conclusion? We must sanctify ourselves, or rather we must allow Christ to sanctify us, *that we may sanctify others.* That is the only way He can be " a light to the revelation of the Gentiles " (Luke ii, 32), for He has willed to let the nations that sit in darkness see the Light, but only the Light which shines forth through us. All this can and must be accomplished simply by doing the one work entrusted to our care with persistent diligence; not two candles but one. The candle of self must burn down to the last flicker; and Christ is Light — is Life. Nor can we excuse ourselves on the ground that the interpretation is too broad. *We are our brother's keeper.* We willingly and cheerfully assumed that responsibility when we hastened to assuage the torments of the Beloved of our soul Who pitifully moaned into our ear as we held Him close, a worm and no man: " *Sitio* " (John xix, 28). *I thirst* — " *Sitio*."

And what is His gratitude for the refreshing draft? Recall a third time: " And the glory which Thou hast given me, I have given to them; that they may be one, as We also are one; *I in them and Thou in Me; that they may be made perfect in one: and the world may know that Thou hast sent me (as the Father hath sent Me, I also send you) and hast loved them, as thou hast also loved Me*. Father, I will that where I am, they also, whom Thou hast given Me, may be with Me; that they may see my glory which Thou hast given Me (and I to them) because Thou hast loved Me before the creation of the world " (John xvii, 22–24).

And what is this glory that Christ wills us to see and possess?

It is the glory of Calvary when the Light of the world apparently went out. On Calvary our light will die.

It is the glory of glories — Christ glorified, and the Beatific Vision — when the Light of the world, the new eternal world, *our* Light, will *never, never fade*, but will shine forth in all men for all eternity, Amen.

VI. *The end of existence: sanctity; union with God*

24. SANCTIFICATION AND COÖPERATION
WITH GRACE

"Be not wise in your own conceits" (ROM. xii, 16)

IT IS well for you always to remember that no two of
you come to prayer with the same gifts of mind and
soul, nor even with the same vigor of body. This thought
should check any motions of discouragement which the
weakness of our nature, often aided by the subtle, poi-
sonous grace of the devil, frequently occasions. Just because someone is more learned, or wittier, or more clever,
or apparently more pious than I, does not prove, does
not at all begin to hint, that he is more apt than I am
where there is a question of simply coöperating with the
Holy Spirit. The Holy Ghost knows far better than we
do of what heights we are spiritually capable. He Himself tells us what these are by the lips of Wisdom, the
Incarnate Word, Whom the Mother-Maid is pondering
in her heart, while He is lulled to sleep by its love-
inflamed beatings: "If any one love Me (poor little
Babe, lonely little Wanderer, far, far away from His
Father's house — could any one hate such a helpless Mite?
And yet — Herod seeks the Child to destroy Him!) — if
any one love Me," the Infant Heart pleads, "My Father
will love him." This must be, for love begets love, even
Infinite Love — "and we will come to him, and will

[263]

make our abode with him " (John xiv, 23). What a promise! And it holds good for everyone, forever, not merely by the indwelling of the Triune God in each baptized soul by grace, but in the most intimate " one-ing " of each soul with its Creator in the perfection of grace. " Thy Kingdom come " (Matt. vi, 10). This is that kingdom for which He taught us to pray, that sovereignty He desires to see established, that truly catholic, universal rule which brought the King of Kings to earth.

But is there no condition? Only the proof of love ᵂhich He asks: " If any one love Me, he will keep My Word " (John xiv, 23), that is, he will do my will in whatever manner it is manifested to him, all day long and the whole night through. For My union with the spirit of man is possible only when he, by his continual actions, can say in all sincerity that word which I lived when on earth, and by which I glorified My Father: " My meat is to do the will of Him that sent Me " (John iv, 34).

Union with God, then, is the spiritual height God calls everyone to achieve — " any one," not only religious, but " any one " who chooses, who *wills* to seek this pearl of great price, who specializes in the traffic of eternal goods, who says " yes " constantly to God the Holy Ghost. Witness Catherine of Sienna, the ecstatic household drudge; and Joan of Arc, the unlettered soldier-heroine, the saviour of her people; Elizabeth of Hungary, the contemplative of a royal court; and countless others — beggars, and peasants, and merchants, and princes. If these out in the world have attained this exalted degree of friendship with God, with what greater reason does He not expect the same of us *who are especially consecrated for this one end,* no matter what the external form of our service may be.

What was it that Our Lord said to Benigna Consolata? "The reason that there are so few contemplatives among religious is because there are so few mortified souls. I long to pour out My graces upon these My chosen ones, My spouses, but I cannot, for their hearts are far from Me." Is not this about the same thing He said four centuries previously to Teresa of Avila? "I have traveled all over the world," He said, "seeking souls on whom to lavish My graces, but nobody wants them, so I am going to pour them all out on you." Evidently the world has not changed much. Back in the early fifteenth century Thomas of Kempis wrote: "And this is the reason why there are found so few contemplative persons, because there are few who know how to sequester themselves entirely from perishable creatures" (Imit. III, 31). No, the world has not changed since the crushing fall in Eden — it was the same yesterday, is the same today, and shall be the same till time shall be no more.

"But," you may argue, "look at the voices heard by Joan of Arc, and the visions seen by Teresa. Who would not be holy with all these extraordinary helps? We cannot measure up to them; it were folly to try."

No, we have not heard the voices that Joan of Arc heard, and the better that we have not. Our ordinary way is much safer for us, and more secure. But we have even more than Joan had. We have the absolutely safe and always audible voice of our superiors and our rule. There is no mistake possible here in knowing the will of God. Joan easily could have slipped. Did we ever really stop to think, though, that it was not the voices that made Joan a saint, not the command to do God's will, but her doing it? Neither will our voices sent by God sanctify us; our persistent, insistent adherence to them, however, will.

This is a point we very easily overlook in the lives of the saints. And it is not always our fault, either. The fault is often the biographer's. So many biographers seem so engrossed in impressing their readers with the authentic and genuinely supernatural sanctity of the saints, that the human element is so far omitted or obscured or distorted that mere man is apparently no longer human. While humanity admires, it is at the same time repelled. The imitation of Christ in the lives of the saints is always possible and compatible with every state of life. The saints did but one thing — the will of God. But they did it with all their might. We have only to do the same thing; and according to the degree of intensity with which we labor shall our sanctification progress. We shall attain that height of glory in heaven that corresponds to the depths of the humility we have sounded on earth. The harder you hit a ball on the ground, the higher it rebounds. The perfection of humility is the annihilation of our will, its absolute submission to the divine in every least detail. That is what made Joan a saint. And Teresa, too. " If thou wilt be perfect " (this is what Joan's voice said to her, and Teresa's visions revealed), " go sell what thou hast and give to the poor, and come, follow me " (Matt. xix, 21). For the Maid it meant the renunciation of her home and kinsfolk; the voluntary acceptance of the hard and unpleasant life of the soldier; difficulties and misunderstandings, and jibes and jeers, and imprisonment and torture, and the stake. She knew it beforehand. The call to follow the Master — *really* to follow — always means Calvary and crucifixion. But the Maid had her answer ready. It came from her heart, as it had come years before from the heart of another Maid: " Behold the handmaid of the Lord: be it done to me according to Thy word " (Luke i, 38). She heard the word; but she did not have to consent. She was free. ' Yes ' or ' no.' A movement of the will; and possibly a movement of the lips. But the ' yes ' meant the salvation of France, and sanctity — but remember the stake. And the ' no '? Ah, who can tell? Who, save God, could measure the undoubted loss?

The Mother-Maid had been free, too. She had heard the word, the voice of the angel. ' Yes ' or ' no '? she can accept or reject. " And thy own soul a sword shall pierce " (Luke ii, 35). He shall be called " a man of sorrows " (Is. liii, 3). " And upon My vesture they cast lots." (Ps. 21, 19). Mary knew beforehand. Mary saw and felt Calvary. But the ' yes ' (and how glad we should be for Mary's courage!), the ' yes ' meant not the salvation of a country, but the salvation of the souls of mankind. And the ' no '? Ah, who can tell? Who, save God, could measure the horrible loss? We can imagine it, faintly. Despair here and hell hereafter! And despair is hell! Thank God for Mary's bravery.

What did the call mean for St. Teresa? She had already renounced her father's house and the goods of the world. " Go, sell what thou hast and give to the poor " (Matt. xix, 21). Apparently she had done so. But " to sell what thou hast " means *all* that thou hast; it means absolutely everything. Not a particle can be retained, if we wish really to follow the Master. The following means Calvary, and crucifixion; — Calvary, " the mount where lovers are made " (St. Francis de Sales).

The Lord our God is a jealous God; He has created the human heart — that is, the soul, for Himself, and He can possess it only when it is entirely given up to Him. Possession means ownership, absolute right over an object, unhampered sovereignty in the matter of use and disposal. " Thou hast created us for Thyself, O God," sings St. Augustine, from the depths of a penitent and sadly experienced heart, " and our hearts are ever restless until they find rest in Thee." Teresa's heart was torn because, on the one hand, she felt urged by grace to give up really *all*, and, on the other, she was tied to earth by an affection for a relative. Therefore she had no rest, no peace. " You cannot serve God and mammon " (Matt. vi, 24) applies equally to a religious as well as to worldlings. But religious have given up the world. For them, then, there is no mammon? Only too much of it, alas! and they perhaps see it not. Mammon — self; disorderly affections for persons, places, things, for self, even; the pleasures and comforts and luxuries of the world, yes, and its gossip, that creep in through every possible crevice of our spiritual armor. St. Teresa had not as yet sold all. In seeking the delights of a human and particular friendship, she was seeking self, not God.

But this did not deter her from becoming a saint. It actually helped her on the way; it gave her a strong impetus, because she had to fight, and fight hard against it. She was selling the last of her goods, and the price of severance was torture, and the fruit of severance was sanctity. She was commanded, as are we, " to sell and give to the poor " (Matt. xix, 21). Who was the poor to whom she gave? She gave to the poorest of the poor — to Christ, the Divine Mendicant. " Behold, I stand at the gate and knock " (Apoc. iii, 20). But if there be noise within, the householder will not hear. The Master has a very gentle knock. He is exquisite refinement. The household must needs be very quiet not to miss the appeal for lodging of this Silent Guest. Else He will pass on and knock at another door. Being thus repulsed, He will again pass on — and on. It is the story of Christmas Eve repeated. " There was no room for them in the inn " (Luke ii, 7). No room for God, no room for the Christ-Child, Who was come to suffer and to die and to sanctify. " He came unto His own and His own received Him not " (John i, 11). What a bitter reproach! Verily, in a literal sense, " A man's enemies shall be they of his own household " (Matt. x, 36).

He came unto His own then. Mary is still pondering

the Word in her heart. He comes unto His own now, His chosen ones, His spouses. And His own — receive Him not? God forbid. Yet not in the manner of the bride in the canticle: " I found him whom my soul loveth. I held him and I will not let him go " (Cant. iii, 4). " I sleep and my heart watcheth " (Cant. v, 2). This is how He wishes to be received, to be held tightly, to be bound fast to the soul of His beloved, for His delight is to be with the children of men. Ah, but the " oneing " means Calvary and crucifixion, and most of us do not care to take our stand with Mary and John and Magdalene at the foot of the cross. We do, yes, in words. Deeds, though, are the things that count. Most of us are content to take our stand with those apostles who " all leaving Him fled " (Matt. xxvi, 56). We prefer with them to watch the crucifixion from afar off. The Master is most forgiving. " I am not come to call the just, but sinners " (Matt. ix, 13); to call the sinners that I may make them just. The apostles really loved Christ, but their love had not yet been purified. When later on it had been, they laid down their lives for Him.

Perhaps our love has not yet been purified by all manner of tribulation. " Every branch in me that beareth not fruit He will take away; and every one that beareth fruit He will purge it, that it may bring forth more fruit " (John xv, 2). With the deserting apostles who shrink from pain because of fear and human frailty, we can yet redeem our cowardice. The purifying process, as you now know, goes on till death. We, too, with the enlightened apostles, must lay down our lives for Him, not superficially and in a half-hearted way, but essentially and with earnestness of spirit. " He that will save his life shall lose it " — this is the threat — " and he that shall lose his life for My sake " — and this is the promise of the Babe in Mary's arms — " shall find it " (Matt. xvi, 25). We who have vowed to follow a crucified God must expect crucifixion. It is the sublime end of our vocation. The crucifixion of the will is the perfection of love, for remember always, we love God with the will. Yet this must occur not simply now and then but constantly, perseveringly.

The reason we have not yet become saints is because we have not understood what it means to love. We think we do, but we do not. To love means to annihilate oneself for the beloved. The self-sacrifice of a mother for her child is only a shadow of the love wherewith we should love the Beloved of our soul. To love is to conform oneself to the Beloved in the most intimate manner of which we are capable; to have no views but His views; no thoughts but His thoughts; no desires but His desires; no likes but His likes; no wants but His wants; no hopes but His hopes; no will but His will. It is to have no joy but in suffering for Him; no glory but in being humiliated for Him; no life but in dying for Him; no death but in living for Him. It is to have no consolation but in ministering to Him; no desolation but in grieving Him; no reward but, as the least of the least, in serving Him.

Oh, if only we could attain this love, this heroic, magnificent perfection of love, what bliss would not be ours! We should have heaven begun on earth. And we

can, if we but so will. The fight will be hard, and the
fight will be long, but the Master is fighting for us, and
He is invincible. Victory will always be ours. Only we
must have confidence. " Do you believe that I can do
this unto you? They say to him, Yea, Lord " (Matt. ix,
28). Then the Almighty Physician will say to us, as He
said to the centurion of old: " Go, and as thou hast believed, so be it done to thee " (Matt. viii, 13). For if we
have faith but as a grain of mustard seed, we shall be
able to remove mountains, even the huge towering
mountain of self. " The right hand of the Lord hath
wrought strength; the right hand of the Lord hath
exalted me " (Ps. 117, 16).

It was this same right hand of the Lord that exalted
St. Teresa when she had given her own into his keeping
with childlike confidence and abandonment. For Teresa,
the final renunciation, the sacrifice of self that had deterred her from winning those remarkable graces which
later God showered upon her with such magnificent
abundance, that torturing severance of which I have
spoken, meant Calvary and crucifixion. Teresa saw it
beforehand, even as had the Mother-Maid, even as must
every soul who deliberately and lovingly wills to follow
in the footsteps of the Babe of Bethlehem. " Yes " or
" no." Teresa was free. But the " yes " meant sanctity,
and the salvation of souls as numerous as those brought
to the Master's feet by the great apostle of the Indies,
St. Francis Xavier. And the " yes " meant illumination
for countless souls through her inspired writings, and an
added glory to the Church. But the " no "? Ah, who

can tell? Who save God could measure the irreparable loss?

So, too, with us. We, who have answered the call of the Divine Beggar, must sell all and follow Him. We have no right to hold back anything which would debar Him from being established as the one and rightful owner of our whole being, body and soul. We have no right, we who are called to perfection, to be satisfied with imperfection. We have no right either in our own name or in that of our brethren, because we may not say to God on the last day, " Am I my brother's keeper? " (Gen. iv, 9). We have assumed that responsibility in the acceptance of the garb we wear — and how gladly and impatiently we awaited it! " You have not chosen me," thus said the remarkable Infant to each of us, " but I have chosen you, and have appointed you that you should go, and should bring forth fruit, and your fruit should remain " (John xv, 16). Suppose Teresa had said " no "? Suppose the Maid of Orleans had said " no "? Suppose — terrifying thought! — the Blessed Virgin had said " no "? I wonder what would have been their meeting with the thwarted God, and what would have been their sentence?

Suppose we say " no "!

25. SANCTIFICATION DURING SPIRITUAL DESOLATION

" — but He was asleep" (MATT. viii, 24)

YOU should now be well convinced that no one need be deterred from attempting the work of his perfection on the ground that the effort is beyond his reach, or incompatible with the duties of his state in life, however active and numerous these duties may be. Since we have no choice in the matter, God having ordained sanctity as the end of our existence, and we having bound ourselves by our religious vows to strive until death to attain it, we should, on the contrary, have all the more reason for absolute confidence in getting there. We would actually fly, not crawl, if only we remembered that it is the Holy Ghost Who sanctifies us, our consent given. But we do not fly because we very, very frequently set up barriers, unrecognized by ourselves, to His free action in our souls. One of the strongest and highest and deepest and thickest, if not, indeed, the superlative of all barriers — sin excepted — is that which we raise when He is asleep.

St. Matthew tells us that " when He entered into the boat, His disciples followed Him: and behold a great tempest arose in the sea, so that the boat was covered with waves, but He was asleep " (Matt. viii, 23–24).

The boat which Jesus has entered is the innermost sanctuary of the soul, the secret citadel of the spirit, where God dwells. The soul itself is the sea. Only the comparison is very imperfect, because the boat is something apart from the sea, and differs from it essentially, whereas the center of the soul, in which God resides, is the very core, if I may so call it, of its being. Bear this distinction in mind, please. This dwelling place of the Omnipotent is so secret that ordinarily it is unknown, it is hidden to the soul itself. But every effort made by the soul to perfect itself, however fruitless it may seem, necessarily and infallibly must bring the created spirit closer to its Uncreated Origin, Who inhabits it in all the amazing splendor of His divinity.

What most of those who are not yet deeply experienced in the spiritual life fail to realize, and therefore fail to understand, is this, in the words of the *Imitation*: " I am accustomed to visit my elect in two manner of ways: namely, by trial and by consolation " (III, 3). And further, the trial far outweighs the consolation. It must, because we are as yet in exile. We are here to be purified, refined, and made perfect. And perfection can be acquired only by suffering. There is no other way. We are not perfect because we are not willing to suffer. " Every branch in me that beareth fruit," — the Divine Infant is the eternally flowering Vine — " he will purge it, that it may bring forth more fruit " (John xv, 2). But the purging is of value only when it is accepted in the manner God's love desires, and one of His favorite, and hence one of His most excellent and efficacious pur-

[275]

gations is this of His remaining apparently asleep. Only the sad thing is we too often do not understand that He is just asleep, and so we proceed to spoil the work that the Life-giving Spirit is accomplishing in us. Do you not know that God is all-powerful, whether He seems near or far, awake or asleep?

In what, though, does this sleeping consist? To answer, we must first distinguish the waking.

"When Jesus is present all is well, and nothing seems difficult," sings the author of the *Imitation* (II, 8). Such, then, is the general condition of the soul when God seems near or awake. It is an absolute pleasure to arise at the first sound of the bell; we are so full of love and zeal that we should like, if possible, to anticipate somewhat the hours devoted to the service of the Lord. Meditation is a positive joy; distractions are few, and when they do come they are easily repelled. There is a great stirring-up of the emotions and a consequent jubilation of spirit — a jubilation mostly animal, though. It is sunshine all the time. We now realize — or rather we *think* we realize — how good we are, and how holy! At Mass and Communion our devotion is rather perfect. We feel — not that we care to confess this feeling, or even to admit an examination in this point, but it is there just the same — that we have really served the Lord manfully, have done something really worth while and at last as it should be done — from our point of view — and for which — and this is the tenderest spot of all and most secret — God is almost under an obligation to us.

You object that this is not so? I will prove it. We

have been acting thus for a good while, and we are also begging God for a favor. Somehow or other He has not granted it, and there are no indications that He intends answering our petitions in a hurry. What happens? We pout. " Here I have been trying to be so good, and I have been, is it not so, Lord? Now when I want something, You will not give it me." Then we begin to think — the devil is in our ear — " Oh, what is the use! Sanctity was never meant for me. I have tried it, and I have not succeeded. I fear someone does not know what he is talking about. I might just as well stop, and let things take their course. As long as I get to heaven, I will be safe." Yes; *there* is another ' saint ' that now must be reckoned among the " possibles."

But I am digressing. All this was just to illustrate that we actually, unknown to ourselves, feel that God is under an obligation to us for the miserable rags of good — not goods — that we do.

But we must continue. How else is this nearness of God, this consolation, made manifest?

It is rather easy to keep silence; to remain recollected. No, we do not want to talk to anyone nor have anyone talk to us. At last we truly despise the world. All work assigned is just the thing we want to do, and we do it with a vengeance — literally. In fact, we are quite perturbed when the recreation bell rings. " Whoever invented recreation, anyway? Why, that is not at all conducive to recollection. Perhaps they did not know exactly what they were doing. It would be much better to be thinking of God and telling Him beautiful things. Here it has been so easy to keep all the good resolutions that I have made, and now I will go in and break every one. Well, it must, I suppose, be endured. This must be one of those trials they talk about." And so, with a sanctimonious sigh and the air of a newly-crowned — or beheaded — martyr, we make our appearance among our brethren.

Of course, our reasoning has not been altogether perfect and in conformity with the fundamental principles of religious existence, but then we hardly can be blamed for not recognizing this defect, our vaunted opinion of ourselves having made us impervious to any contrary and contradictory opinion, no matter how authoritative. The trouble is, we would be masters before we have been scholars, and that would never do. We are not as yet qualified to prescribe for ourselves for any of our spiritual ailments. Truly, the medicine is not to our liking, and because it is bitter we imagine it destructive. And this is precisely where we go astray.

But who doses out this unpleasant tonic? Only He Who is the Healer of soul and body, the Master Physician. And how is it done?

"But when Jesus is absent," continues Thomas of Kempis, " everything is hard " (II, 8). Such is the general condition of the soul when God seems far away or asleep. It is absolutely detestable to hear the first strokes of the rising bell. It is rather hard to distinguish the voice of God in those harsh clangs. Why, we have not been asleep a minute — at least that is the way we feel. Once we are up (and here is a secret we will whisper aloud — we did not get up as though the house were on fire) our eyes insist on closing, and our fingers become all thumbs, and strings tangle, and clothing gets mixed up, and our temper is just a little bit on edge, just a little bit. Here we have given God hardly half a thought. But, then, we will make good at prayers and meditation.

"Amen." It is the last. We come to with a thump. Prayers are finished — and where have we been? All over creation. The meditation begins. We nerve ourselves to listen. "What are they reading? Greek or Sanskrit? It might just as well be either. Nothing penetrates. We stifle the tenth yawn. Yes, we are ashamed to confess it, but we have been nodding. But God certainly cannot expect us to do impossibilities. If we have not slept all night — we are fully convinced of this now — He will not blame us for giving in just a trifle. He understands. Besides, were we not told *not* to *strain* after perfection? *not* to *strain* in any of our spiritual exercises? It might result in a fatal or nearly-fatal rupture. That would never do. And since we are not to strain — (the seventeenth yawn) — and the meditation is finished.

Mass begins. How it drags! (God forgive us!) Were we ever at Mass before? How unintelligible it all is! The Host is uplifted. "My Lord and my God" (John xx, 28). We say the words mechanically. Are we stupid, or simply in a stupor? The Host is laid on our tongue. We swallow It. Our thoughts are far away. We kneel. Our knees are leaden. And so is our head. Did we really receive God? "Have mercy on us." It is the last response. We look up. The priest is leaving the altar. That *penetrates*.

We go to table. Everything is too hot or too cold; nothing seems to satisfy.

We go to our work. Were we ever told to do *anything* that was *really* to our liking? And — pardon me — we are not very gentle in doing things. We just do not care. " Let them know it." A dish, or a book, or a desk-top, carelessly handled, reveals to others our inward sentiments. We would feel more relieved if we could say a few things to someone. And we do. They are not very gentle things, either. And so it continues.

Suddenly a thought strikes us. We have not been very recollected, have we? Recollected? " Just talk to me about recollection, and I will ———." But wait a minute. Was it not only yesterday that you did not want to talk to anyone, or have anyone talk to you, or to recreate, or ——— ? " Was that I? " " It could not have been. I must have been insane. Who could be recollected with a million and one things to do, and no time in which to do them, and no one to help? That is well enough for those who have leisure. But do not talk to *me* about recollection."

The recreation bell does not have to ring. We anticipate it. We have much to say, and though it has been said before, it can bear repeating — with half-conscious additions. It is thundering all the time. It must be a great storm. The signal for silence is given — and we still have not finished our grievance. *And we do.*

We examine our conscience. Yes, we have been impatient, and angry, and sullen, and resentful, and uncharitable, and ———. " Lord, I'm sorry." — Stop a minute, though, and dig down into the cause of these faults. Ah, but we do not. That is one reason why we are not yet saints. If we did dig down, they would not happen so often, and after a short time they would hardly happen at all.

What was the real difficulty? We failed to submit to God's providence. We failed to be resigned to His will that had been marked out for us. Why? ". . . but He was asleep." God withdrew the consolation, the sensible fervor we had yesterday, to see how we would act. Yesterday it was He Who really did all for us. And today, when we had only the stick left after having eagerly consumed the candy, we made a face, and pouted. The candy had been tasty and sweet, but the stick was hard and stiff. Yet, if we had disposed ourselves properly we might have found a few grains of the sweet adhering to the stick, or at least a hint of the original flavor. For — and this is the mark of a truly spiritual man whom the winds of sensible consolation do not bowl over — " the flavor continues," that is, the relish for God's work continues in the midst of darkness and desolation: the adhesion of the will to His, its steadfast turning to Him, is not lacking in the minutes, — and there may be sixty in each hour — when everything goes awry.

But all this is only a small troubling of the waters of the soul. What of the time when the storms of temptation and doubt and painful anxiety blow up strongly? Blow up they certainly shall for everyone who follows in the wake of the Master. The more earnest, the more persevering, the more intimate the following, the darker, the fiercer the tribulation of the winds and waves. What happens then? There is nothing to fear; there is all the more cause for confidence, for the Master is in the boat, and He knows the condition of the sea, and is therefore permitting it — " but He is asleep " (Matt. viii, 24).

What are we going to do?

And His disciples " came to Him and awaked Him, saying: Lord save us, we perish. And Jesus saith to them: Why are you fearful, O ye of little faith? Then rising up He commanded the winds, and the sea, and there came a great calm " (Matt. viii, 25–26).

What are we going to do? Are we going to act like the timorous disciples who trusted not when they saw the Lord God in their very midst? But that is what we have been doing, I fear. That is why our advance has been so slow.

Just because distractions are thick and heavy, duties irksome, spiritual exercises abhorrent, commands distasteful, temptations foul and plentiful, prayer is a thing from which to run away, the world beckons, the devil is in our shadow — just because these signs of tribulation make known to us the distress of the soul is no reason for throwing up our hands in despair and thinking ourselves on the road to perdition. The game is not lost. *This is the very time to be most punctual and exact in the least details of rule and custom, to be most punctual and exact to the commands of superiors, and to the interior practices which we formerly followed.* Why? It is the golden hour of spiritual progress, more precious to the soul than days of consolation.

But how is this? God is testing the soul to discover whether it love Him for Himself or for His gifts. That He must know before He can admit it further into the garden of delights which is Himself. He wants to find out whether the soul's love is a selfish love, or a pure love. The way we act under fire tells Him all. Remember *we love God with the will, not with the feelings.* God designedly takes the feelings away to discover our real self to us and to Him. If we are in earnest, if our love of God is pure, if we love Him for Himself *alone,* we shall be more than careful in time of darkness to show Him all those proofs of affection we showered on Him when the sun was shining brightly. But if our love is a mixture, then *we give up the struggle before we have really begun,* because we have been seeking self; we have been seeking the delights, yes, the spiritual delights, which God can and does give. We were certain that we had been loving God for Himself, but the test shows that we had been loving Him for ourselves. *The selfish soul will never arrive at intimate union with God.* The selfish soul will never arrive because it shrinks from suffering. *And suffering and sanctity are synonymous.*

But how are we to persist when the desolation lasts not one day but a week, not two weeks but perhaps months, not one year but five or more — God only knows how many — with very little consolation in between? With God all things are possible. And God is with us, within us. St. Teresa says that God and I are a majority. This is infallibly true. We must expect that the darkness is going to last longer, much longer than the sunshine. We are here to be purged, purified, refined, made Godlike. And the more there is to be cast out, the more exalted the degree of union we shall with God's all-powerful grace attain, the longer and more soul-searching will the cleansing be. There is nothing to fear, for He Who has overcome the world is at our right hand, His arm around us.

Many people get up to this point and never get beyond it, because they act like the shrinking disciples. "Lord, save us, we perish" (Matt. viii, 25), they cry, awaking Him. They think themselves lost, because all sense of feeling is gone. He awakens and says to the turbulent waves; says sadly and with wistful face: "Peace, be still" (Mark iv, 39). Immediately there comes a great calm. The soul is satisfied, and thinks it has gained much, because it feels that all is well with it.

But what would you think of a servant who had lived for years and years with a kind and loving Master Who had gone to take a much-needed rest. While the Master was asleep, a strange and ferocious dog entered the yard and began to bark. And the Master still slept. But the servant, wishing to get rid of the pest, went and awakened the Master that He might tell him what to do — or rather do it Himself. And the Master, expelling the dog, went back to rest. (Now, this Master never gave orders not to be disturbed. He was too courteous and loving for that.)

Shortly thereafter, the servant, hearing a knock, went and opened the door. (He was an incautious servant, for instead of opening it just a little he opened it right wide.)

A strange and savage-looking merchant entered, who wished the servant to traffic with the goods of the Master for his own gain. The servant, instead of becoming indignant at the proposal and sending him forth, went and awakened the Master. And the Master, expelling the ' serpent,' went back to rest.

Again, after an interval, the sun darkened. Heavy clouds rolled along the sky. There was crashing thunder; blinding lightning; pelting rain; rattling hailstones! And the servant awakened the Master for the third time — awakened the Master Who had control of all the elements.

What would you think of that servant? Think it — think it hard — and to yourself.

Why did the servant act in this manner? *Because he kept his eyes fixed on himself, and not on the Master.*

We, too, are prone to worry too much about our spiritual progress, and we are prone to worry too little. Too much in this sense: we begin manfully to serve the Lord, and when He falls asleep, as has just been explained, we begin to fret and fume and get harassed and perplexed and make difficulties for ourselves a thousand times more numerous than the Lord ever intended. We want to know why this distraction persists, and where it came from; what we ever did in the past to be tempted in this fashion; we try to unearth in ourselves, for the coldness we experience, a hundred faults that never existed; we question God as to the reason for His conduct; we show curiosity as to what it may mean; we complain to Him of the chastisement. All this shows lack of confidence

[285]

and trust in God. There is no need to let our imagination run away with us just because we are undergoing interior anguish.

Let us look at the problem as though it were the case of someone else. Have I really tried to put out the distractions as best I could? Yes. Very well! Am I responsible for them through curiosity of the eyes, ears, mind, tongue? No. That is good. Have I played or trifled with the temptations? Goodness, no! Have I paved the way for them by placing myself in the occasion of sin of grave imperfection? No. I have not. When I realized my tepidity and dulness and want of attention at spiritual exercises, did I tell God I was sorry, and ask Him to help me to improve? Yes. Excellent. You have been serving Him with all the strength of your being and He is delighted. " Oh, but I feel so unhappy and discontented! " That is well. That is just where the shoe pinches. Are you serving God for Himself or for His gifts? " For Himself." Are you certain? Then why the secret sensitiveness which you do not like to confess even to yourself? That is just what He is trying to kill. Tell Him " thank you " for letting you see it, and promise to help Him in the work. That is the way to get ahead — to work with Him. *But face the truth squarely.*

I said a moment ago that we are apt to complain to Our Lord about this chastisement. Is it wrong to do so? Oh, no. But it is rather imperfect love. Does a mother complain to her child of all the sufferings she has endured out of love for it? To her they all seem as nothing, and she is willing to endure others a thousandfold more severe. Her love is self-forgetful, generous, and pure. She has her child in mind, not herself. And the love a mother bears her child is but a faint shadow of the love wherewith we should love the Beloved of our soul. Instead of complaints and murmurs, He should hear from our lips an unending " Deo Gratias " and " Gloria." Why should He not? We do not realize the wonderful privilege it is to be the very least menial in the house of this great King. But to be chosen to be His spouse! He has a right to expect us to console Him. It is the place of the bride to hide her griefs and lighten the burden of the bridegroom. When the heavenly Bridegroom, Who sees all, perceives how selflessly His bride is seeking His good pleasure alone, what can He do but to incline towards her with an outpouring of excessive love? Oh, if we only could learn to think of Him *always*, and forget our miserable, worthless self!

On the other hand, we worry too little about our spiritual growth. Many of us are apt to undertake it but haltingly. And we will get out of it only what we put in. To be consistent, the fighting must be persistent — if we want to accomplish anything. Applying ourselves now and again, " when we feel in the mood," will never obtain results — at least, not very many. *Remove all consideration for feelings and all feelings of consideration for self.* It sounds easy, but try it. Remember, he who has God, has *everything plus* what he needs.

A word of warning must here be given. Do not confuse visions and revelations and locutions and ecstasies and the gift of tears with the essential part of perfection.

All these things mentioned are accidental to the state —
that is, they are not necessary. Perfection consists in the
" oneness " — or rather I should have said, in the " oneing " — of our mind and will with the Divine Intellect
and Will. And here is another point. It is possible for a
soul to have attained this end and not be conscious of it.
It is not necessary. God has His own reason for disclos-
ing to a soul its state of intimate union with Him, or
withholding that knowledge until it is in the added possession of the glory of the Beatific Vision. Remembering this, our hope and desire should be as vast as — God
Himself. But one thing is necessary — faith, and faith,
and faith. And sanctity is the perfection of faith. You
do not understand? God grant that some day you will.

26. THE PERFECT TREASURE OF THE SOUL — UNION WITH GOD

"For where thy treasure is, there is thy heart also" (MATT. vi, 21)

A TREASURE is something very precious, something we prize very highly, the possession of which delights, forming the chief source of our joy; the absence of which pains, creating a void commensurate to the depth of the previous gratification. A treasure is a secret thing; it is a treasure only because it is secret and guarded. Once the ownership, or even the use of the cherished object — for example, a book in which I find great solace — is shared with another, it ceases to be a treasure, for it is no longer hidden from the sight or knowledge of men. Secret delectation in an extremely precious secret something constitutes the essence of this our wealth. "For where thy treasure is, there is thy heart also" (Matt. vi. 21).

Our Lord never once gave a command, or counsel, or precept, which He Himself had not first realized in His own life, public and private; else how could He, the Eternal Truth, say "Follow me" (Matt. xvi, 24); "for I have given you an example, that as I have done to you, so you do also. Amen, amen, I say to you: The servant is not greater than his lord; neither is the apostle greater than he that sent him. If you know these things, you shall be blessed if you do them " (John xiii, 15–17). Had He acted other than as He had taught, how could He, Unfathomable Sanctity and Exquisite Justice, solemnly and publicly question: " Which of you shall convince me of sin? " (John viii, 46).

Our Lord, then, taught, and taught efficaciously only because He had already lived His doctrines. Moreover, He continues living them and will do so for all eternity. " For where thy treasure is, there is thy heart also " is equally true by force of living example in God's life today as it was the day He first uttered this word.

" Where," you may ask, " is Our Lord's treasure? " " Where is His Heart? " Only by studying Him shall we see how far we have misinterpreted His precept in its application to ourselves, for He is our radiant Mirror in which we are continually reflected. Although we are quite frequently unconscious of this reflection, this is, nevertheless, the one mirror before which we may, and must, scrutinizingly stand, because it is the one alone which being Virtue Itself, rejects all defects, and shows them clearly forth in all their deformity. Our principal object in life is this: that one day, after painstaking and faithful effort, as we stand before this Mirror, Christ's image will be reflected in Christ. Having clothed ourselves with Christ, we will manifest Him alone in all we think, or say, or do. Looking into our souls, which, made to the image and likeness of God are living mirrors of the one Resplendent Mirror, He, the Uncreated Spirit, will see His eternal likeness beam forth in all that dazzling purity He destined it to have — dependent, of course, on the soul's coöperation — when He created it.

To clothe ourselves with Christ we have but to despoil ourselves of ourselves; the clothing following naturally the stripping. In fact, to clothe we have but to strip. It is precisely because the outer layer of self is laid on so thickly over our souls that Christ, Who is the life and center of the soul is not and cannot be visible. In proportion as the stripping, the denudation of self progresses, section by section, in like ratio the garmenting with virtue, the clothing with Christ, makes itself manifest. Most of us wear our virtue in patches. We all possess some goodness, some small degree of similarity to Christ since no man is essentially bad. It is just as important not to ruthlessly tear off the patches, in our ignorance foolishly deeming them as anything but ornamental, as it is for us to peel off the large layers of selfishness, the main portion, perhaps, of the image as it now shines forth. Selfishness means everything that has its root in self-interest, no matter how hidden to others, and more lamentably to ourselves, that perennial plant of self-love may be. Viewing ourselves in Christ, the Light Transcendent, we see in their proper relation both the good and the bad; the good in one sense, the bad in another. In this manner we shall clothe as we strip, divesting ourselves of the old Adam that the new may be revealed.

Why is it, then, that though we stand before the mirror, quite scrutinizingly too, the work of stripping goes on so slowly; perhaps, the wrong way; perhaps, not at all; perhaps, not at all because the reflection is rather satisfactory, according to our estimation of values? Why? Simply because some of us look continually, others occasionally, into the wrong mirror — the mirror of the world — the devil's mirror. We look once. It is not as bad as I thought. We look again. It is quite good, well, *rather* good. In fact, there is just the slightest suspicion of a halo indicated. A third look — and a pleased smile results. I was *not* mistaken. There are signs of a halo, without a doubt. Two more glances, and the effulgence of the nimbus is so overpowering that we are struck blind on the spot, yet not so soon but that we caught a lasting impression of a very perfect, superior creature, our own magnanimous self — seated on a pedestal.

Pitiable blindness! Is there anything more blinding, more deadly, more eternally blinding, than the light of self-admiration? Yes, one thing alone: *secret* self-admiration, which stalks abroad as the essence of a positively respectable, decent, super-genuine humility. God preserve us from this truly devilish humility!

What has this to do with the questions proposed some time ago: Where is Our Lord's treasure? Where is His Heart? Where is it? It is here. We have just been looking at it. But where? It is inside of you — it is your soul — the real ' you.' You are made to the image and likeness of God, Life Eternal. You are, in a sense, part of His Spirit, part of Himself, for though not eternal, you are immortal. In this regard only are we children of the Father by nature. What does a man hold dearer than himself, than his life, his very soul? Nothing. So also is it with God. You are that very precious something, that

tory response is ever on our lips: We have left all for God. But have we in reality?

Mere isolation — or in the case of active religious, segregation — from a contaminating influence does not preclude the possibility of desire, even virile desire for that very evil from which we have been removed; nor does it necessarily mean that that same pestilential atmosphere may not, unknowingly to us, perhaps, gain entrance into the mansion of the soul. There is no hermitage so remote which the devil cannot infest with all the insidious disorders of a sensuous and sensual world. On the other hand, thank God, there is no life of activity so distracting but what the Divine Spirit can convert into the only true hermitage — a life hidden with Christ in God. We who are engaged in active labor for God must of a truth hold intercourse with the world. We are they for whom Christ, in His sublime prayer to His Father, pleaded thus: " I pray not that thou shouldst take them out of the world, but that thou shouldst keep them from evil " (John xvii, 15).

In a special sense, we are those very disciples whom Christ willed to be *in* the world, but not *of* it. For what did He pray? " That thou shouldst keep them from evil " (John xvii, 15) ; from that greatest of evils — a backward glance, at first unwitting, then through successive curiosities, ultimately deliberate, into the mirror of the world — Satan's mirror. By almost imperceptible shiftings we swerve from our position before the Radiant Mirror of Life, until we have our back completely turned to our gentle Saviour, the meek Lamb of God,

the divinely-sensitive Spouse of our soul, and are looking
scrutinizingly into that noxious pool of foul-smelling
vapors, which we profess to have long since abandoned.
Woe to us if we have done so! Let us not be like the
Jews, who, fed with the manna which rained down from
heaven, yearned for the fleshpots of Egypt. Or like the
Jews, again, when, with the vision of the Promised Land
in the distance, they forgot the bountiful Lord Who
had miraculously delivered them from bondage, and
Who continued to protect and preserve them; and so,
after the fashion of His faithless people, His chosen
people, to make for ourselves a golden calf as an idol.
What treachery more perfidious!

This is rather strenuous language; nevertheless, truth
admits of no deception, however veiled or honeyed. Beyond a doubt many will scout what has been said as
preposterous, smiling the while in superior wisdom,
which, whether they like it or not, is certainly not born
of God. But does all this, in reality, smack of that exaggeration attributed to it by extremely prudent scoffers?
Let us look into the matter disinterestedly.

"For where thy treasure is, there is thy heart also."
If we discover by thoughtful considerations where our
heart — our affection — is, we shall have no difficulty in
determining the place of our treasure, since the one conclusion suffices. Our heart is simply the compass that
follows magnetically the north star of desire. To locate
my treasure I have but to unearth the lodging of my
desires. Do my desires arise, develop, and cease in God?
Do they? Always? I wonder. I wonder if there be not

in me a restless craving for knowledge of what is passing on in the world; a growing yearning for intercourse with former friends and companions; a too ready acquiescence, mayhap invitation, in their all too numerous visits; an absolutely unnecessary perusing of worldly books and papers; a cheerful fostering of boon individuals, with an explosive negation of the existence of this cultivation (the very deadliest indication of its actual being); a pair of gluttonous eyes and ears; a devilishly comfortable attitude relative to the observance of rule; a broad-minded disregard of conventual custom; an asinine opinionatedness; a deft proneness for seizing at any occasion, or even creating opportunities, for prowling abroad; a strangling adhesion to my own will (not in the essentials of obedience to superiors — goodness, no, not outwardly, at any rate — which, after all, means no kind of obedience, but in certain inviolably prudent consequences inevitable to my religious dignity and priority); a smug complacency in my own personal goodness, in comparison with, let us say, " the common herd " (the halo, originally self-adjustable, and guaranteed to fit any sized head, now requires assistance to slip into position); an overweening tenderness for self, for my own poor, tired, overworked self which *absolutely* requires at least trifling comforts (and yes, let me whisper it aloud, luxuries); a feverish anxiety under the fuming illusion of a white-hot zeal to acquire all sorts of information, really indispensable, perforce, to the labor in which I am now engaged; a facile tongue in admirable working order; a hint of presumption in the demands made upon seculars; a laxity of religious decorum in confidences with relatives; a distracted weariness in the performance of spiritual exercises; an eager predilection for congenial occupations and most impatient aversion for distastful ones; a constant dwelling in thought upon creatures (which means upon any person, place, or thing, past, present, or to come); an apogeal, most active sensitiveness, somehow rather strangely unfeeling when the susceptibilities of my neighbor are affected; a patronizing superciliousness which disdains trifles as contemptible, while embracing sublime visionary achievements that pertain to the really " big things " of life; an " obtuse-angled " view of God, which includes His mercy but precludes His justice; in brief, a prosperous self-love of a microscopic organism magnified disgustingly to the nth degree.

Why certainly we have left the world! Oh, yes, we do everything for God. " All for Thee, sweet Jesus." It sounds almost blasphemous. God, You Who once said something about " whited sepulchres full of dead men's bones " (Matt. xxiii, 27) forgive me. In my sinful pride, I thought I was a religious; and I fear — I am only a religious habit. I feasted, and gave You the husks fit only for swine. I feasted, and grudged You even the crumbs cast carelessly to dogs. I vowed to be poor in spirit; to belong to You body and soul; to make You absolute Master of my dearest possession, my will — and " this people honoureth me with their lips, but their heart is far from me " (Matt. xv, 8). God, it is I — I. In my madness, I thought myself wise, forgetting that " the Lord knoweth the thoughts of men, that they are vain " (Ps. 93, 11); that He " catcheth the wise in their craftiness " (Job v, 13); that to become wise I needed to become a fool for the sake of Christ. My God, my God, why have I forsaken You!

Poor child, " know you not that you are the temple of God, and that the Spirit of God dwelleth in you? " (I Cor. iii, 16). Behold, I have stood at the door of your heart, and knocked — one year, two years, three, five, ten, twenty, yea thirty — years. " Have I been so long a time with you and have you not known Me? " (John xiv, 9). So long a time have I been with you, and you have not known — because you did not care — that " God is a Spirit, and they that adore Him must adore Him in spirit and in truth " (John iv, 24). In spirit, interiorly, in your heart, where I, your forgotten Treasure, your well-beloved, your Spouse, always am — neglected, forsaken, despised for that world on which you have riveted your gaze, your desires, your affections; for that world which gratifies the least whim of nature; for that world you have made the secret treasure of your heart, in which you find your secret delectation; for that world which dispossesses Me of the chosen dwelling place I have created for Me — your heart. Again, as when I lived on earth, can I truly say " the foxes have holes and the birds of the air nests, but the Son of Man (your Spouse) hath not where to lay His head " (Matt. viii, 20), for you " that eateth bread with me (My Bread, My very Flesh) shall lift up his heel against Me "

(John xiii, 18) and " have turned their back to me " (Jeremias ii, 27).

The light of My truth is too strong for your cowardly nature because it lays bare your real self in all its miserable deficiencies and weakness; yet I wound only that you may be healed, and live. But you, in your folly, have caught the lure of the world, have cast a backward glance after contemplating Me, your Radiant Mirror; and so, little by little have swerved from your position before My face because of the satanic halo you glimpsed enveloping you in that mirror of fetid iniquity — the world. You " strain out a gnat, and swallow a camel " (Matt. xxiii, 24). Blinded by secret pride and self-love, your life has been a glorification of self under the veil of zeal for the honor of My Father's house. " My house shall be called the house of prayer, but you have made it a den of thieves " (Matt. xxi, 13). My treasure house, the temple of your soul, should be the house of continual prayer, the unceasing activity of a mortified will united to My Father's and Mine.

The temple of your soul, you whom I have espoused, should be open, unfaithful spouse, to Me alone. " But I say unto you, that whosoever shall look on a woman to lust after her, hath already committed adultery with her in his heart " (Matt. v, 28). Is this infidelity, sinful in natural conjugal intercourse, to be considered of no moment in the supernatural? What of the lusts of your senses which you have taken no pains to subdue? " If you live according to the flesh, you shall die " (Rom. viii, 13). What of the buying and selling you carry on daily in My temple, the trafficking in disorderly affections whereby you freely substitute my creatures for Me? " Thou shalt love the Lord thy God with thy *whole heart* " (Matt. xxii, 37). What of the lingering, straining glances into that foul mirror of corruption? " No man putting his hand to the plough, and looking back, is fit for the kingdom of God " (Luke ix, 62). What of the thieves — lukewarmness, selfishness, inconstancy, pride — which you wantonly have allowed access through the loopholes of inordinate desires? " The thief cometh not, but for to steal, and to kill, and to destroy " (John x, 10). " If the good man of the house knew at what hour the thief would come, he would certainly watch, and would not suffer his house to be broken open " (Matt. xxiv, 43). What though it be *one* sense left unguarded, *one* creature for whom you cherish a secret attachment, *one* glance you have riveted on the devil's looking-glass, *one* thief that has gained admittance into the innermost shrine of your soul — " where thy treasure is, there is thy heart also " (Matt. vi, 21). Once the ownership, or even the use of the cherished object, that secret something, is shared with another, it ceases to be a treasure, for it is no longer hidden from the sight or knowledge of men. Do you, My spouse, dare to call Me your treasure, if you presume to share My dwelling place with even one unmortified passion? " You cannot serve God and mammon " (Luke xvi, 13). Mind what you are about, for I have appointed you that you should bring forth fruit by faithful labor in My vineyard. " For by the fruit the tree is known " (Matt. xii, 33), for men do not "gather grapes of thorns or figs of thistles" (Matt. vii, 16).

What fruit have you brought forth? "If any man will come after me, let him deny himself, and take up his cross daily, and follow me" (Luke ix, 23). But the sensual man, you whom I have chosen and deigned to elevate to the dignity of spouse, perceive not these "things that are of the Spirit" (Rom. viii, 5); for it is foolishness to you, and you cannot understand because it is spiritually examined. "And why call you me Lord, Lord; and do not the things which I say?" (Luke vi, 46). "He that despiseth me and receiveth not my words hath one that judgeth him; the word that I have spoken, the same shall judge him in the last day" (John xii, 48).

Lord, what wilt Thou have me to do?

"Take these things hence" (John ii, 16). Make to yourself a scourge of little cords and drive out from the temple of your soul the thieves who have desecrated it — them that buy and sell, and the changers of money; and overturning their tables, cast all their belongings boldly forth; and locking the door, give Me the key, your will, that I may no longer stand knocking, knocking in vain. "Amen, amen, I say unto you, — he that entereth in by the door is the shepherd of the sheep; — he calleth his own sheep by name, and leadeth them out. And when he hath let out his own sheep, he goeth before them. ("I am the way." — John xiv, 6.) And the sheep follow him, because they know his voice" (John x, 1-4). But the lambs, His spouses, he carrieth in His arms that they may hear the beating of His heart; be enamored of the beauty of His countenance; thrill to the melody of His voice; feel the power of His protecting presence; be quickened in the loving fire that glows tenderly in His consuming glances; — for these, His chosen lambs, are the dearest treasures of His sheepfold. Only be passive, My dearest spouse, in My embrace, and resist not the inspirations of My desire, " for my delights were to be with the children of men " (Prov. viii, 31).

" Arise, make haste, my love, my dove, my beautiful one, and come. For winter is now past, the rain is over and gone. The flowers have appeared in our land, the time of pruning is come: the voice of the turtle is heard in our land. The fig tree hath put forth her green figs: the vines in flower yield their sweet smell. Arise, my love, my beautiful one, and come. My dove in the clefts of the rock, in the hollow places of the wall, shew me thy face, let thy voice sound in my ears; for thy voice is sweet, and thy face comely. Catch us the little foxes that destroy the vines: for our vineyard hath flourished. My beloved to me, and I to him who feedeth among the lilies, till the day break, and the shadows retire " (Cant. of Cant. ii, 10–17). Amen.

Litany of Love

Lord, have mercy on us;
Christ, have mercy on us.
Lord, have mercy on us;
Jesus, hear us;
Jesus, lovingly hear us.

God, the Father of heaven, have mercy on us.
God, the Son, Redeemer of the world, have mercy on us.
God, the Holy Ghost, have mercy on us.
Holy Trinity, One God, have mercy on us.

This Litany, with the prayer that follows, is published
as the private composition of Sister Miriam Teresa, who
used it for her personal devotion. It is not the intention
of the editor to present it as an approved litany.

Jesus, my Well-Beloved
Jesus, my Strength
Jesus, Light of my mind
Jesus, Power of my will
Jesus, Fire of my love
Jesus, Life of my life
Jesus, Life of my soul
Jesus, Soul of my life
Jesus, Soul of my soul
Jesus, my Ceaseless Delight
Jesus, my Rapturous Bliss
Jesus, my Infinite Joy
Jesus, True Peace of my soul
Jesus, my Only Existence
Jesus, my Own
Jesus, my Heaven
Jesus, my Magnificent Love
Jesus, my Eternal Repose
Jesus, my Vehement Desire
Jesus, my Crucified Spouse
Jesus, my King
Jesus, my God

I love Thee.

Glory be to the Father and to the Son and to the Holy Ghost; as it was in the beginning, is now, and ever shall be, world without end, Amen.